ENGINEER DEPARTMENT, U. S. ARMY.

REPORT

OF A

RECONNAISSANCE

OF THE

BLACK HILLS OF DAKOTA,

MADE IN

THE SUMMER OF 1874.

BY

WILLIAM LUDLOW,

CAPTAIN OF ENGINEERS, BVT. LIEUT. COLONEL U. S. ARMY,
CHIEF ENGINEER DEPARTMENT OF DAKOTA.

WASHINGTON:
GOVERNMENT PRINTING OFFICE.
1875.

TABLE OF CONTENTS.

ILLUSTRATIONS AND MAPS.

OFFICE OF THE CHIEF OF ENGINEERS,
Washington, D. C., May 17, 1875.

SIR: I have the honor to submit herewith a copy of a report by Capt. William Ludlow, Corps of Engineers, of a reconnaissance of the Black Hills of Dakota.

Captain Ludlow was attached to the military expedition under the command of Lieut. Col. G. A. Custer, of the Seventh Cavalry, who penetrated this interesting region in the summer of 1874; and his report, including the reports of Prof. N. H. Winchell on the geology, and Mr. George Bird Grinnell on the paleontology of the country, contains much valuable information.

I have respectfully to recommend, therefore, that it be printed at the Government Printing Office; and that 2,500 copies be furnished on the usual requisition.

By direction of Brigadier-General Humphreys, and in his absence,

Very respectfully, your obedient servant,

GEORGE H. ELLIOT,
Major of Engineers.

Hon. WM. W. BELKNAP,
Secretary of War.

Approved:

By order of the Secretary of War.

H. T. CROSBY,
Chief Clerk.

WAR DEPARTMENT, *May* 19, 1875.

HEADQUARTERS DEPARTMENT OF DAKOTA,
OFFICE OF CHIEF ENGINEER,
Saint Paul, Minn., April 28, 1875.

SIR: I have the honor to forward to-day my report of the reconnaissance of last summer of the Black Hills of Dakota.

Accompanying the report are those of Professor Winchell and Mr. Grinnell, (the latter including drawings and descriptions of new fossils discovered on the trip,) a summary of the daily readings of the thermometer and barometer, the distances marched, the altitude, latitude, and longitude of each camp. A set of observations in four of the principal camps is also inclosed.

Three maps are presented, one showing the entire reconnaissance; one, more in detail and on a larger scale, representing thehills and their vicinity; and one geological map of the Black Hills, prepared by Prof. N. H. Winchell.

Very respectfully, your obedient servant,

WILLIAM LUDLOW,
Captain of Engineers, U. S. A.

The CHIEF OF ENGINEERS, UNITED STATES ARMY,
Washington, D. C.

REPORT.

HEADQUARTERS DEPARTMENT OF DAKOTA,
OFFICE OF CHIEF ENGINEER,
Saint Paul, Minn., April 28, 1875.

SIR: I have the honor to submit herewith my report of the reconnaissance of last summer to the Black Hills.

Accompanying the report are those of Prof. N. H. Winchell and Mr. Geo. Bird Grinnell, and a summary of the daily instrumental observations, with deduced altitudes, and the latitude and longitude of each camp, distances traveled, &c.

Two maps are submitted; one, of the whole reconnaissance; the other, more in detail, of the Black Hills themselves.

ORGANIZATION OF THE EXPEDITION.

The expedition was organized in compliance with the following order, the provisions of which were subsequently slightly modified, as far as they related to myself, by Special Orders No. 127, of June 19, which directed me to accompany the expedition, and take six instead of three of the enlisted men under my command.

[Special Orders No. 117.]

HEADQUARTERS DEPARTMENT OF DAKOTA,
Saint Paul, Minn., June 8, 1874.

1. In pursuance of instructions from the Headquarters of the Military Division of the Missouri, an expedition will be organized at Fort Abraham Lincoln, D. T., for the purpose of reconnoitering the route from that post to Bear Butte, in the Black Hills, and exploring the country south, southeast, and southwest of that point. The expedition will consist of the six companies of the Seventh Cavalry, now stationed at Fort Abraham Lincoln; the four companies of the same regiment now at Fort Rice; Company I, Twentieth Infantry; and Company G, Seventeenth Infantry; and such Indian scouts from Forts Abraham Lincoln and Rice as the commander of the expedition shall select.

Lieut. Col. G. A. Custer, of the Seventh Cavalry, is assigned to the command.

The expedition will start from Fort Abraham Lincoln as soon after the 20th instant as may be practicable. Lieutenant-Colonel Custer will proceed, by such route as he may find to be most desirable, to Bear Butte or some other point on or near the Belle Fourche, and thence will push his explorations in such direction or directions as in his judgment will enable him to obtain the most information in regard to the character of the country and the possible routes of communication through it.

Lieutenant-Colonel Custer will return to Fort Abraham Lincoln within sixty days from the time of his departure from it. Should, however, any unforeseen obstacles render it necessary or advisable for him to return from any point of his contemplated march, even before the Belle Fourche is reached, he is authorized to do so.

Capt. William Ludlow, Chief Engineer of the Department, will report to Lieutenant-Colonel Custer as engineer office of the expedition. He will be accompanied by his civil assistant and three enlisted men of the Engineer Battalion.

* * * * * * *

By command of Brigadier-General Terry.

O. D. GREENE,
Assistant Adjutant-General.

GENERAL ACCOUNT OF THE COUNTRY.

Some general account of the country to be explored will be useful in order to a full understanding of the objects of the expedition as set forth in this order.

The Black Hills are an outlying portion of the Rocky Mountains, covering an area about equal to that of the State of Connecticut, included between the forty-third and forty-fifth parallels of latitude, and the one hundred and third and one hundred and fifth meridians of longitude. They lie, therefore, mostly within the borders of Dakota, but trench also upon those of Wyoming.

On the north, east, and south sides, they are surrounded by the open prairie, and are accessible only by a journey of a hundred or more miles from the nearest point which even frontier civilization has reached. This region had been skirted by Lieutenant Warren, of the Topographical Engineers, in 1855, 1856, and 1857, and by Captain Raynolds, of the same corps, in 1859 and 1860, and the maps and reports of these officers nearly summed up our knowledge of it, if we except the vague and sometimes highly-colored reports from Indians and stray frontiersmen.

The North and South Forks of the Big Cheyenne River head nearly together on the west side, thence, spreading widely apart, embrace the hills between them, uniting in longitude 102° 20′, to flow eastward and discharge into the Missouri.

The immense reservation secured to the various bands of Sioux—now the most numerous and warlike of the northern tribes—by treaty of April 29, 1868, lies between the one hundred and fourth meridian of longitude and the Missouri River. It is bounded on the north by the forty-sixth and on the south by the forty-third parallel, the Keya-Paha River, (a branch of the Niobrara,) and the Niobrara itself, to its confluence with the Missouri.

This immense tract, inclosing nearly forty-three thousand square miles, the greater portion of which, however, is bare and often arid prairie, destitute of every attraction for the settler, and only capable of supporting a scanty population of hunters, has for its choicest and most valuable portion the Black Hills, lying on its western border. All reports agreed in describing this as a mountainous, heavily-timbered tract, abounding in game, and containing within its unexplored interior an open, fertile, and well-watered region.

In case, at any future time, complications with the Sioux, or the advancing needs of bordering civilization should make it necessary to establish military posts upon this Indian reservation, indications all pointed to the Black Hills as the suitable point, both on account of their geographical position and of the abundance of wood, water, and grass to be found there. To explain the value of its position, it should be stated that the trails from the camp of the hostile Sioux on the Yellowstone, to the agencies near the Missouri, where live the reservation Indians and whereon the issues of annuities are made, lead by a southeasterly course through the hills, the abundance of game and ample security of which, make them a ready refuge in time of war, and a noble hunting-ground in time of peace.

It was therefore considered desirable to gain positive information regarding them, and to connect them as well by reconnaissance with the posts of Lincoln and Laramie. To accomplish these results was the object of the expedition.

The *personnel* of this consisted of ten companies of the Seventh Cavalry, one each of the Twentieth and Seventeenth Infantry, a detachment of Indian scouts, together with the necessary guides, interpreters, and teamsters, in all about one thousand men. The wagon-train consisted of about one hundred and ten wagons and ambulances, while the artillery was represented by three Gatlings and a 3-inch rifle.

Previous to leaving Saint Paul I had engaged the services of Prof. N. H. Winchell, State geologist of Minnesota, as geologist of the expedition. He would also make such notes as his time would admit on the flora, in which Dr. Williams, surgeon, U. S. A., kindly promised to assist.

Mr. George Bird Grinnell, of New Haven, accompanied the expedition as a representative of Professor Marsh, of Yale College, and I arranged with him to furnish me a report on the paleontology and zoology. The valuable reports of these two gentlemen are appended, and special attention to them invited.

A photographer was engaged in Saint Paul, and furnished with a complete apparatus for taking stereoscopic views. He agreed, in consideration of using Government material, and being furnished with other facilities, to make six complete sets of pictures upon return to Saint Paul to accompany the official reports. About sixty excellent views were taken, illustrating vividly the character of the country. But one incomplete set of pictures was furnished me, which is forwarded herewith. The photographer failed, and subsequently refused, to furnish more, and an attempt to compel him to do so was defeated.

For surveying purposes my detachment of six engineer soldiers was employed. The two sergeants, Becker and Wilson, each with one man as an assistant, kept separate trails with prismatic compass and odometer—one with an odometer-cart, a two-wheeled vehicle specially constructed for the purpose, the other in an ambulance. Two odometers were read on each vehicle, and the compass-notes made as full as possible. Two chronometers (mean solar, 1362, Arnold & Dent, and sidereal, 202, Bond & Sons) were carried by the fifth man in a basket, while a record of thermometer and aneroid barometer readings was made by the sixth man during the day.

The additional instruments were a small Würdemann transit, No. 94, and a Spencer, Browning & Co. sextant, No. 6536. The general topography during the day was taken as thoroughly as possible by my assistant, Mr. W. H. Wood, and myself, and night observations were made whenever practicable. The positions of all but ten of the camps were astronomically determined. A summary of these is appended.

The direct course to Bear Butte, which is a well-known point north of the Black Hills, is south 39½° west, and the air-line distance two hundred and two miles. As it was known that the intervening country was dry and woodless, General Custer considered that, by inclining westward toward the divide east of the Little Missouri and then turning south, a better road would be found than by pursuing the straight course. Prairie travel resembles that by sea, which indeed the landscape not unfrequently suggests. The compass is the guide, the direct course is not always the best, and the probabilities of finding wood, water, and grass, and a good road, compare with those of obtaining favorable and moderate winds and a smooth sea.

The Dakota prairies have been often described, but their general characteristics may be briefly stated: a rolling and at times a hilly country, destitute of wood, except small quantities in the eroded valleys of streams, and covered with short grass. The horizon, bounded everywhere by the undulating outlines of the surface, and varied occasionally by some more dominating elevations which constitute the landmarks for the traveler, and are called buttes. (In pronouncing the word the *u* is sounded as in tube.)

The summer sun shines from a generally cloudless sky; the purity of the air gives its rays great power, and the thermometer frequently rises above 100° in the shade. Water is scarce, and almost invariably alkaline, even in running streams, from the presence of a salt which forms a component of the clayey soil. The rivers are small streams of great comparative length, which, from absorption and evaporation, shrink in their downward course, and are frequently dry at their mouths while flowing freely a hundred or two miles above. The seasons of spring and fall are exceedingly brief. The winter snows are rapidly disposed of in the spring, and rain-falls are unfrequent until cold weather in the fall, which soon again merges into winter. By July 1 the grass is fully grown, and in another month has turned dry and yellow, cured to hay upon the ground and readily burned.

The whole country was once ranged over by enormous herds of buffalo whose trails are everywhere visible, but which are now seldom or never found east of the Little Missouri; and the only game animals inhabiting the vast waste are antelope, numbers of which were seen during every day's march. The grasshopper having proved himself to be one of the most serious obstacles to the future successful colonization of the country, is worth brief mention.

Previous to the departure of the expedition, and while still in camp near Fort Lincoln during the last days of June, the grasshoppers were very numerous. I counted twenty-five one morning on what I judged to be an average square foot of ground; a brief calculation gives at that rate over a million to the acre; and as they are often much more numerous than then observed, and are exceedingly rapacious, their capacity for destruction to living vegetation may be imagined. Their powers of sustained flight, too, are wonderful when one considers the build of the creature and compares it with that of a bird. They appear able to keep the wing the whole day, always moving with the wind, and filling the air to a vast height. By shading the eye from the direct rays of the sun, and still looking near it, an idea of their numbers can be gained. The wings reflecting the light make them appear like tufts of cotton floating lazily with the wind, and apparently increasing in numbers upward as far as the eye can reach. They will journey thus all day long for several days, settling to the ground at night-fall. In descending through the slanting rays of the sun, they resemble a fall of huge snow-flakes. In one of our camps there must have been a hundred to the square foot. They were crowded as thickly as they could stand upon the ground, and every blade of grass bore several. No successful means of destroying them or mitigating their ravages have been yet discovered; and the serious consequences of a visitation from them were seen last season in many portions of the West.

The course determined upon by General Custer was successfully pursued. The expedition left Fort Lincoln at 8 a. m. of July 2, steering at first southwesterly toward the bend of Heart River; thence, July 7, across the North Fork of the Cannon Ball, a fine stream, 30 feet to 75 feet in width, and 1 foot to 2 feet in depth, flowing with swift current over a shaly bed through a well-wooded valley from 100 feet to 200 feet deep, and 500 to 1,000 yards wide; thence, July 8, across the South Fork, also called Cedar Creek, a smaller stream, 20 feet wide and 18 inches deep with a rocky bed, banks from 10 feet to 12 feet high, and valley 100 to 200 yards wide, scantily furnished with wood; thence over the Belle Pierres Hills, so called from the colored pebbles abounding there. Here, bending nearly westward, the trail gradually sloped into the valley of North Fork of Grand River, in which we camped July 9. The stream was about 25 feet wide and a foot in depth, with a rapid current of muddy sweet water from recent rain above. The valley is level, from one to two miles wide, defined by low hills, and supports a scanty growth of thin grass and weeds. Wood is very scarce.

The next day's march (July 10) was still west, and a little north, up the valley, in which we again camped. The grasshoppers were in immense numbers during these two days.

From this camp the trail bore strongly southwest, to enable us to explore a cave, of which the guides told wonderful stories. We found it, after an uphill march of twenty miles over a sterile country covered with cactus, in the eastern side of a ridge several miles in length and covered with the first pine timber we had seen. With regard to this ridge and the cave, the following is a note from my itinerary: "The ridge presents a peculiar appearance, having a level cap of light friable sandstone, which has washed and weathered into the shape of battlements and towers. The exterior presents the appearance of a scarp, and suggests strongly the ruins of an old fortified city fairly laid out with bastions and curtains, with sally-ports guarded by towers. The tendency in places is to wear into holes large and small, which, often of regular size and arrangement, give the idea of embrasures and loopholes. The scarp varies in places from 3 feet to 20 feet in height, against which lies the talus derived from the breaking down of the sandstone walls and the washing of the superjacent clay. The 'cave' is a hole washed out of the sandstone 200 feet or 300 feet in depth horizontally, with an entrance 15 feet by 20 feet, and proved to possess no special interest other than that imparted to it by the superstition of the Indians." From the Cave Hills the route led southwesterly across several bends of the South Fork of Grand River, through a rather difficult and arid country, to the camp of July 14, in a well grassed and watered valley, through which flowed a small wooded branch of the Little Missouri. The view here was so attractive, in comparison with the landscape recently passed over, that General Custer names the place Prospect Valley. Here the first halt was made for the purposes of rest and washing, much needed after a march of two hundred and thirty miles, and a mail was dispatched back to Fort Lincoln by Indian scouts. The camp lay between two ranges of pine-covered hills, from the southern extremity of which, and due south of us, the Black Hills loomed up high and dark, and, although sixty miles away, some separate peaks and elevations could be identified. The Short Pine Hills are of a soft arenaceous marl, very light in color, some 400 or 500 feet above the valley and covered with pine from 20 feet to 40 feet in height, except on the level top, which is seven or eight miles long by two to three and a half miles wide, and shows a heavy growth of grass. Slim Butte, which has been in sight to the southeast and east for several days, appears more like a high wooded plateau than a butte, and is presumably of the same formation as the Short Pine Hills. Information from the guides indicates that a branch of the South Fork of Grand River separates it into two portions. On the west side of the Short Pine Hills some fossils were discovered, regarding which the following is my note: "Descended from the hills into the Little Missouri Valley and passed by a range of bare hills of the same character as the larger ones. Examined them for fossils, and Winchell discovered two vertebræ (saurian) and a couple of turtles of great size. Vertebræ preserved, but turtles were too much decayed. A thigh-bone of one was 2 inches in diameter, and the carapace 1¼ inches thick. From

Prospect Valley the trail led around the northern extremity of the Short Pine Hills into the valley of the Little Missouri, which proved to be an inhospitable country enough. No grass could be seen, the vegetation was all cactus and weeds. The train watered at a bend of the river, and taking some wood struck off southeast. Finding a little grass we finally camped, after a hot and dusty march of thirty and a half miles over the most unattractive country we had seen."

The Little Missouri is a rapid stream, 30 feet to 40 feet wide and 18 inches deep, over a gravelly bed. The banks are steep and 40 feet in height, and the valley is several miles in width, with small cottonwood in the lower levels. Information from the guides pointed to the northwest corner of the Black Hills as the most favorable point of entrance, although they still insisted that an exploration was impossible, except on foot. The camp of the 16th of July being on the one hundred and fourth meridian, but little additional westing was required.

The next day's travel (July 17) led south, over a rolling prairie tributary to the Little Missouri, and partaking of the characteristic features of that valley; very little grass; cactus and prickly pear prevailing; the soil a loose, dry clay, into which the foot sank. Camp was made on the edge of a bluff facing south, overlooking a very rough and much-tumbled country, with the Black Hills in full view, fifteen or twenty miles distant, and Bear Butte rising from the prairie forty miles away to the southeast. During the night heavy clouds and lightning appeared, and, toward morning, a severe wind-storm routed us from sleep and covered us with sand.

Crossing the broken country, which was deeply washed and gullied, noon of the 18th brought us to a small branch of the Belle Fourche, timbered with burr-oak and pine, and strongly impregnated with iron. The cause of this was soon explained. Just beyond we found iron-ore covering a large surface and heaped up in mounds. The landscape suggested the waste-banks of an enormous iron-furnace, and showed that we had entered upon the outer edge of the geological disturbance which had culminated in the formation of the Black Hills. Passing the iron country the valley of the Belle Fourche was reached, and two or three hours were spent in looking for a practicable descent. The hills are 500 or 600 feet in height, deeply scarred with ravines, pine and burr-oak covering the slopes.

Camp was favorably selected in a clear level opening, 25 feet or 30 feet above the river, with abundant wood, water, and grass.

The Belle Fourche, or north fork of the Cheyenne, has a rapid current, in a shaly bed 30 feet to 50 feet wide, and from 1 foot to 4 feet deep, with water slightly alkaline. The rocks have been strongly tilted and metamorphosed. The river valley is from a half mile to a mile in width and well timbered. Captain Raynolds's trail of 1859 passed along the crest of the hills in rear of camp. The guides continued to proclaim the uselessness of attempting to take wagons farther, and if they possessed any knowledge which would be valuable to us refused to impart it. They have hitherto supposed we would skirt the hills without seriously attempting an entrance. Finding their monitions falling on deaf ears, they realized our intention to see all we could.

July 19.—The command remained in camp. The distance marched from Lincoln was two hundred and ninety-two miles, an average of eighteen and a quarter miles per day. Heavy rain fell until 4 p. m., and the huge camp-fires were a luxury all day. Toward evening the precaution was taken of moving the wagon-train across the river, in view of a possible rise during the night.

July 20.—The first day's journey was made into the hills. The morning opened threateningly, but subsequently cleared. Crossing the river and bending to the westward, a winding and easy ascent was made of the opposite hills. Reaching the summit the course was southerly, over a high, gently-rolling prairie, heavily grassed, with clumps of oak and pine beautifully interspersed.

A ravine cut into the shingle by a small stream was passed. From the sides of the cut exuded some salt of sulphur, and the water was strongly impregnated with alum, and possessed a decidedly inky flavor and astringency. Pursuing the southerly course the high table narrowed to a ridge and suddenly turned to the left; the trail descended into a valley thickly wooded with oak and pine. The change from the hot, dry, burned-up landscape north of the Belle Fourche was wonderful. The temperature was delightful; the air laden with sweet wild odors; the grass knee-deep and exceedingly luxuriant and fresh; while wild cherries, blueberries, and gooseberries abounded, as well as many varieties of flowers. All these advantages, combined with that of an abundance of pure cold water, were ours, with rare exceptions, until the final departure from the hills.

Over a narrow ridge into a small grassy park, thence into another and another, the trail led to camp facing a lofty sandstone range of hills through which a narrow pass had admitted us, and at the foot of which a small stream of pure water flowed eastward.

Soon after leaving camp next morning, (July 21,) the trail winding southeast among high wooded hills, emerged upon the valley of the Redwater, a branch of the Belle Fourche. The valley seemed comparatively level; the soil a bright brick-red in color; the cuts made by small streams exhibiting the same hue; traversed in places by broad white bands of gypsum; the grass a bright green, but not luxuriant. Owing to the ravines and cuts the valley was found difficult to travel, and recourse was had to a narrow ridge of hills on the right, finally descending from which we camped in the valley on a small creek issuing from a spring of 45° temperature, and flowing a stream a foot wide and several inches deep. This water, delightful from its clearness and coldness, proved to have been impregnated by the gypsum-veins, and to be endowed with highly medicinal properties.

July 22.—The course led southward up the Redwater valley, which is from four to ten miles in width, and bounded by high hills heavily timbered with pine. The gypsum appeared in enormous quantities. One of the guides took me off to the right to see a huge mass of it, crystallized and shining beautifully in the sun. The Indians, for generations, have, in passing, split off pieces for ornaments, and by degrees cut a shoulder several feet deep on it at the level of the ground. Inyan Kara was in sight all day to the southward, approaching which the trail turned to the left around two igneous-looking peaks, and reached camp on Inyan Kara Creek, so called from flowing west past the foot of that peak. A heavy well-marked pony and lodge trail led up the Redwater valley southeasterly to the Red Cloud and Spotted Tail agencies.

July 23.—The command remained in camp while a party started out to make the ascent of Inyan Kara, about five miles distant. It resembles a lunar mountain, having a rim in shape of a horseshoe, one and a half miles across, with an elevated peak rising sharply from the center. The rim, 1,142 feet in height above the exterior base, has a sharp edge at the summit, and falls steeply on both sides. The central peak, towering 170 feet above the rim and resembling a formation of basaltic columns, was gained by means of a narrow spur projecting from it to the southwest. A small spring flowed from the foot of the peak out northward through the opening in the horseshoe rim. The inner space between peak and rim was heavily wooded with pine and clumps of aspen. In the open places were found in abundance strawberries, raspberries, black and red currants, june-berries, and a small red whortleberry. From the summit an extensive view might have been obtained, but the Sioux had fired the prairie to the south and west. After two hours of waiting, the smoke having only grown denser, we returned to camp.

July 24.—The trail led up the creek-valley a short distance, then turned abruptly east, climbing the hills, and winding among a succession of wooded heights and open valleys. After several hours of waiting, while search was made for a practicable descent, we started again and dropped suddenly into the valley of a small stream flowing northward into the Redwater. Ascending a few miles the stream became more full and camp was pitched.

July 25.—The course ascended the valley to the southeast; the hills were limestone covered with pine, and from 150 feet to 300 feet in height. The valley, from 100 to 300 yards wide and filled with the greatest profusion of wild flowers, in almost incredible numbers and variety, General Custer named Floral Valley. As we ascended, through these beds of color, the hills became lower, and tamarack and spruce appeared on the slopes. A beautiful spring was passed, with a temperature of 44½°. The valley rose rapidly, but smoothly, and the visible stream increased to 4 feet in width and 8 inches or 9 inches in depth, of a beautiful clearness and very swift flow. Farther up it disappeared to re-appear again. It seemed to terminate in several springs, above which a dry bed only was seen. An old and deeply cut lodge-trail ran up the valley, and, halting the command, the valleys leading out of Floral Valley were explored. The trail is said by one of the guides to be the old voyageur pack-trail, and is one of the regular routes between the hostile camp on Tongue River and the agencies. Near the highest point many old camps and abandoned lodge-poles were seen. Pursuing the lodge-trail a spring was reached, the waters of which flowed north and east. The fog, which had been sweeping up from the eastward, became very dense. The flowers were if anything more abundant than in the morning, the hills but 30 or 40 feet in height, covered with pine and aspen, tamarack and spruce. The wood and open seemed to share the country about equally. All vegetation was luxuriant and fresh, and we had no doubt that a portion, at least, of the park country we were in search of had been reached. The valleys radiated in all directions, connecting with each other, and a more beautiful wild country could not be imagined. Signs of bear and deer were abundant, and the woods frequently resounded with the clangorous cry of the crane.

July 26.—Still ascending Floral Valley, the divide was reached, and we almost insensibly passed into the valley of another stream, falling rapidly to the southeast. The hills became gradually higher and the valley wider. The beaver had made frequent dams, and their labors occasionally added to those of the pioneers in making a road for the wagons. In the afternoon occurred the first rencontre with Indians. A village of seven lodges, containing twenty-seven souls, was found in the valley. The men were away peacefully engaged in hunting; the squaws in camp drying meat, cooking, and other camp avocations. Red Cloud's daughter was the wife of the head-man, whose name was "One Stab." General Custer was desirous they should remain and introduce us to the hills, but the presence among our scouts of a party of Rees, with whom the Sioux wage constant war, rendered them very uneasy, and toward nightfall, abandoning their camp, they made the escape. Old "One Stab" was at headquarters when the flight was discovered, and retained both as guide and hostage.

From a high hill near camp, the first well-defined view was gained of Harney's Peak, twenty miles to the southeast. The position of this peak, on the southeast slope of the hills, was known from Warren's map. We were nearly in the heart of the unexplored portion of the hills, and the results of energy and good management had been shown in the entire success of the expedition.

The high limestone ridges surrounding the camp had weathered into castellated forms of considerable grandeur and beauty, and suggested the name of Castle Valley. The valley itself was luxuriantly rich and grassy, a fine stream meandering through it. Just below camp was seen a mica schist on the bank of the creek, in bed with a nearly vertical tilt, indicating the geological depth we had reached, while pebbles and bowlders of quartz were scattered over the surface in great numbers. By the courtesy of General Custer, Lieut. Edward S. Godfrey, of the Seventh Cavalry, was this day detailed to assist me in topographical work, and rendered most valuable services.

July 27.—The command remained in camp, to give time to examine the neighboring country, and the gold-hunters were very busy all day with shovel and pan exploring the streams. Several surveying-parties were sent out in various directions. Each tributary valley had its springs and little streams; was heavily grassed and often filled with flowers. The grass in places was as high as a horse's shoulder. This portion of the Black Hills evidently never suffers from drought. No arid places are seen except on the summits of the limestone ledges. Springs are numerous and very cold and pure. The soil is everywhere moist, and vegetation marvelously luxuriant and fresh. The altitude is great, as compared with that of the prairie, and is sufficient to materially lower the average temperature. The warm currents of air from the plains condense as they ascend the slope of the hills and are robbed of their moisture in fog, rain, and heavy dews which occur nightly. The clouds almost invariably formed in the afternoon and interfered greatly with astronomical observations.

July 28.—The valley below us was rather too marshy for the wagons, and the easterly course lay up the hills to the left out upon a high rolling prairie, crossing which the Castle Valley Creek was again encountered, here flowing northward and contracted into a wooded and impassable cañon, 500 or 600 feet in depth, with another creek and valley coming in from the westward to join it.

A huge pile of elk-horns of ancient date, and of which the Indians disclaimed any share in the construction, was found on the northeast part of this prairie, and suggested the name for it. No camp could be made there, and partly retracing our steps, we camped again on Castle Valley Creek, a few miles below the camp of the day before. Another creek coming in from the south, promised a road for the next day. The following note is given: "After dinner made a reconnaissance with General Custer up the creek below camp. A good road was found up the valley, which is heavily grassed and flowered for two and one-half miles. Then ascended a hill on the left and reached, through some timber, the open prairie I was on in the afternoon."

Harney's Peak was visible from the top of a high, bare hill, and the sun having just set, we were in a few minutes well rewarded for the ride of five miles. The moon was rising just over the southern shoulder of Harney, and masked by heavy clouds. A patch of bright blood-red flame was first seen, looking like a brilliant fire, and soon after another so far from the first that it was difficult to connect the two. A portion of the moon's disk became presently visible, and the origin of the flame was apparent. While it lasted the sight was superb. The moon's mass looked enormous and blood-red, with only portions of its surface visible, while the clouds just above and to the left, colored by the flame, resembled smoke drifting from an immense conflagration. The moon soon buried herself completely in the clouds, and under a rapidly darkening sky we returned to camp.

July 29.—The course led southeasterly up the valley examined the evening before, finding heavy grass with wild oats and barley and many flowers. An old, deeply-worn Indian trail led up the creek, following which took us across a high prairie exhibiting bowlders of quartz. Crossing a ridge the head of a stream was reached, flowing southeasterly. Following the new creek for some miles, the valley was found uncomfortably narrow, frequent bridging of the stream being necessary. Recourse was had to the hills on the right, and camp finally made on another creek, also flowing to the south and east.

July 30.—We traveled all day through a beautiful pastoral and agricultural country, half wood, half glade, full of deer and abundantly grassed. Harney's Peak was passed eight or nine miles on the left. A few high hills were scattered about, but most of them were low. Granite appeared for the first time, and the range of which Harney is the chief, appeared granitic and very rugged. Our proximity to the outer plains in the east was evident as camp was neared. The air was milder, the grass drier, and the streams contained less water. Grasshoppers appeared, and a rattlesnake was captured in camp. All strong indications of the vicinity of the prairie.

July 31.—The command remained in camp, while surveying-parties were sent out, and the gold-hunters redoubled their efforts. General Custer and myself, with Professors Winchell and Donaldson and Mr. Wood, escorted by a company of cavalry, set out to ascend Harney. A rough ride of eight or nine miles over high hills and heavily-timbered ravines, in some of which birch was seen for the first time, brought us to the foot of a granite elevation with a creek flowing eastward. Wild raspberries, unexcelled in size and flavor, abounded; and in the dark wet bottoms the june-berry bushes grew to a height of 10 or 12 feet, and hung full of fruit. Leaving the horses at the foot of the clear granite, the ascent was made on foot. Halting to rest and lunch, another summit, two or three miles west, was seen, rising higher than the one we were on. Reaching the summit of this, still another, several hundred feet higher, and a mile more west, showed that we had more work to do. A stiff climb brought us to the top, whence nothing more lofty could be seen, and we stood on the most elevated portion of the hills some 9,700 feet above the sea, except that alongside us rose a mass of granite 40 feet in height, with perpendicular sides that forbade an attempt to scale them without the aid of ropes and ladders. A stunted spruce was growing under its protection, and a few ferns and harebells obtained sustenance near by. The view was superb, extending over the intervening peaks and hills to a broad expanse of prairie from north by east round to southwest. The course of the Forks of the Cheyenne could be distinctly traced, and a dim line visible to the southeast was even thought to be the hills of White River, fifty or sixty miles distant. Bear Butte, forty-odd miles to the north, was again seen over the wooded ranges; and all but Inyan Kara of the principal peaks were in view. Two of the prominent ones I have named for General Terry and General Custer.

The return to camp was a struggle against almost every possible obstacle—rocks, creeks, marshes, willow and aspen thickets, pine timber, dead and fallen trees, steep hillsides and precipitous ravines. Every difficulty multiplied by the darkness, and only the stars for a guide, camp was finally reached at 1.30 in the morning.

August 1.—Camp was moved a short distance down the creek for fresh pasturage.

August 2.—Command still in camp. There is much talk of gold, and industrious search for it is making. I saw in General Custer's tent what the miner said he had obtained during the day. Under a strong reading-glass it resembled small pin-heads, and fine scales of irregular shape, perhaps thirty in number. The miners expressed themselves quite confident that if they could reach bed-rock in the valleys at a favorable place, plenty could be obtained by use of the pan.

General Custer determined upon a rapid scout south to the South Fork of the Cheyenne, for the purpose of examining the intervening country, while another party should go southeast, following the creek upon which we were encamped to its junction with the same stream. These two explorations would cover considerable country and complete the examination of the south and southeast portion of the hills.

August 3.—The headquarters, with five companies of cavalry and a few pack-mules, leaving the train and the balance of the command in camp, started on the reconnaissance, and Lieutenant Godfrey, with an escort of two companies, left at the same time to follow down the creek. The headquarters trail led south and southwest through the park country, until the head of a creek flowing southwardly was reached. This was pursued all day, leading us at first into a narrow valley, hemmed in by high wooded hills. The character of the country changed gradually as we went south. The valley grew broader, the hills lower, grass dryer, and timber more and more scarce. Crossing the red-clay belt which encircles the hills, the creek increased in size and plunged into a cañon 500 or 600 feet in depth, containing cottonwood and box-elder, with scattering pine on the hills. Emerging from this into smoother country, we halted for the night a few miles from the South Fork, having accomplished a march of forty-five miles. *

Reynolds, a white scout, was dispatched late at night with a mail. He had about seventy-five miles in an air-line to make to Laramie alone, through a country infested with Indians, with the additional disadvantage of crossing their probable routes at right angles, and coming upon them suddenly. We were greatly relieved to learn afterward that his trip had been successfully made, though not without privation.

August 4.—A ride of three miles down the creek brought us to the South Fork. We found it a shallow stream with a flat, stony, and sandy bed about 30 feet wide and a few inches deep, though evidently much broader in wet seasons. The water was alkaline with a metallic gypsum flavor. The bordering hills low, with a few stunted pines. Going down stream two or three miles the course turned abruptly to the left and struck due north, passing over a high dry prairie with occasional valleys and ravines. We entered and crossed at right angles the Red Clay Valley, finding as usual a gypsum stream in the middle, and here flowing east. Having crossed another valley tending southeast, deeply cut out of the red clay, we entered pine timber again on the north side, and finally halted near some big pools and springs. The day had been excessively hot. The ride of thirty miles succeeding another of forty-five was very fatiguing, and many of the horses gave out. We enjoyed, however, a fine camp, with excellent grass, water, and wood, and rolling ourselves on the ground in our blankets slept without dreaming.

August 5.—Course was still northerly, through timbered, hilly country, which rapidly improved into "Park" with bright little brooks, beautiful grassy valleys, and abundant game. Granite knobs and peaks occasionally emerged from among the trees, and at half past 9 we passed a huge knob, resembling a turbaned head, some 200 feet in height, which we had seen off to the eastward on the first day of the reconnaissance. About noon the permanent camp was reached, after a march of twenty-five miles that day, and one hundred miles in three days. Lieutenant Godfrey had already returned, but had failed to reach the South Fork on account of the tortuous and cañony character of the stream he was pursuing. He had, however, been clear of the hills, and mapped the creek so far as he went.

August 6.—Camp was broken for the return trip. General Custer determined, instead of going eastward upon the prairie, to partly retrace his steps, and examine into the practicability of a route northward through the hills, emerging somewhere near Bear Butte, and so complete the examination of them. The old trail was accordingly run back with some slight divergence, and camp was reached just beyond the high prairie passed over July 29. A heavy thunder-storm came up during the night, and the echoes among the hills were exceedingly grand.

August 7.—The storm of the night before had swelled the brooks, but the old trail furnished a good road. Crossing Castle Valley we passed over Elk Horn Prairie again, and bearing north and west crossed a creek and ascended a small valley in which the beaver had been at work, thence through a heavily wooded tract into the valley of another creek flowing eastward. Passing down this for a few miles, further progress was barred by a cañon, and turning sharply to the left over a

*NOTE.—No instruments were taken on the trip, as the column moved without wagons, and the sextant was needed in the permanent camp.

W. L.

slight ridge we camped on the bank of another creek. Two grizzly bears were killed near this camp, and the first grasshoppers seen in the hills in any numbers were swarming in both creek valleys.

August 8.—The morning opened with thick fog, which cleared about 10 a. m. The course was north and east, crossing several creeks leading eastwardly. One deep valley gave considerable trouble to the wagons, crossing which, we traveled over a high, rocky ridge, with schist projecting from the surface nearly vertically, and made a fine camp in the next valley.

August 9.—The course lay down the valley, which was in possession of the beaver, for several miles, then turned to the left over a ridge. The hills were high and wooded; and from an occasional open spot glimpses of the open prairie a few miles away were caught. The creeks flowed eastward, and in piercing through the outward range of hills had cut deep cañons, which were often blocked by bowlders and fallen trees. Several were explored, but none affording a practicable route for wagons were discovered. Springs were abundant, of clear, cold water, with a temperature of 46°. The heavy pine forests on the hill-sides were full of deer. In all the open glades grass was luxuriant.

August 10.—The route was southerly, crossing a low ridge, and taking the head of a creek flowing a little east of south. It is remarkable and characteristic of the hills that, in whatever direction we have wished to go, a creek-valley has always furnished a road. Following down the valley, we found it enlarging to a broad fertile meadow luxuriantly grassed, through which wound the creek, a fine rapid stream 10 feet to 12 feet wide, flowing over a rocky bed. We were continually looking for trout in these streams, which seemed as though made expressly for that fish, which requires an unfailing flow of cold pure water. There could be no finer trout-streams in the world than these were they once stocked. As it was, we found nothing but some small chub, and a species of sucker of perhaps a pound weight. The neighboring hills were 600 or 700 feet in height, capped with 50 feet of bare limestone, resting upon Potsdam sandstone. The meadow terminating and the stream entering a cañon, camp was pitched.

August 11.—Taking advantage of the command remaining in camp while General Custer made exploration for a road eastwardly, I returned to the camp of the day before with a surveying party, for the purpose of measuring a base line and locating with the transit the important elevations. A base of 3,200 feet was carefully laid out, whence two hills were located, from the summits of which Bear Butte, Harney, Terry, and Custer Peaks, and many minor hills could be seen, and their azimuths determined. ~~Lieutenant Warren spent a week in camp in 1859 near Bear Butte. Regarding that as properly located, Harney, on Warren's map, is too far east by six or seven miles.~~ Returning to camp, I found that several elk had been killed during the day by the hunters.

August 12.—Camp was moved down the creek a few miles into a very pretty and luxuriant valley, at a point where another large creek joined it from the westward. Judging from its size and direction, this must be the Castle Valley Creek, upon which we twice encamped, (July 26–'7 and July 28,) and the hills portion of what is called Box Elder on Warren's map.

August 13.—Lieutenant Godfrey, with an escort, was dispatched down the creek, to determine its course and ascertain his position from bearings to Bear Butte and Harney when clear of the hills. The main trail turned north across the creek, and, following a narrow ravine for a few miles, then turning east and south through open timber and a second growth of pine, emerged upon an open, rolling park of great extent, where camp was made. The open prairie was visible, separated from us by a wooded ridge, which, though not high, was deeply cut by ravines. Elm trees were seen in the vicinity of camp, and a plantation of hops was reported.

August 14.—A favorable road was found through the intervening ridge by making several abrupt turns among ravines filled with oak and hills covered with pine, and early in the day we suddenly emerged from the hills into the encircling red clay valley, which at this point is closely bordered by the open prairie. The scorching suns and hot, dry breath of the prairie, covered with yellow grass, bore instant witness to the change in our surroundings, recalling vividly the coolness of air and freshness of vegetation, the abundance of pure, cold water, the noble camp-fires, and quantities of game, which had made our stay in the hills a daily delight, and compelling us to contrast with them the dry, dusty journeys, the warm alkaline water, and scanty wood which awaited us on the return march of over three hundred and eighty miles. The course lay up the red clay valley to the north and west. The numerous creeks in the hills reaching the prairie sunk beneath the gravel and shingle of their beds and disappeared; some of them re appeared briefly in the form of springs in the red clay valley, which was from two to three miles in width. On account of these springs and the occasional marshy ground, the trail broke through the low hills separating the valley from the prairie on the east, and bore straight for Bear Butte. Camp was made on a creek named for the butte, and six or seven miles south of it.

August 15.—The command remained in camp reloading and refitting for the return journey. During the day a party made the ascent of the butte, which is an igneous-looking elevation, rising out of the rolling prairie 750 feet in height and 1,200 feet above the camp. Standing clear of the hills as it does, it is a well-known landmark, and its summit affords a wide prospect, notwithstanding its inferior height. The principal peaks were visible from it, as well as the buttes rising from the prairies northeast and southeast.

August 16.—The course lay northward, to the right of Bear Butte, over a rolling prairie and across some small creeks. We found the Belle Fourche, when crossed, to be a rapid stream, in a shaly and gravelly bed, 80 feet wide and a foot deep, the banks low, and cottonwood abundant. Four Cheyenne Indians were met en route to the agencies from the hostile camp on Tongue River, and reported that Sitting Bull, five thousand strong, was preparing to intercept us at the Short-Pine Hills. Camp was made near the headwaters of Crow Creek, with good water and grass, but no wood.

August 17.—The course was still northerly, to the left of Slave Butte; the name of which is derived from the fact that the Sioux killed some Snake captives there many years ago. The Butte is capped with sandstone, and the top is about level with that of Bear Butte, although the height above the base is only about 250 feet, the ground having risen steadily from the Belle Fourche. The country offered no inducement to linger. There was little grass, weeds and sage-brush prevailing. The soil was dry and porous, and cracked into hexagons and octagons of perhaps a square foot in area. Small plates of gypsum were scattered over the surface. Passing a branch of Moreau or Owl River, with miry, alkaline banks and water, camp was pitched on the main stream, in whose bed water stood in pools; willow and cottonwood in the bottoms.

August 18.—The course bore for our old camp of July 14 and 15, between the Short-Pine Hills, in Prospect Valley, which was passed and camp made five miles farther on, having seen nothing of our promised interceptors.

August 19.—A long march of thirty-five and one-half miles was made; at first along the divide parallel to the Little Missouri, seven or eight miles distant. The prairie was rolling and hilly, with fair grazing, but water very scarce. Interrupted by the Bois Pommes Blanches Hills and adjacent Bad Lands, we bore to the northeast, and camped against the northern end of the Cave Hills, on one of the headwaters of Grand River, with plenty of fair water and good grass.

August 20.—Traveled north and west across several heads of Grand River, and over a rolling prairie, which the Indians, to embarrass our march, had thoroughly burned. Finding no camp on the prairie, which was black as far to the northward as the eye could reach, a rapid descent was made into the valley of the Little Missouri, where, among the Bad Lands, wood, water, and grass were found.

August 21.—The command remained in camp. We had averaged nearly thirty-one miles per day for five days, having marched one hundred and fifty-three miles from the camp on Bear Butte Creek. The Bad Lands of the Little Missouri apparently began at this point. We could not see much of them to the southward, but down the river they were heavily massed on both banks. The stream was some 50 feet to 75 feet wide and a few inches deep; bed sandy and gravelly, valley from one-half mile to one mile in width, with occasional bluff peaks, exhibiting the bare, rounded clay surfaces, and broad horizontal bands, colored from black to white, through the browns, reds, and grays which characterize what are known as the "Bad Lands" or *Mauvaises Terres*. The water was alkaline, and the timber cottonwood.

August 22.—Breaking away from the Little Missouri, we traveled north over a prairie, level at first and then rolling, but all thoroughly burned. In this vicinity, I was informed that Captain Fisk, in 1865, with a train of one hundred and fifty wagons and a company of infantry, bound for Montana, was attacked by the Sioux and driven back with the loss of seventeen men and several wagons. Camp was made near a spring, in a spot of unburned grass, which we were fortunate enough to find.

August 23.—The course was north and east, over a high rolling prairie, until the Yellowstone expedition trails were encountered; following which eastwardly, we camped among the Bad Lands, on a small branch of the Little Missouri, near the Big Bend of that stream, where the grass had escaped the fire. These Bad Lands are extensive; do not compare in height with those of the Yellowstone and Missouri, which are sometimes 600 or 800 feet high; these being but from 50 feet to 150 feet. They make, however, a very striking landscape, and usually are impassable to wagons. The clay hills, of a purity which renders them incapable of supporting vegetation, are absolutely naked and stand thickly crowded together, with rounded summits and steep sides, variegated by broad horizontal bands of color. The black and brown stripes are due to veins of impure lignites, from the burning of which are derived the shades of red, while the raw clay varies from a dazzling white to dark gray. We found the ravines near camp full of ash and box-elder, and affording shelter to quantities of black-tailed deer. The remaining homeward journey was at first north-easterly, across a barren, burned plain, to a camp on one of the headwaters of Heart River; thence easterly, across the river, whose valley was one-fourth mile wide and 100 feet deep, stream 30 feet wide and a few inches in depth; thence over a rolling prairie, which would have been well grassed had the Indians not burned it. The camp of August 26 was near Young Men's Butte, at the head of some ravines filled with oak, whence spring the headwaters of Knife River, flowing north and east into the Missouri; thence, to Fort Lincoln, traversed a fine rolling prairie, well watered, and ordinarily well grassed. Gradually working out of the burned district on the 27th, the final crossing of Heart River was made at noon of the 30th. The stream was similar to where we crossed it above, being somewhat broader, flowing through a wider and deeper valley, heavily timbered with cottonwood. Fort Lincoln was reached at 4.30 p. m. of August 30, the sixtieth day of the trip. The wagon-train had traveled eight hundred and eighty-three miles, and, adding the various reconnaissances, the total number of miles surveyed was twelve hundred and five.

Whatever may ultimately be determined as to the existence of large amounts of precious metal in the Black Hills—and the evidence gathered on the trip I conclude was on the whole discouraging to that supposition—the real wealth and value of the country are, beyond doubt, very great. Utterly dissimilar in character to the remaining portion of the territory in which it lies, its fertility and freshness, its variety of resource and delightful climate, the protection it affords both against the torrid heats and arctic storms of the neighboring prairies will eventually make it the home of a thronging population. To this, however, the final solution of the Indian question is an indispensable preliminary. The region is cherished by the owners both as hunting-grounds and asylum. The more far-sighted, anticipating the time when hunting the buffalo, which is now the main subsistence of the wild tribes, will no longer suffice to that end, have looked forward to settling in and about the Black Hills as their future permanent home, and there awaiting the gradual extinction which is their fate. For these reasons, no occupation of this region by whites will be tolerated; nor, so long as the majority of the Indians live beyond the control of the United States Government, can any treaty be made with them looking to the relinquishment of their rights of ownership which will command observance by the hostile tribes. Even if, under the authority of reservation Indians, occupation of the Black Hills should become possible, settlements there could only be protected by force and the presence of a considerable military power. Hostile incursions would not be unfrequent nor an occasional massacre unlikely, and these are conditions unfavorable to a rapid and permanent increase of population. The Indians have no country farther west to which they can migrate, and only the Saskatchewan country north of the United States boundary, and which is still the range of the buffalo, offers them a possible home. It is probable that the best use to be made of the Black Hills for the next fifty years would be as the permanent reservation of the Sioux, where they could be taught occupations of a pastoral character, which of all semi-civilized means of subsistence would be most natural and easy for them, and result in relieving the United States Government of the burden of their support.

There are forwarded herewith the reports of Professor Winchell and Mr. George Bird Grinnell; also a tabular statement giving the record of daily marches, the thermometrical and barometrical reading during each day, the deduced altitude, and latitude and longitude of each camp. My thanks are due to all the officers of the expedition, and in particular to General Custer and the other officers at headquarters for constant courtesy and kindness, and every needed aid in the discharge of my duties. To Lieutenant Godfrey I am greatly indebted for valuable assistance, cheerfully and intelligently given. To Professor Winchell and Mr. Grinnell, especially, my obligations are very great. Without their valuable reports, based on unwearying and constant work of observation, nothing like an adequate exposition of the interesting country explored could have been made. While profiting by their labors, I have to express regret at Mr. Grinnell's comparative disappointment in not securing a larger collection of fossils, his failure being due to the facts that our marches were necessarily rapid, the time being limited to sixty days, and that the country traversed was nearly barren of the objects of his search.

The attempt to reach the south fork of the Cheyenne from the camp near Harney's Peak, if successful, would probably have repaid him.

The computations of latitude and longitude were made by my assistant, Mr. W. H. Wood, the work of observing being shared between us, and I owe him thanks for valuable aid, well performed.

In locating the longitude of the various points in and near the Black Hills, I was disposed at first to accept the position of Bear Butte, as given on Raynolds's and Warren's map, as fixed. But finding that the surveys of the Northern Pacific Railroad moved Powder River about four miles west of Raynolds's longitude for it, and that my determination of Bear Butte was two miles west of Raynolds's, I concluded to adopt my own throughout, feeling quite confident of its correctness. The two chronometers did excellent service, as a comparison of rates previous to starting and after the return fully showed.

Very respectfully, your obedient servant,

WILLIAM LUDLOW,
Captain of Engineers, and Chief Engineer Department.

The ASSISTANT ADJUTANT-GENERAL,
Department of Dakota.

GEOLOGICAL REPORT.

BY N. H. WINCHELL, STATE GEOLOGIST OF MINNESOTA.

THE UNIVERSITY OF MINNESOTA,
Minneapolis, Minn., February 22, 1875.

SIR: During the expedition to the Black Hills of Dakota the past summer, under General G. A. Custer, all my geological and other notes were made in the form of a daily journal, dated and referred to the nearest camping places, or to some prominent object of topographical importance, in order that the localities spoken of could be accurately referred to by comparison with the general map, containing the tracing of our route and daily camping-places. In the present state of our knowledge of the geology of the region through which we passed, the observations I made will be of more value to science, if they are carefully recorded and preserved with little or no attempt at generalization. Then the work of future geologists will not be prejudiced by inferences that might not be well grounded, and my observations will go to augment the general knowledge of the country, and to assist future observers in intelligently deciding its geological character and age. Hence, in making this report, it is thought best to preserve something of a journalistic form, and to give facts in the order in which they were observed. My notes in Dakota begin with the crossing of the Red River of the North.

FROM THE RED RIVER OF THE NORTH TO FORT ABRAHAM LINCOLN.

June 24.—The Red River flats may be said to extend to at least the first beach-line, which is twenty-five miles, more or less, from Fargo. Within that distance there is no observable variation of level, but on passing that line, where the cut of the railroad shows gravel, the surface begins to have gentle undulations. These become more and more marked to fifty-two miles from Fargo, where we reach a divide, and the first curve in the railroad west of Fargo occurs. This divide is three or four miles east of the Cheyenne. In descending to that river stratified materials are seen in the railroad cuts underlying the drift, probably belonging to the Cretaceous. This observation was made in passing on the train, and I cannot be certain but these loose materials pertain to the Post-tertiary. There are no visible bowlders on the surface in the Red River flats, but they gradually appear west of the first beach. The Cheyenne Valley is about a mile wide, and deeply cut, not terraced. The country remains a rolling prairie to the Missouri River. The so-called "Coteau du Missouri" is, so far as can be observed at the crossing of the Northern Pacific Railroad, a misnomer. The whole country is rolling. There is, of course, some point of highest divide, but it is not very noticeable. The soil is very nearly everywhere a gravelly hardpan, (*i. e.* a stony and gravelly unstratified clay,) with large bowlders. In the valley of the James River, and also on approaching the Missouri, some loam is locally overspread. The alkali is seen in some marshes, and about some lake-shores. Sometimes half-desiccated alkaline surfaces, blackened by dirt, but shining as if moist, extend fifty or a hundred rods, or even more, from the real beach lakeward. About ten miles west of the James River the Northern Pacific Railroad Company have sunk a well for water, going down by shaft 100 feet and boring 205 feet farther, without getting any. The materials thrown out, both by the shaft and by the bore, consist of hardpan drift entirely, of the usual blue color, containing small pieces of lignite.

June 25.—At the "landing" at Bismarck I see a hundred boxes, each holding about a bushel, filled with hard lignite, being transported for use in that way. It is from this portion of Dakota, and comes from the Cretaceous. It appears like the better portion of that seen on the Cottonwood and Redwood Rivers, in Minnesota. It is cracking and crumbling in the air.

June 26.—At Fort A. Lincoln, near the water, may be seen the following downward section of the Cretaceous:

No. 1. Shale, thickness unknown.	
No. 2. Sandy shale	2 inches.
No. 3. Shale	4 feet.
No. 4. Impure lignite, about	6 feet.
No. 5. Shaly greenish clay, about	6 feet.

Near the top of the bluff, at the fort, is an exposure of sandstone by the roadside. The whole amounts to about 15 feet, but it is intersected both horizontally and sometimes obliquely by layers of varying thickness of argillo-siliceous limestone, which is gray and hard. These layers are lenticular and vanishing, but are sometimes 18 inches in thickness. The sand in which they are inclosed is loose, but contains washed shells, uncemented and not decomposed, but very frail. There is one turreted shell about 1¼ inches long and a bivalve resembling Unio, with fragments of others. There are no evident vegetable remains, but indistinct impressions that may be of fiber. Silicified wood is common in the drift, particularly among the small stones on the surface near the brow of river bluff.

FROM FORT ABRAHAM LINCOLN TO THE BELLE FOURCHE.

Camp, July 2.—Fourteen and three-fourths miles west of Fort A. Lincoln. The country passed over the first day after leaving Fort A. Lincoln has been a rolling prairie, and heavily drift-laden. The bluffs, however, sometimes show a squareness of outline near their summits that shows the presence of rock in outcrop, which can sometimes be seen at a distance with a field-glass. I take it to be the same sandstone as that seen in the bluff of the Missouri River near the fort.

Camp, July 3.—Fourteen miles from the camp of yesterday. The march during the day has been through a very broken country, in which the square and flat-topped buttes, which may be seen on either hand in the distance, show the continuation of a similar geological structure to that of yesterday. Yet just at camp, which is in a wide plain, below the general level of the country, those buttes have disappeared from view, bringing a change very noticeable over the face of the country. The hills and bluffs are smoother, lower, and more grassy, without bowlders. During much of the day we have traveled on high ground, a sort of divide between two large drainage valleys, one on the north and one on the south. This high land is closely underlain by the sandstone already mentioned, and is strewn with foreign bowlders. Just at camp this sandstone seems to have run out, and can only be seen in one or two distant buttes that stand isolated.

Camp, July 4.—On Dog Teeth Creek. This creek is a tributary of the North Fork of the Cannon Ball River. The country from our last camp has been undulating and rolling, but less so than during the march of yesterday. Have seen to-day but one small exposure of rock, that of sandstone, in a low mound. We are here in the midst of the Dog Teeth Buttes, according to "Goose," our Sioux guide, but none of them are visible from our camp.

Camp, July 5.—We have marched to-day about seventeen miles west from our last camp, and are now on a creek named by Goose, "Where the bear stays in winter." It is a flowing stream of clear water. There are here a few oaks, and good grass. The country passed through to-day has been perhaps the finest yet seen, much of it being level or nearly level prairie, with large grass. Occasional square-topped hills expose a rusty sandstone, the probable continuance of that already seen. At our camp, the bluffs of the creek are in this sandstone. Distributed at irregular intervals in it, is a fine-grained, hard, argillaceous limestone which occurs as nodules or lenticular beds, somewhat concretionary. They are usually not more than an inch in thickness, but sometimes are six inches. When broken, they are gray inside. When fallen down and long exposed to the weather, they become coated with hard hematitic iron, probably derived from the surface-water that flows over them. They have a deceptive appearance of clay iron-stone. They are as heavy as iron, and have a sharp and almost vitreous fracture. No fossils found.

Camp on the North Fork of the Cannon Ball.

July 6.—We have passed through a fine country to-day, with good grass, crossing two or three little streams. The aspect of the country is much the same as that of yesterday, but we are evidently passing over a different geological horizon. There are occasional buttes, but of less height than those mentioned. There is a yellowish, rusty sandstone, sometimes only in dislodged masses about their summits. These seem to be the running-out aspect of the sandstone which has been mentioned, a lower formation giving rise to the difference of surface features. At the river near our camp, the lower portion of this loose sandstone is seen in the upper portion of the bluffs, underlain by a thickness of at least 150 feet of bedded shale, or clay, as follows:

Descending section on the North Fork of the Cannon Ball River.

No. 1. Sandy clay or sandstone, friable and weathering rusty, with large shaly and calcareous concretions. This forms the general level of the country just here, but the surface rises a hundred or two hundred feet before reaching the level of the low buttes, several miles from our camp .... 30 feet.

No. 2. Shale, bedded, greenish, with similar concretions. I notice in these concretions, which show no concentric structure, an indication of their sedimentary origin. When broken with the bedding, there are, on the freshly broken surface, scattered, rusty, angular specks, showing some striation. Nothing else can be distinguished, owing to the fineness of the parts. No other evidences of fossils are visible either in this or in the last. Seen .... 150 feet.

The geological age of this rock is uncertain. There is here a total absence of fossils, and has been since leaving Fort A. Lincoln. Judging, however, from the topography and the continuance of certain features, there is no great change in the geological age of the underlying rock since leaving the fort. A series of sandstone-capped buttes has nearly or quite disappeared by receding from our route of travel, while the general surface has become smoother. Between the sandstone of those buttes and the rock of this section there is an unobserved interval of one or two hundred feet, embracing one small lignite bed, (15 inches,) and some light clay. Dr. Hayden has mapped this as Fort Union Tertiary,* but I am inclined to continue the Cretaceous as far west as this point, and to make the rock included in the foregoing section a lower portion of the Fox Hills group of Meek and Hayden with the upper part of the Fort Pierre.

Over the surface of the country, pertaining to the drift, are scattered fragments of beautifully silicified fossil wood, one of which, seen to-day, was two or three feet in diameter. It had the appearance of being a large stump. This silicified wood is associated in fragments near our camp with a gray quartzite, having the appearance of a highly siliceous limestone. This wood is also attached to such limestone. I have seen none of this limestone, perhaps more properly called a quartzite, in place, and cannot yet give its probable age. Near our camp the above sandstone (No. 1 of the last section) is washed off and a "bluff" deposit, perfectly comparable to that of the Missouri, lies on the shale, having a thickness of about 15 feet. Between the "bluff" and the shale is a layer of coarser drift made up of washed pieces wholly of local origin. The drift itself is much attenuated or wholly wanting.

Camp, July 7.—On the south fork of the Cannon Ball. This is called Cedar Creek by our Indian guide. Our camp is thirty-two miles from that of yesterday. Throughout the latter part of this day's march, and perhaps through the whole of it, the water we have passed is alkaline and the grass is short. The surface is always turfed, unless it be on the immediate rock exposures, which are not common. Double Buttes, which we passed to-day, so named by General Custer, are perhaps 250 feet in height. Their tops are of sandstone, and the sides, where bared of turf, were of a light, marly clay. I could find no fossils in them. The sandstone on their tops was about 25 feet thick. At another point, about eight miles before reaching camp, this same clay was seen exposed in a low bluff, with some light-colored sandstone beds, the whole dipping about 15° or 20° to the northeast. The water of a little stream running near, or standing near, as all the streams are very slow, was whitened almost like milk with leachings from this marl.

* See his geological map accompanying the final report on the United States Geological Survey of Nebraska.

There is no foreign drift, as I also noted yesterday, but there is a good thick soil and a heavy local drift. Often the surface is strewn with fragments of a very hard, gray, siliceous limestone, which has already been mentioned. This passes almost to a flint. Indeed there is very much silica in all the fragments from the local rocks. Silicified wood is also common, a fact which requires some cause for its distribution different from that assignable for the distribution of the usual foreign drift.

July 8.—Two miles west of camp. In a butte, sandstone in horizontal beds returns. This sandstone is characterized here by very large and harder masses, which are concretionary; and after the stone has all crumbled away these lie intact and cover the ground. The beds here are horizontal, and of the same material for 45 or 50 feet from the top and till the butte becomes turfed. It is, then, 100 feet above the level of the country on each side.

Rising out of the valley of the Cannon Ball, and looking across toward the north, we see a series of white spots on the opposite bluffs, made by the exposure of the marl or clay mentioned in yesterday's notes. These bluffs must be ten miles away; a fact that indicates the magnitude of the clay beds and their importance in the topographical structure of this portion of the Territory. In front of us is what Colonel Ludlow denominates White Clay Butte, a very prominent object, rising higher in the horizon than any other object in that quarter.

There is still no foreign drift, but the ground is stony with the siliceous limestone (or gray quartzite) already mentioned, and with beautiful pebbles and stones, including fossil wood, with many flinty pieces wholly of local origin. The origin of these flinty, gray, limestone fragments, so abundant, is still involved in uncertainty.

Overlying the above white clay is a sandstone. We rise on to the level of the top of this sandstone and travel on a plateau for several miles, when we reach Bois Caché Creek, so named by the early French explorers, from the fact that a little wood, mostly *Negundo*, grows on the side of a bluff, along the base of which runs the creek. The bluff protects this vegetation from the prairie-fires, on one side, and the creek on the other. Our camp is on the north side of this creek.

Camp, July 8.—On Bois Caché Creek, a branch of Grand River. The low bluff opposite our camp is composed, so far as can be seen, of sandstone, but whether above or below the white clay is unknown. It is considerably lower, topographically, than the sandstone seen in the buttes overlying the white clay. There is here an apparent, though not actual, dip southwest. About 40 feet can be seen, the rest being turfed. There are similar low buttes and mounds visible on either hand, their summits being irregular and not so flat as many others seen a few days back, and diversified with tumbling fragments and large loosened concretions.

Wolf Butte is a sharp conical butte, about five miles southwest from our last camp. Its very top is of light sandstone, the same as already mentioned, though it has not elsewhere appeared so white. The top is of bare rock, not more than 40 feet in length by 25 feet wide. Swallows in great numbers build in the overhanging angles, the sandstone below 25 or 30 feet weathering out faster than the top.

Eagle-Nest Hills are the bluffs along the south side of Grand River, plainly visible from Wolf Butte. White Clay Butte is in the fork formed by Grand River, with the creek we camped on last night. Lodge Butte is 20° south of west from Wolf Butte, and consists of a series of sharp teeth-like points.

Eagle-Nest Hills are rocky near their tops, and on a level with Wolf Butte. The top of these is flat, and spreads out in a plateau which is visibly two miles (more or less) in length east and west. The country from Wolf Butte, on all sides, presents a rough aspect, except toward the northwest. Low mounds rise on all sides, overstrewn with the problematical siliceous limestone fragments, with here and there a mound caused by the worn-down sandstone, large displaced fragments being on the top.

Bald Hill is about a mile and a half north of Grand River, and about four miles west of Wolf Butte. It is a singular, isolated butte, almost devoid of turf; nearly circular, and bowl-shaped. Its base is about 30 rods in diameter, and its top is about 40 feet across. Its strata dip slightly to the north, so as to show that it overlies entirely the sandstone of Wolf Butte, &c. I get the following section in descending order. No fossils anywhere.

Section in Bald Butte.

No. 1.	Light yellow marl, or argillaceous marl, with thin shingle of arenaceous, sometimes siliceous, limestone, irregularly imbedded, and ocher concretions; passing into the next, about	35 feet.
No. 2.	Black shale in thin laminations; carbonaceous, and having silenite crystals	5 feet.
No. 3.	Massive, hard shale, carbonaceous and black; less finely laminated than the last.	4 feet.
No. 4.	Hard, gritty clay, with fine gypsum crystals; bedded, weathering bluish	25 feet.
	Total	69 feet.

Although this dips slightly to the north and overlies the sandstone which overlies the white clay before mentioned, yet to the north, six or eight miles, a belt of light, glittering exposures in the bluffs indicates the same light-colored clay. Bald Hill itself would be denominated white at a distance, as contrasted with surrounding objects. Toward the south, however, nothing but irregular knobs and buttes of broken-down sandstone can be seen.

About a mile before reaching our camp on Grand River, in going down to the bottoms, I take the following section. This is near the level of the bottoms:

Descending section on Grand River.

No. 1.	Sandy marl, (about)	20 feet.
No. 2.	Lignite and lignitic shale	6 feet.
No. 3.	White, massive sand	15 feet.

The buttes and bluffs between here and Bald Butte are less rocky and much more turfed. This is probably due to the advent of sandy clays and sands.

Camp, July 9.—On a wide bottom on the north side of the Grand River. This wide bottom extends up and down the river a great distance. Since passing Bald Butte we have not seen much rock, a few exposures along the banks of the river like that last mentioned being the only ones. The hills and buttes are all rounded off and turfed over even to their tops.

July 10.—The same features of country continue in passing up the valley of Grand River for nine miles, where we cross to the south side. At the place of crossing, in ascending the low bluff on the south side, I meet an exposure of fine white sand, the same as at the bottom of the section near last night's camp. The whole bluff seems to be of this sandstone, but almost completely turfed over on account of the friable nature of the rock. There are still some portions that are more enduring, having a thin stratification. These fall down with the weathering out of the friable parts, and lie on the surface in huge rusty lumps.

Camp, July 10.—On the north side of Grand River. We are about twenty-four miles above the camp of last night. The river is muddy, like the Missouri, and has considerable current. The country through which we have passed to-day has been the same as that described at our last camp. About half a mile below our present camp I took the following section:

Section on Grand River.

No. 1.	Light-brown bedded clay, with argillo-calcareous concretions	30 feet.
No. 2.	Lignite	3 feet.
No. 3.	Impure lignite	2 feet.
No. 4.	Sandstone, white, massive, seen	4 feet.
	Total	39 feet.

The lignite included in the foregoing section was also seen exposed in a similar way near the water of Grand River, about two miles below our camp, at our place of recrossing.

Leaving our camp of July 10, we travel over the same kind of country for about eleven miles, no rock being seen, except the gray siliceous limestone pieces, that are strewn like bowlders over the surface. In the distance ahead of us can be seen a cluster of conical hills that look like upheaved strata, but on reaching them we found no rock exposures. Everything is smoothly turfed over, except where the siliceous limestone fragments are too large and too numerous. Yet, before getting entirely past them, I see several burnt, red spots, which present much the appearance of local disturbances of the strata, with accompanying metamorphism. Scoria-like masses, varying in texture and color from red to dark-brown and almost black, are strewn over the little knolls. On searching further, however, I saw that near some of these burnt mounds in the ravines a white, massive sandstone lay undisturbed, and it became necessary to account for this fusion in some other way. That I was enabled to do, on discovering that just above that massive sandstone is a bed of 6 feet of lignite. In weathering down, this lignite has taken fire by some means, and, when in isolated mounds admitting plenty of air on all sides, has burned with heat enough to bake the adjoining strata so as to make the appearance of occasional brick-yards, every piece being of some shade of red.

Passing on farther southwest, this lignite can again be seen in several ravines, and especially about a mile and a half before reaching camp. It is in all cases observed underlain by a massive white sandstone. This lignite seems to have above it a thickness of fine sandy clay, which cannot be well determined, owing to its being generally weathered away. Over that is a rusty sandstone which, at our camp, holds Ludlow's Cave and forms extensive castellated bluffs, which are wrought by the elements into very fantastic forms. The top of this sandstone is separated from the top of the lignite by an interval of 175 feet, measured at our camp by barometer and by Locke's level.

Camp at Ludlow's Cave, July 11.—Rising another elevation back of the brow of the sandstone bluff near our camp, which holds Ludlow's Cave, I find a solution for the problem of the scattered siliceous limestone fragments. Here, about 80 feet higher than the measurement already given to the brow of the sandstone of Ludlow's Cave, is a gray siliceous, very hard limestone in place. It is only a foot or two in thickness, and is very rough on the surface, which it forms, over an area of about a hundred or more feet square. The full section at this place, and including the observations for two or three days, may be summarized as below, in descending order:

Section at Ludlow's Cave.

No. 1. A descent of 10 or 15 feet; rock not seen	10–15 feet.
No. 2. Siliceous limestone, mostly gray and very hard, but sometimes porous and of a lighter color; very rough; containing silicified wood and impressions apparently of bones. This rock, as seen in fragments, is mostly purely silica, and might be styled a quartzite	1–2 feet.
No. 3. Whitish, sandy marl	50–60 feet.
No. 4. Reddish sandstone, with many irony concretions	40 feet.
No. 5. Sandstone of Ludlow's Cave, rusty and castellated, about	40 feet.
No. 6. More argillaceous and calcareous sand, white	15 feet.
No. 7. Bedded blue clay, seen at a distance, like that in the base of Bald Butte	35 feet.
No. 8. Interval unseen to the lignite, (No. 9)	85 feet.
No. 9. Lignite	5–6 feet.
No. 10. Massive white sandstone	
No. 11. Top of Bald Butte	
No. 12. Light-yellowish, argillaceous marl, with ocher concretions, about	35 feet.
No. 13. Carbonaceous shale, with selenite	5 feet.
No. 14. Carbonaceous massive shale	4 feet.
No. 15. Hard, gritty clay, weathering bluish	25 feet.
No. 16. Sandstone and sand of Wolf Butte	
No. 17. White clay? (seen only at a distance)	

From the bluffs at Ludlow's Cave, where there are a few scattered Norway pines, we get the first views of the Black Hills and of Slave Butte. We can also discern what our guide names "the rock with a hole in it," and the bluffs beyond the Little Missouri.

Camp, July 12.—In the midst of hills and buttes. After a wearisome search for a route through these hills passable for the train, we have camped within seven miles of our last camping-place, though the odometer records a distance traveled of eleven miles. The country is a series of hills and ravines. The geological section is the same as that last given. The sand-rock affords very frequent exposures. Notwithstanding a vigilant search for fossils, none have been seen to-day. The bed of lignite in outcrop in front of our camp last night is seen to-night in outcrop just back of our camp. These bluffs, in weathering down, pass through a great variety of forms, and give a great deal of roughness to the landscape, while affording a geological interest I have not before observed.

July 13.—Immediately on leaving the camp we pass near several sharp buttes that show the effects of burnt-out lignite. The section of one, hastily taken, is as follows:

No. 1. Sandstone, reddish; one butte has been semi-fused, near the top	15 feet.
No. 2. Sandy, laminated shale	10 feet.
No. 3. Conglomerate, as if from fusion, showing cinders, ashes, and sulphur	local.
No. 4. Black shale or clay	3 feet.
No. 5. Sandstone, local; included in—	
No. 6. Sandy shale	40 feet.
No. 7. Lignite	6–8 feet.
No. 8. Sand, or sandy clay, seen	10 feet.
No. 9. Turfed	80–100 feet.
Total	164–186 feet.

Immediately on leaving these buttes, we come down on to the formation underlying, which proves to be a heavy layer of blue clay, without much variation in composition or aspect, at least within the first 30 feet. This is both geologically and topographically lower, and even lower than the lignite mentioned as occurring at our last two camping places; though the first below the lignite in some places is a sand or a sandy clay for the first eight or ten feet.

We travel (July 13th) across a wide, undulating plain, underlain by various strata of the above, alternating and varying horizontally with sandy clay and sand. The last is often massive. Along our right, a few miles north, occasional buttes rise, showing the composition and external features of those last described, and from which sections have been taken. This indicates that the level of the plain does not sink very much into the clayey formation. On our left, however, no such buttes are seen. In the distance, perhaps twenty miles ahead of us, can be seen a belt of white bluffs, forming a continuous square shoulder, having at this distance a different aspect from the shoulders and table-lands formed by the sandstone. The plain over which we are traveling shows no siliceous limestone fragments. In the banks of the ravines which we cross are seen occasional irony concretions, but no fossils.

Camp, July 13.—There has been no noteworthy change in the country since leaving the sharp buttes near camp this morning from that described in the last note. This plain is largely devoted to sage-brush and cactus. The latter is a low, spreading form, or that has flat branches two or three inches across, with frequent joints and changes of angle.

July 14.—At Castle Butte, ten miles from camp, we find the first vertebrate fossils. They were discovered by Mr. G. B. Grinnell. They are in the northeast side of the butte, about 15 feet above the base, which is 20 feet below the general level. The butte itself is cut into very fantastic shapes, the general form resembling an immense castle, from which we gave it the name. One spindling spire rises from the southwest side nearly as high as the body of the butte, and is capped with a thin piece of rusty sandstone. The section of the butte is about as follows:

Section of Castle Butte.

No. 1. Sand; friable, but with perpendicular walls, that rise on all sides, making it impossible to reach the top. This contains courses of obliquely-bedded rusty sandstone, and iron-covered, calcareo-argillaceous concretions, the latter strewing the surface below with iron balls, about	50 feet.
No. 2. Rusty sandstone in one course of oblique beds	2–3 feet.

No. 3. Plastic clay, yet bedded, of a dark color, containing iron-ball concretions and occasional wood-impressions and charred woody fiber. This also contains veins and irregular deposits of a curious bone-like substance, which much resembles the decomposing ivory of Mastodon tusks, often found in the drift. The grain of these deposits is always nearly upright. Spots on the otherwise uniform bluish surface of a lighter color indicate them, and the fiber, or that which resembles fiber, stands an inch or two above the floor of the terrace on which they occur. They show no cellular structure. They are solid and heavy, but crumble and decompose, or are washed away with the rains. They are probably of crystalline origin.* This clay also contains the vertebrate remains seen by Mr. Grinnell, seen about............ 110 feet.

Total.. 163 feet.

Over the clay of No. 3, above, we have traveled to-day and yesterday, crossing a dusty, cactus-covered, undulating plain. No. 1, above, is supposed to be that which occurs below the lignite of the general section at Ludlow's Cave.

Camp, July 14.—Fourteen miles from the camp of last night. In Prospect Valley. We have continued to march to-day over the undulating plain caused by the sands and clays below the lignite bed, mentioned in yesterday's notes, till near the close of the march, when we came among the clay buttes, which have been visible in the distance ahead for a day or two. This is a remarkable range of buttes and conical and castellated hills, entirely devoid of vegetation, that runs north and south, in common with the valleys of this region. They constitute a region of Bad Lands. It is in these buttes that the vertebrate bones were found to-day. We had some difficulty in finding an ascent of this range of hills fit for the train. When once on the top, we find that instead of descending again we are on an undulating table-land, which is beautifully grassed hard and easy for the train. Traveling on this plain about a mile, we come to a most pleasant grassy valley, eight or ten miles wide, which opens before us, gently descending from the plain, and bounded on the opposite side by a range of low hills and buttes. There seems to be also an easy ascent from this valley on to the hills on the other side. It extends as far to the south as we can see, and to the north it is tributary to the Little Missouri. The hills on the other side of the Little Missouri are plainly seen in the distance toward the northwest. Through the middle of this valley runs a little stream of water, which is outlined by a few bushes and small trees. This valley General G. A. Custer appropriately named Prospect Valley. Here we have wood, water, and grass, all abundant and convenient. This valley is in the sand overlying the clay of Castle Butte, and the contrast between it and the plain, which is on the underlying clay, is very noticeable. We have seen, to-day, none of the siliceous limestone fragments, nor any pebbles or stones. There is no foreign drift here. The surface consists entirely of the weathered-down detritus from the sands and clays of the rocks, and the soil varies with every change in the formation. The change of soil is accompanied with a corresponding change in the common vegetation. There can be no better exemplification of the dependence of the agricultural character of a region on its geological.

The disappearance of the siliceous limestone fragments on the surface is a fact worthy of attention. They were seen for several days strewn over the ground, and particularly on the summit of rounded hills. When we reached the buttes and hills of Ludlow's Cave, they were especially abundant, and on the tops of those buttes they were associated with more porous, calcareous pieces, as well as with smaller and lighter-colored, more numerous fragments. I am satisfied that the place of origin of these pieces is very near the summit-level of this sand. I even found this limestone in place there, as described in notes on that place. We descended abruptly down on to the clay lying at the base of these buttes, and in coming west, and from that time to this, we have seen no more of those fragments. Their occurrence toward the east is an evidence of the former extension of the rock of that age intact, over the whole country, although the beds are now almost entirely demolished and wanting, the level of the country being one or two hundred feet lower than these. If the clay over which we passed to-day and yesterday lies really below the sandstone of

*This mineral is heavy spar, sulphate of baryta.

Ludlow's Cave, and so below that bed of siliceous limestone, why have not those fragments also been seen on this side of the place where the limestone-bed was seen *in situ?* There was certainly every appearance of a similar breaking down of the overlying sandstone, a fact which was noted at the time, and an occasional sandstone-capped butte on our right confirmed the opinion that we were traveling on a lower geological horizon. There are three ways in which to account for the absence of these fragments:

1st. The superposition of the beds that I have given may be incorrect, and the clay that forms the undulating alkaline plain may really lie above the sandstone of the buttes, conformably, although there is also a clay that I could not distinguish from this, found in the bases of those buttes, and although in descending from those buttes toward the west, we came down on to that clay and on to the alkaline plain. This supposition I regard very improbable.

2d. This clay may belong to a later deposit than the rock of those buttes, being Tertiary, while those buttes may be Cretaceous, and so may lie unconformably on the older rocks; *i. e.* those buttes may have formed a shore-line, or a lot of islands in the Tertiary sea, and all the broken-off pieces of the siliceous limestone on the west would thus have been buried in the Tertiary sediments, as far west as the Cretaceous layers ever extended. This clay, in that case, is not the same as that seen near the bottom of the buttes and hills at Ludlow's Cave. This supposition is the more probable, and it seems to me will satisfactorily account for the disappearance of the siliceous limestone fragments to the west of the bluffs at Ludlow's Cave, but it does violence to the observed composition of those bluffs and the succession of parts in passing from them toward the west. No observation could be more satisfactory than that of the infraposition of this great clay formation below that sandstone.

3d. The layers of the bluffs at Ludlow's Cave may never have extended further west along our line of march than they now do, and hence the overlying stratum supposed to have been the origin of these fragments could not have been stretched over this lower plain, and could not have distributed them there. In that case we are descending into the Cretaceous rocks as we go west, instead of ascending upon the Tertiary. This is in harmony with my observations along our route, though on our right a line of low buttes was supposed to indicate the extension of the sandstone, also as far west as our present camp.

Doctor Hayden extends the Tertiary as far east in this latitude as nearly to the Missouri River, as shown by his general map accompanying his final report on the geology of Nebraska. Again, a few miles south of my route, he has indicated the Cheyenne Valley as lying in a belt of Cretaceous, extending from its headwaters to the Missouri. I have not yet seen any reason to limit the Cretaceous along this route to any narrower area than required by the last supposition.

July 15.—Remained in camp, preparing dispatches to send by Indian couriers to Fort A. Lincoln.

July 16.—Leaving camp, the train takes a northwest direction round a point of hills and range of bluffs, facing our camp toward the east, and so enters the immediate valley of the Little Missouri, while an exploring and reconnoitering party, under Colonel Ludlow, passes, with one company of cavalry, over the ridge, calculating to intercept the command on the opposite side, after they turn south. These hills, formed of horizontal strata, have scattering Norway pines, many of which are dead from fire and tempest. They are mostly confined to the gullies and ravines. The tops of these hills are in an arenaceous, chalky limestone of a white color, which disintregrates readily, but few fragments being found on the surface below. It might, perhaps, be properly styled an arenaceous marl, indurated. Sometimes it is rather firm, and of a gray color, but always arenaceous. Nothing but the upper 15 feet can be seen, the slopes being turfed. This marl overlies the clay of Castle Butte, as well as the sand that forms its top. Above the foregoing, which rises, perhaps, 200 feet above the valley which we have crossed, and in which was our last camp, rises a bench or terrace about 50 feet higher, the top of which is similarly composed, and the slope turfed. These hills are known as Short-Pine Hills. The valley of the Little Missouri can be seen toward the west, the meandering of the river being marked by an interrupted line of trees and shrubs.

Traveling three or four miles southeast on this plateau-ridge, we find more Norway pine than before. It grows on the brows of the bluffs and in the ravines. We finally reach a place where the plateau descends or breaks off perpendicularly toward the south, forming bald escarpments of rock, showing buttes and bluffs with ribbed sides, wrought in the marl and sandy limestone. Just here the uppermost member seen consists of harsh, arenaceous limestone, that perhaps ought to be styled a sandstone with lime-cement. This is all white and overlies a massive sandstone that appears to be that forming the top of Castle Butte. It is about 200 feet.

An immense valley lies here before us, extending toward the southeast, south, and west, the Black Hills being visible in a long range before us, including Bear Butte, Slave Butte, Crow Butte, Deer's Ears Butte, Blue Earth Butte, Topknot Buttes, toward the southeast, and Lodge Buttes in the Black Hills.

In returning to the train we descend from this plateau to the valley on the west side, and pass northward along the foot of the ridge to its northern extremity, where we encounter the Little Missouri River. Up this valley the train having passed, we follow it toward the southwest, and overtake it after traveling about ten miles farther.

Referring again to this plateau-ridge, known as Short-Pine Hills, we found it about eight miles long and from three-fourths of a mile to perhaps two miles wide. It is nearly flat on the top, and covered with good grass. There are in it a few secluded and densely wooded ravines, but generally the pine is very thin. The trees are small or short. There is nothing that will ever be valuable for pine lumber. Geologically, we found the composition of the ridge to be as follows:

Descending section in Short Pine Hills.

No. 1. White arenaceous marl, indurated, varying from a harsh arenaceous limestone to a sandstone with limy cement, cracking into small conchoidal blocks, that soon crumble into soil in the air; contains but little iron, but has a few argillo-calcareous concretions, about	200 feet.
No. 2. Massive, rusty sand, weathering into pinnacles and isolated peaks. This is the same as that seen on the top of Castle Butte	50–75 feet.
No. 3. Blue clay, locally varying to sand, seen	110 feet.
Total height	360–385 feet.

There are several interesting features connected with this clay, No. 3, above. 1st. It contains at different horizons what appear like concretions of sand. They are laminated, and the laminæ are concentric, though the sandy masses are usually somewhat elongated. The sand on the outside of these masses is loose and friable, but the interior is firm, and in most cases the inside of the mass is very hard, appearing darker-colored and close-grained, passing into an argillaceous limestone. These masses or balls were not observed to contain any fossils. They are entirely isolated in some cases, closely impacted in the clay, but usually lie in an interrupted course, having a parallelism with the stratification of the clay. They are apt to be coated with iron or an argillaceous iron-ore. 2d. A substance occurs here in a regular layer that was described as occurring in irregular patches in the clay of the Castle Butte, and ascertained to be heavy spar or sulphate of baryta. It has a fibrous grain or lamination, somewhat radiated, and in some places reminding one of the character of cone-in-cone, though never so perfect. This soon disintegrates in the air, and rolls down the bluff in angular pieces of an inch or two in diameter. It pertains specially to a certain horizon about 75 or 100 feet below the top of the clay, and is sometimes associated with a little calcite. 3d. Iron: This occurs as coatings to fine-grained, hard concretions, of a dark color, which have no other concentric arrangement. The interior of these lumps, which are generally less than six inches in diameter, is apparently an argillo-siliceous limestone. There is not enough of this iron here to make it economically valuable, 4th. In this clay I found two vertebræ of what appears to be *Hadrosaurus*, Leidy, and a variety of turtle-bones. The vertebræ are about five inches in diameter, and are preserved. The turtle-remains were too fragile and incomplete to be of much value. I also found the ball of a large ball-and-socket joint, its assignment being uncertain, and remains of wood. There is a gentle dip of these beds toward the south, so that the overlying sandy marl, of a white color, which has a great thickness at the southern end of the ridge of Short-Pine Hills, is entirely denuded at the northern extremity of that ridge, the underlying clay and sand being bared of vegetation and wrought into a series of "bad-land" buttes. The rest of the day we traveled over a plain on this clay toward the south and southeast, the train having made thirty-one miles.

Camp, July 16.—In view of the Black Hills; on high ground; among the cactus; poor grass, no water; a hard day's work.

Camp, July 17.—We have come in a nearly south direction about nineteen miles, over an undulating plain, where grassy tracts have alternated sparingly with Artemisia and Cactus wastes; water scant, but generally pretty good to-day. The surface has been hard and smooth till reaching our camping-place, where we come to a very different tract of country; the whole prospect before us, as far as visible toward the Black Hills, being roughened by a net-work of ravines and alternating clay hills. The latter are usually bare, their lower slopes being very scantily clothed with grass, the eroded and washed sides being entirely bare. These little eminences are of all heights up to 25 or 50 feet, the ravines being dry. After the day's march it was not thought best to enter upon this tract, although we set out for the Belle Fourche this morning, as the air is dry and hot, and there is little appearance of water ahead.

About three miles out of camp to-day I picked up a lot of black, limy concretions, filled with fossils, such as the following, identified by Mr. Grinnell: *Aturia biangulata*, M. & H.; *Nucula planimarginata*, M. & H.; *Pteria linguiformis*, Ev. & Shu.; *Vanikoro ambigua*, M. & H.; *Scaphites larvæformis*, M. & H. (?); *Actæon concinnus*, M. & H.; *Amauropsis paludinæformis*, M. & H.; *Baculites ovatus*, Say, *Terebratula*, (Sp.?) These concretions show no concentric lamination. They are hard, but part readily by a blow from the hammer along certain angular predetermined weather-cracks. Although these lay on the surface, they have not been far transported, there being no drift in this region, and must have originally pertained to some of the denuded overlying strata, probably to No. 3 of the section taken at Short-Pine Hills.

Slave Butte is flat-topped, like nearly all others, but Crow Butte and the little one near it on the east are irregular and dark colored, appearing at this distance as if eruptive.

To my surprise I saw to-day on the march a number of siliceous limestone fragments, exactly like those seen so numerously before reaching Ludlow's Cave. They lay on the open plain, though on a slight eminence above the general level. There were also a very few on the sloping ascent from the east in going up Short-Pine Hills. These are the only points at which they have been seen since leaving Ludlow's Cave Buttes, a distance of about sixty miles. East of that point they are strewn generally over the whole country. They may occur here by reason of a demolished outlier of the sandstone of Ludlow's Cave, the eminence on which they lie being the ruins of that outlier, nothing else pertaining to it being so indestructible.

Camp, July 18.—On the Belle Fourche. Captain Reynold's trail passes near our camp, made fifteen years ago. He camped a few miles below this point.

Immediately on leaving camp this morning we entered on a series of "bad-lands," consisting, as already described in yesterday's notes, of short ravines and small weathered-down mounds. Toward the Black Hills these change to larger and longer mounds, and finally to ridges, some of which, rising about 50 or 100 feet, are scantily clothed with Norway pine. The intervening valleys are sometimes beautifully turfed. These alternating changes in the prospect are very cheering and agreeable. I also noticed, on setting out from camp this morning, that the shale or clay over which we were traveling was very much darker colored and in places somewhat fissile, becoming a shaly slate. This change continued to become more marked to our present camp. Just before reaching the Belle Fourche we come on two or three more prominent ridges, bearing pine and some scrub-oak, which, with the intervening eroded valleys, are perhaps 250 feet high. In these ridges I see the rock is slaty and that it dips perceptibly away from the Black Hills. There has been a great deal of iron on the surface, throughout the whole of the march to-day, some of it being in large lumps. I have seen nothing, however, but clay-ironstone of a gray color, coated with a peroxide.

The bluffs back of our camp, which is on the northeast side of the Belle Fourche, are 350 feet in height, those on the opposite side being much less abrupt and less high. This altitude is got by aneroid in a slow rain. This thickness of strata consists almost entirely of grayish and blackish, fissile, slaty shale, without fossils, but contains two or three beds of marl, or what appears like marl, each three to five feet thick. These beds of marl, in their outcrop, are very conspicuous in contrast with the shale, which, on being wet, is nearly black. Some of this marl is of a light ochery color, and when powdered is free or nearly free from grit. By these light belts I can see a few miles below our camp, in hills farther east, that the dip is in the opposite direction in some places, such belts crossing the bare sides of the hills on the west, though I am not sure but this is rather apparent than real. The actual dip may be but little changed. There are, a few miles farther south, a few higher hills, evidently composed of about the same strata, that may have modified the local dip at this place, changing it a little from the normal direction.

I presume the beginning of this slate to mark our point of entrance upon the Fort Benton, or rather upon the metamorphosed condition of the Fort Benton. Whether that member of the Cretaceous extends farther east and north I am unable to say, but am disposed from the evidence as I have observed it to believe it does. At our last camp there was a very marked transition to this dark, slaty shale, the rock that immediately overlies it being a thin stratum of about 15 feet of rusty sandstone which extends toward the southwest no farther than that camp. The strike of that stone there followed the outline of a little ridge overlooking a wide prospect, toward the southwest, across which the strong westerly winds swept clouds of dust and sand. From that point to this we have traveled over the Cretaceous, probably some of its lower strata. These beds correspond in lithological characters very closely with the Fort Benton group of Messrs. Meek and Hayden. There is evidence here, however, of some change by metamorphism, occurring probably at the time of upheaval.

July 19.—Remained in camp. It rained all day.

ENTRANCE INTO THE BLACK HILLS—FROM THE BELLE FOURCHE TO HEENG-YAKA-GA PEAK.

Camp, July 20.—We are in the midst of sandstone hills, the layers of which dip north at an angle of about 8°. We struck this sandstone formation about eight miles from camp this morning, having traveled till then, after crossing the Belle Fourche, on the overlying blackish, blue, and gray fissile shale mentioned in the notes at the Belle Fourche. We have traveled about eighteen miles, but probably are not that distance from our last camp.

To the northwest of our camp rises one of the highest of these hills, distant about three-fourths of a mile. This seems to be made up of sandstone, at least all that can be seen is sandstone, of a light color, weathering rusty, pinkish, and reddish. Within it is not red. No fossils seen. Some very thin layers are of an arenaceous marl, but the mass of the whole is quartzose sandstone, showing a thickness of several hundred feet. It sometimes holds angular fragments of soft shale. It has some clay-ironstone and other irony concretions. There is a talus of perhaps 100 feet that cannot be seen. The whole height of this hill is 500 feet, measured by aneroid. Bear Butte, toward the south, can be seen from this bluff. Among these hills are a few Norway pines and gnarled burr-oaks.

July 21.—Immediately on leaving camp this morning, I discovered a deeper red color in broken spots in the sandstone of some of the little mounds and in the ravines, indicating the approach of what had been denominated the *Red Beds*, supposed to be of the age of the Jurassic. In that case the sandstone measured near our last camp would belong to the Dakota group of Cretaceous.

A little farther on I see exposures of red marl and sandstone to the extent of about 40 feet, the whole dipping east at the usual angle, which is not more than 8° or 10°, yet the height of the little mounds which here take the place of the flat-topped sandstone bluffs, shows that the formation must be considerably thicker and largely composed of more friable and probably marly rock. The rock immediately underlying this red sandstone here is a bed of white sandstone having a thickness of at least 3 feet. Large masses of the overlying light-colored sandstone lie on the flanks and bases of these red mounds, tumbled down from their summits with age.

Casts of the interior of a belemnite are numerously strewn over the natural, somewhat turfed surface, along a belt about 10 feet thick, just below the tops of these little hills. This is taken for the *Belemnites densus*, M. and H., characteristic of the Jurassic, though it seems to occur here above the supposed base of the Cretaceous. These casts are composed of calcite, of a gray or ashy-gray color, having a radiated, fibrous crystallization.*

At a nice little creek, about ten miles from camp, flowing easterly, red sections are exposed,

*See the Smithsonian Contributions to Knowledge, No. 172. Paleontology of the Upper Missouri, by Meek and Hayden.

both in the creek banks and in the hills to the west, the dip being west. I obtain here, by uniting both, the following downward section:

Section in the Redwater Valley.

No. 1. White sandstone, massive; firm, but tumbling down in large blocks by the disintegration of the underlying shale; seen	18 feet.
No. 2. Green shale, laminated, fine, containing crystals of gypsum, about	45 feet.
No. 3. Fossiliferous conglomerate. This has quartz pebbles, pieces of greenish shale, and fragments of bivalve fossils, (*Camptonectes bellistriata*, Meek,) and fragments of *Gryphæa*	2 feet.
No. 4. Purple shale; laminated, fine, toward the top arenaceous	10 feet.
No. 5. Snowy gypsum	4–6 feet.
No. 6. Red, massive, or indistinctly bedded, arenaceous marl, weathering into a slope; seen about	75 feet.
Total exposure	156 feet.

No. 6, above, holds a few thin layers or veins of gypsum. This section probably covers the line of superposition of the Cretaceous upon the Jurassic. This section occurs just after crossing the first creek, after leaving camp, and within the valley of the Red water.

In camp, July 21.—We are in a valley made by the excavation of the soft Jurassic beds, with a range of bare, red bluffs toward the north—indeed, in nearly all directions about us. On the west, however, a higher range, capped with the Cretaceous, can be seen over their tops, the sandstones at the base of the Cretaceous forming an important geological cause for prominent topographical features. In some places the Jurassic is broken away entirely to the Cretaceous hills toward the west.

A beautiful spring of hard water, with a temperature of 45° Fahrenheit, is situated within the camp. It is so copious that it furnishes water for nearly one thousand men, with their horses, and six hundred and fifty mules. The water, however, has a cathartic effect on those who drink freely. It rises from below a layer of white gypsum, about a foot in thickness.

Fig. 1.

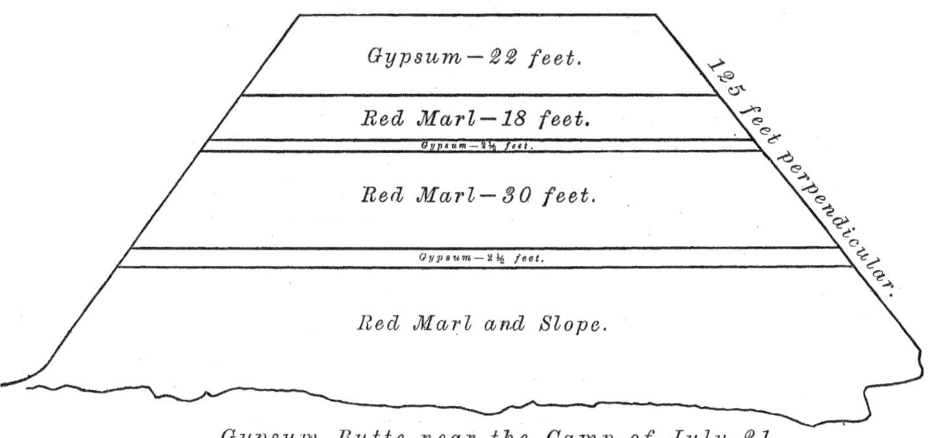

Gypsum Butte near the Camp of July 21.

In this little valley are slight evidences of a foreign drift. There are pebbles of a quartzite and of a gray feldspathic rock, as well as dioritic, in the bed of an arroya just south of our camp.

On the surface of the valley in which we are camped, sometimes half a mile from the range of sandstone bluffs formed by the Lower Cretaceous, are seen very large quartzite bowlders. These can be referred without much hesitation to the sandstone of that range, as they show sometimes a gradation of characters to the characters of that formation. These large masses show several interesting features, due, probably, to subaërial causes. 1st. They are much harder and sometimes a little redder than the sandstone from which they were derived. They do not disintegrate by crumbling, as that sandstone sometimes does, but by parting into blocks. 2d. They are metamorphic, changed to a vitreous quartzite, in which the arenaceous composition is greatly obscured, if not entirely lost. 3d. Their upper surfaces are often very smooth, as if polished. There seems to have been an epoch between the Dakota Group of the Cretaceous and the Drift, when silicification of surface-lying fragments was one of the effects of atmospheric agents.

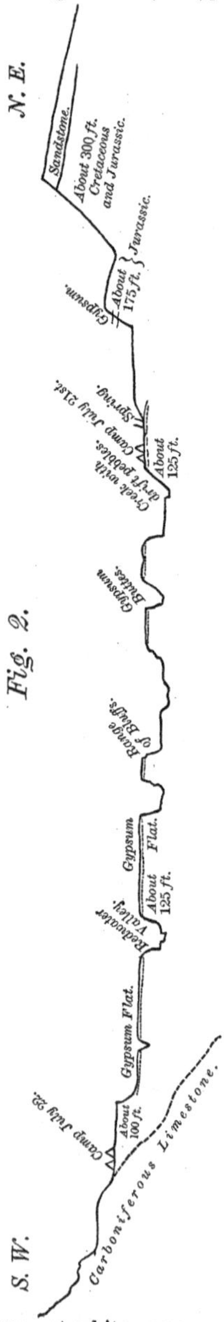

July 22.—On leaving camp, toward the south, we enter a vast gypsiferous region. I had noticed a whiteness of the surface and a white rock capping the buttes and hills in the direction we were to travel before setting out from camp, and even yesterday before camping, and had presupposed a change in the formation, some lower beds, perhaps, rising to the surface; but had afterward surmised this peculiar color might be the effect of gypsum, yet had not by far estimated the amount of actual crystalline gypsum to be what it is. It dissolves easily and surcharges the water that falls as rain on the surface, and is afterward redeposited as an efflorescence, especially on bare rock or marl surfaces. Here are a number of beds, the thickest of which forms a capping to a range of buttes and bluffs running east and west, and can be seen two or three miles. This lies below the gypsum beds I have already mentioned, but forms the floor of the flat on which we camped yesterday, and hardens the water of the spring at that place.

A butte which lies just south of our last camp, about a mile distant, affords the first good opportunity to take a section of these gypsiferous beds. This is but one of a number that lie on either hand. It rises boldly and pyramidally above the flat in which it stands, and, with its white cap and its narrower white belts, constitutes at once a remarkable illustration of the effect of atmospheric agents in demolishing these Red-Beds and exposing the contained mineral to the cupidity of man, and of the impunity with which nature displays her treasures when none but the shiftless Indian beholds them.

The level of the top of this butte forms the level of the country after ascending the range of hills about three-fourths of a mile further south. Figure 1 gives the section of this butte and shows the accessibility of the gypsum, which is purely crystalline and white.

Figure 2 is a profile of the march of July 22 and a portion of that of July 21, intended to show the manner of occurrence of the gypsum in the Red-Beds.

Camp, July 22.—We are camped four or four and a half miles east, 5° north, from *Heéng-ya Ka-gá*,* and on a ravine, with water, a short distance below where Lieutenant Warren camped. Although Jurassic hills surround us and hide our view, except the top of Heéng-ya Ka-gá, yet the Carboniferous limestone, which immediately underlies the Red-Beds, forms the floor of the plain on which we are situated, and is exposed in the bed of the creek half a mile above our camp.

In our march to-day we have passed over millions of tons of the purest white gypsum, which occurs in the tops of the Jurassic bluffs. This remarkable gypsiferous horizon is about 60 feet above the Carboniferous limestone, as seen near the end of to-day's march, but near the camp of yesterday it lay over 100 feet above it. The Triassic, (or Jurassic,) lying

Fig. 2. *Profile of the March of July 22, showing the surface Erosion in the Gypsiferous Red Beds, (Jurassic.)*

N. E. — Sandstone. — About 300 ft. Cretaceous and Jurassic. — About 175 ft. } Jurassic. — Gypsum. — Camp July 21st. — Spring. — Creek with drift pebbles. — About 125 ft. — Gypsum Buttes. — Range of Bluffs. — Gypsum Flat. — About 125 ft. — Redwater Valley. — Gypsum Flat. — About 100 ft. — Camp July 22. — Carboniferous Limestone. — S. W.

---

* The name "Inyan Kara," given to this mountain by Warren and Raynolds, is a corruption of the Indian word given above, which I carefully obtained from our guide, Cold Hand.

unconformably on the Carboniferous, causes a great variation of the relative position of the horizon of the gypsum in regard to the highly-tilted beds of the Carboniferous.

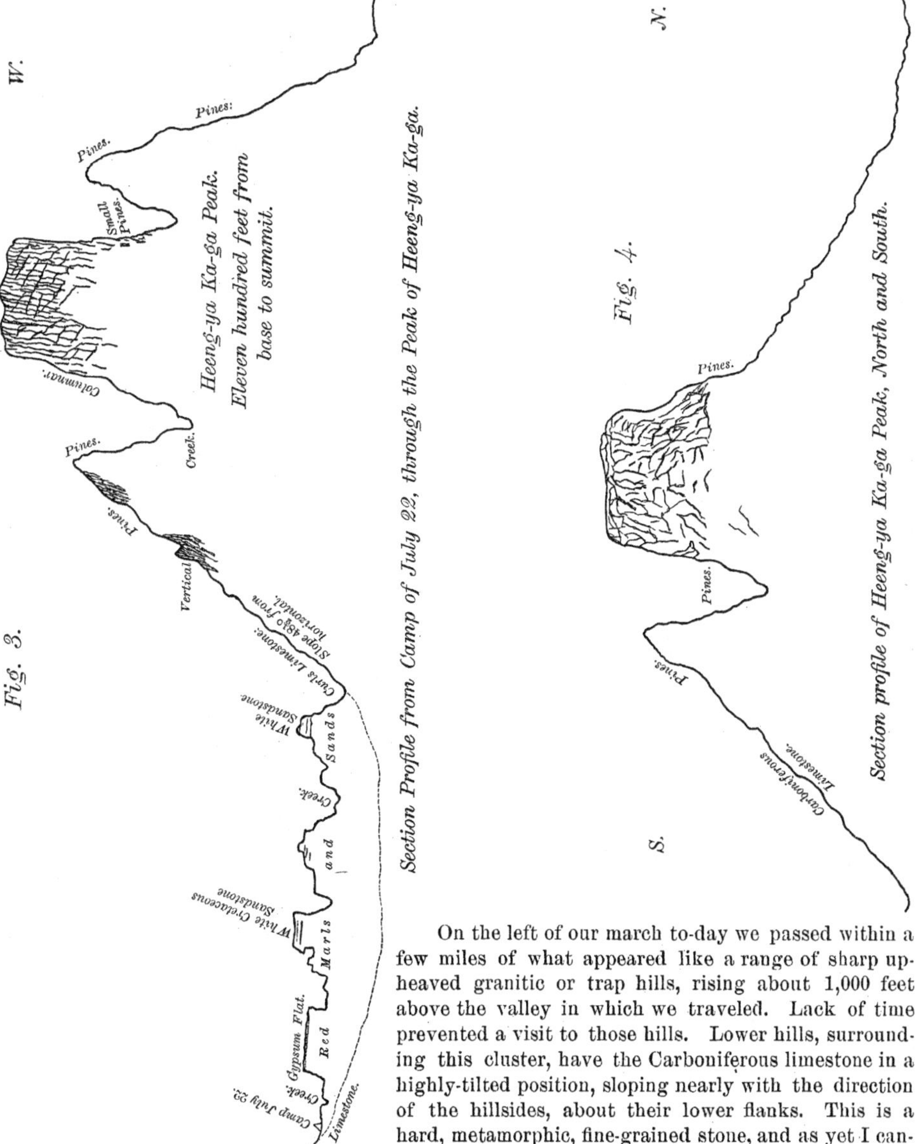

Fig. 3. Section Profile from Camp of July 22, through the Peak of Heeng-ya Ka-ga.

Fig. 4. Section profile of Heeng-ya Ka-ga Peak, North and South.

On the left of our march to-day we passed within a few miles of what appeared like a range of sharp upheaved granitic or trap hills, rising about 1,000 feet above the valley in which we traveled. Lack of time prevented a visit to those hills. Lower hills, surrounding this cluster, have the Carboniferous limestone in a highly-tilted position, sloping nearly with the direction of the hillsides, about their lower flanks. This is a hard, metamorphic, fine-grained stone, and as yet I cannot make out more than 40 feet of it. It is closely involved with the upheavals.

July 23.—Visit to Heeng-ya Ka-ga.—This isolated mountain, which has been visible in our front for several days, has, at a distance, a characteristic form. Its summit, which rises high enough to mark it as an important peak among the hills that surround it, has the shape of an inverted saucer, with another smaller inverted saucer lying on the top, and covering its central third part. This visit was made in company with General Custer, Colonel Ludlow, and two companies of horse as escort. Before reaching it we pass over three or four foot-hills, composed of Jurassic and Cretaceous, the latter usually more sparsely represented and capping the hills when we come near the foot of the main hill. These formations are not greatly disturbed by the uplift, but still show a very perceptible dip away from the mountain. Just at the foot of the mountain we leave the cavalry. Here we enter upon the Carboniferous limestone, which has a dip of about 30° from a horizontal, varying from 20° to 60°, sometimes presenting shoulders that have a confused dip, or stand vertical. Over this we climb to a height of about 500 feet to the top of a circular ridge which incloses the main colummar center of the mountain. Passing along this ridge toward the south a short distance, one party turns to the right and ascends the mountain from the east or northeast, while I, with Professor Donaldson and Bear's Ears, an Indian guide, cross the gorge separating us from the central mass. Crossing a wooded glen, where we find a refreshing stream of cool water, we ascend the peak from the south and find ourselves the first on the summit. From here we see the shape and structure of the peak. The shape of the summit, which at a distance has the aspect of a small saucer lying on a larger one, both inverted, is caused by the central mass rising above the rim or ridge, by which it is nearly surrounded. The only opening in this rim is toward the north 10° east, where it is entirely wanting. This ridge is about three-fourths of a mile distant from the central mass, in all directions, and gives the outline of the larger saucer. It does not rise as high as the central mass. Its main axis runs about north and south, varying a little east of north. The intervening space is occupied by a dark valley, narrow, and shaded with Norway pines. It is very difficult, and in many places impossible, to pass from the ridge to the center across this gorge, the rock rising sheer up on nearly all sides about the central mass. Figures 3 and 4 exhibit profile sections through the mountain, the former from our camp toward the west, and the latter north and south. With a spirit-level we can see there are higher hills toward the east, rising, perhaps, 500 feet above this peak.

As to the geology of this mountain, it comprises a single isolated outburst, which occurred after the deposition of the Carboniferous limestone, and before that of the gypsiferous Red-Beds. The former was greatly tilted and shattered by the disturbance, and the latter are but little displaced, probably not more than can be attributed to elevations that subsequently raised the country above the Cretaceous ocean. The Carboniferous limestone seems to be warped into a wave-like surface, when exposed on some of the lower flanks, a fact also noticed at other places, and lies at a high angle of incline all about the mountain's base. The mountain itself consists of a light-colored basaltic rock resembling phonolite or clink-stone. It is tough and heavy, ringing under the hammer. It is sparingly but not crypto-crystalline. It has no distinguishable free quartz. It is apparently feldspathic, but not porphyritic. It has fine disseminated folia of mica, and occasional larger fibrous masses of what appears like chlorite. It is not well characterized. While it cannot properly be denominated trap, it still is an igneous rock, thrust through the sedimentary strata. It may have resulted from the fusion or partial decomposition of the lower sedimentary rocks. It contains very little iron.

There is a very marked system of perpendicular jointage-planes, that cut the main ridge east and west, the individual planes being about 10 inches apart, or closer. Another system runs northeast and southwest, the planes being four feet apart, and tipped (their tops) toward the southeast about 10°; while a third system runs perpendicular to the last, and has the tops inclined toward the northeast about 10°. These larger divisions of the rock cause, on being weathered, the columnar structure seen all about the sides of the central mass. There is, besides, on the western side of the central mass, a fourth system of joints, that slope toward the west at an angle of about 45°, which gives the whole mass at that point the appearance of being a heavy-bedded, upheaved sedimentary rock.

This central *coulée*, which has the form of a horseshoe, since it is inclosed by the outer ridge of that shape, has exactly the contour and opening required for the formation of a local glacier. There can be no doubt but that toward the close of the Glacial Epoch glacier-ice did pass northward from this mountain. The evidence of transportation of drift has already been noted, (see notes on July 21,) lying to the north and directly in line from this coulée and its outlet.

The east side of the horseshoe ridge is made up of much the same kind of rock, but weathers whiter. It is very much cut up by divisional planes, and stands up in vertical dike-like ridges in some places on the east and southeast. It seems to hold more of the alkaline earths than the central cone.

Camp, July 23.—In the same place.

THROUGH THE CENTER OF THE BLACK HILLS—FROM HEENG-YA KA-GA PEAK TO HARNEY'S PEAK.

July 24.—We set out from camp nearly east, and at once ascend the slope underlain by the Carboniferous limestone. This undulates in small knolls, having a changeable dip in all directions, with often smooth, bare surfaces for about a mile, when pieces of a different kind of limestone appear on the surface, demonstrating a change in the underlying rock. These lie on a gently-ascending inclination and are coincident with the beginning of timber, the area of the Carboniferous limestone already mentioned being generally without timber. These pieces are of a coarse, granular, magnesian limestone, having the lithological characters of the Lower Magnesian Limestone of Minnesota. They are stained with pinkish spots and white calcite crystals. They are weathered rough, and are nearly white. They seem to be, or have been, constituted of substances of different degrees of hardness, as they have become cavernous under the weather; at least they show thimble and pot-hole depressions, though not so regular as these words denote. They are harsh to the feel, even arenaceous. They hold greenish, apparently argillaceous, often angular blocks. They show no fossils.

The first ridge we pass over has a very steep descent toward the east, and is about one hundred feet high and a fourth of a mile across. It seems to be caused by this limestone, but is covered with a considerable soil, that supports the best pines we have yet seen. The overlying limestone, already named as the Carboniferous limestone, seems not to be separated from this very widely, as it forms no distinct ridge, but disappears imperceptibly in making the ascent of the first ridge.

We pass on east about a fourth of a mile, nearly across the strike of the rocks, when we got down another step, about 100 feet, through a grove of small trees and shrubs, (*Populus tremuloides*, mostly,) when we turn southeast down this valley. I soon discovered a good exposure in the bluff on the right, made up of limestone and white, loosely-cemented sandstone, as follows, in descending order:

No. 1. Magnesian limestone	8–10 feet.
No. 2. White, loosely-cemented sandstone	20 feet.

There is also a very steep talus below the sandstone, of about 75 feet, hid by turf, probably made up of the same sandstone. Dip, west, 25° to 40°.

On the opposite side of this valley, which here is not more than 300 yards across, the same sandstone occurs, exposing about 50 feet, but it is here very much stained with iron, and brecciated, showing a rough exterior, with purgatory openings. It is deeply fractured and parted. No dip is ascertainable. This is no doubt a portion that has been tossed up and down a number of times. Some large portions of this are white and massive, indicating the original condition of the whole.

Ascending the east side of this valley, we pass again over the foregoing sandstone, magnesian limestone, and Carboniferous limestone, and reach a flat very similar to that on the other side of this valley, the surface of which is very closely underlain by the Carboniferous limestone. Over this flat we travel several miles, when we descend again into a perfectly similar ravine, where we find water; and, finally, ascending from it, we travel again over a flat of exactly the same sort for about four miles toward the east, when we descend again by steps, caused by the same formations, into the third valley of exactly the same kind. This is handsomely turfed and green, with no shrubs in the bottom.

Viewed from the bluff, before descending into it, it forms a long serpentine belt of green among the trees of darker foliage, somewhat suggestive of a slowly-winding river. The high, rocky bluffs that appear among the pines on one side and the other detract nothing from the general semblance of a great river-valley. The flats before mentioned are difficult of travel for a train. There are a few standing sound pines, but there seems to have been here, as in many other parts of the Black Hills region, very extensive fires, that have burned the former forest and left the charred trunks and limbs scattered on the surface. Among these have sprung up a perfect mesh of shrubs and small deciduous trees, mostly trembling aspen. We have to this place passed some pretty good Norway pine, but by far the greater portion is small, and not more than 12 inches in diameter, and low-branched. A great many of the trunks are scarred by former fires, and may be unsound.

Camp, July 24.—We are camped in the third valley already mentioned, and about five miles from where we first struck it, toward the southeast. On reaching this valley, General Custer turned to the right, ascending it toward the center of the main mass of the Black Hills. It is narrow, not being generally more than one or two hundred yards wide, though it spreads sometimes to three or four. It is at this time very profusely ornamented with flowers in bloom, from which circumstance General Custer gave it the name of Floral Valley, although the Indians call it Minne-Lusa Valley, on account of a clear and rapid stream which we encountered about half a mile above the point where we struck it. This stream seems to sink into the earth, and becomes larger as we ascend.

The rocks of the notes of this morning, which lie nearly horizontal over a wide extent of country, judging from the aspect of the hills and ravines, as seen from some of the bluffs toward the north, and form the immediate surface, continue on both sides of this valley, affording occasional exposures of sandstone, to this camp. The sandstone presents the same cavernous and iron-stained exterior as already described. We have advanced to-day, with great difficulty, about ten and a half miles, though but seven in a right line.

July 25.—Leaving camp we pass on up the same valley, crossing the stream occasionally, as it swings from one side to the other. We find it the same as yesterday, very profusely covered with flowers. The timber of the hills is Norway pine. In the valley, bordering the grass belt, is trembling aspen, some of which is 4 to 6 inches in diameter, but the greater portion very shrubby. The pine is rather small, and will not be molested for a great many years.

After passing about nine miles from camp up this valley, a change occurs in the contour of the hills, and indicates a corresponding change in the rocky structure. At the same time I see the first of a species of spruce, (*Abies alba*, or *nigra.*) The sandstone is here seen to form, in the distance of a quarter of a mile, a synclinal, the opposite angles of slope being plainly exhibited in the face of the left-hand bluff. Very soon a very prominent upheaval of limestone also appears on the left, dipping also at an angle of about 20° down the valley, (northwest.) This holds fossils, among which have been identified the genera *Streptorhynchus*, *Athyris*, and *Zaphrentis*, by Mr. Grinnell; the specific characters not being preserved. The stone is nearly white, crystalline, subsaccharoidal, and coarsely granular when weathered and hard. It has somewhat the aspect and texture of a crinoidal limestone, but without stem-sections of crinoids. Twenty-five feet seen. As this is entirely a new development in respect to the geology of the Black Hills, (see United States Geological Survey of the Territories, third annual report, p. 12, F. V. Hayden,) and being somewhat uncertain about the relation of this limestone to the foregoing sandstone, having passed an interval of non-exposure, (nearly three-quarters of a mile,) I returned and repeated my observations. Noting carefully every indication of dip, and watching the float-pieces on the hillsides, I came to the conclusion that this limestone underlies the foregoing sandstone. This I shall designate the *Minne-lusa Sandstone*, from the Indian name of the valley in which it was discovered.

Going on up this valley, which now could more properly be styled a cañon, cut out as it is in a rock so hard, with such high and rocky walls on both sides, this limestone is seen to appear in vast proportions. It reaches a thickness of at least 245 feet, that being the height from the valley to the top of the hills, measured near this point by aneroid. In the face of the bluff at the place measured, this limestone is not constantly exposed. The principal exposures are in the form of shoulders, separated by taluses which may conceal other rock. Thus, near the top, and for 20 or 25 feet downward, a perpendicular wall of horizontal beds of limestone faces the valley. This limestone can be seen to extend to other adjoining hills to the north and northeast in a horizontal position, forming their crests, its white serpentine line marking the summit level of several divides between tributary valleys. Below this, after passing over an interval of little or no exposure of 30 to 50 feet, bestrewn with large fragments, there is another line of exposure which forms a shoulder in the hillside. This is also about 20 feet high, of the same kind of hard crystalline limestone, often porous. The third line of exposed rock is about 75 feet below the last, and is of a close-grained and argillaceous character, and of a drab color. It is very hard, and stands in perpendicular faces, with broken-down places filled up with talus, this line being the last exposed. This, also, forms castellated and isolated bluffs and pinnacles. From the tops of the hills, which are flat-topped and sparsely overgrown with stunted pines, can be seen a wide extent of country, having about the same level, very rough and rocky, cut by a net-work of ravines and cañons into a series of the most forbidding ridges, knolls, and valleys, undulating before the eye, but shining with the reflected sunlight from the white spots of exposed limestone, and bristling with scattered and stunted pines. These cañons, and the short intervening areas of table-land, are very similar to those passed over the day we entered Floral Valley, but are far more deeply cut and less wooded. Along this valley here, the dip of the rock being in general toward the northwest, there is a noticeable difference in the aspect of the two sides, the left-hand side, as we go up, being rocky, and the other timbered and with very little rock exposure. Farther down, however, in the area of the sandstone, where the strata seemed nearly horizontal, this contrast is not observable.

This limestone has a great resemblance, both in its own lithological characters, and in the castellated, weathered exposures along the valley, to the Upper Silurian, as seen along the east side of Green Bay of Lake Michigan. The fossils mentioned as found in its lower portion this forenoon, will admit of its being of the Silurian, Devonian, or Lower Carboniferous.

The beautiful stream, from which the Indians call the valley Minne-Lusa, or Running-Water Valley, disappears again about three miles above the place of appearance of this limestone formation, and simply an overland, dry channel can be seen. On searching, I find the stream, which carries as much water as the Belle Fourche where we crossed it, rises in a series of springs within the area of half an acre. The channel, however, about a mile above, has again a little water, and here we make camp, about twelve miles from last night's camp, the road having been all day rapidly ascending, but obstructed by necessary crossings of the creek.

Camp July 25.—In the Minne-Lusa Valley.

July 26.—We travel on up this valley, the stream becoming very small and at last disappearing, to a divide, four miles from camp, where the valley widens out, and the timber, which has all the morning largely been made up of spruce, is smaller and somewhat mixed with aspen. Here is a flat about half a mile over, though there are low hills, made up of the same limestone, on each side, that are more smoothly rounded off, and inclose and continue the valley right over the divide, and down again on the other side. Here the train begins a descent. At the divide, which occurs in the great limestone formation, the bottom of the valley is about seventy feet below the top of the formation, which forms the surface of the country over a vast extent in this quarter. Before leaving the divide, I choose a conspicuous, treeless hill, about one-half mile from the valley, as a point of observation, lying on the left of our route. From here I see the same fossiliferous limestone as that seen yesterday, forming the very top. When I say fossiliferous, I mean that it has traces of fossils only, and that very rarely a fragment can be got that is sufficient for identification. From this hill the country appears to be of the same character as noted yesterday, no prominent hills being visible, except far to the north, very blue in the distance, the whole being a limestone region with narrow valleys or cañons. The country is here densely wooded with spruce and Norway pine, the former being larger than the latter, and making nearly one-half of the whole. The limestone here shows a coral structure. This structure consists simply of small circular pores, opening perpendicular to the weathered surface, about an eighth of an inch apart.

This morning ice was formed at camp. The air is cold, sky is clear, wind is south, and my aneroid stands on this hill 23.17. This, compared and corrected by a mercurial barometer at Minneapolis, and referred to the ocean, gives an elevation of —— feet above the sea.

Passing down this valley, the bluffs continue to show the same composition, the light-colored limestone forming their summits as far as any rock is exposed, the height of the inclosing bluffs gradually increasing till near the place of camping, when I ascend the bluff on our left hand, and find its aggregate height to be 646 feet by aneroid. In ascending I make notes and measurements. These summarized, and placed in descending order, become as follows:

Section of the bluffs of Castle Valley.

No. 1.	Perpendicular cliff of light-colored, magnesian, crystalline, compact limestone....	60 feet.
No. 2.	Talus to the brow of second perpendicular cliff..................................	28 feet.
No. 3.	Perpendicular cliff of light-colored, crystalline, magnesian limestone............	94 feet.
No. 4.	Talus to the brow of the third perpendicular cliff................................	59 feet.
No. 5.	Hard, reddish-gray limestone, with chert..	18 feet.
	[*Note.*—No. 5 was found at other places in this valley to hold cyathophylloid corals and crinoid stems.]	
No. 6.	White, coarse sandstone, with small, rounded, quartz pebbles; conglomeratic....	20 feet.
No. 7.	Red sandstone with glauconitic particles; seen..................................	10 feet.
No. 8.	Talus to the top of a turfed shoulder..	44 feet.
No. 9.	Talus to the bank of the creek. In this talus a greenish shale is indicated by fragments thrown up by gophers, its thickness being 40 or 50 feet probably......	313 feet.
	Total height of the bluff...	646 feet.

This bluff is but one of a series of equal height, that, like immense castle-tops, seem to inclose and guard the valley, whence it was named Castle Valley.

Camp, July 26.—We are camped about a mile below the high bluffs above noted. A short distance below our camp we encountered a small party of Indian hunters, with their families. Getting into difficulty with our Indian scouts, they suddenly decamped. They belonged to the Red Cloud agency, and were not aware of the expedition.

July 27.—Opposite our camp, on the east side of the valley, is an outcrop of very fine-grained, homogeneous, dark, garnetiferous mica schist, which rises by aneroid 270 feet, if a talus above be included, over which pieces of the same are scattered. This is the rock comprised in the lowest talus, at the point where the bluffs were last measured. This schist rises in almost perpendicular slaty sheets, which have their tops tipped north, 10° east, though there are jointing planes that cut it into rhombs. The bluffs here rise about 80 feet still higher. This amount is made up of conglomerate and sandstone. The only exposure of these beds that can be seen comprises about 20 feet of light, loose, coarse sandstone, somewhat conglomeratic, exactly like that seen in the bluff about a mile farther up yesterday. In the slope above this, although no rock is visible *in situ*, are seen surface-pieces, which contain a species of *Lingulepis*. These pieces are thin and shingle-like. They are glauconitic, and were doubtless embraced in a loose and easily destructible rock, as the original beds, whatever they were, are all weathered down, and the surface bears some turf and trees. Back of this hill rises another bluff, separated from it by a deep ravine, which is capped with limestone, and is the equivalent of that measured yesterday.

Half a mile below camp this mica-schist becomes more a talcose slate, holding isolated beds and pockets of quartz. These quartz deposits are here conformable with the bedding; indeed, they make up a part of the bedding of the rock, having been segregated at the time of the metamorphic change.

The general dip of the Silurian for a number of miles back is very gentle to the north. Indeed, it seems almost to be zero, the descent of the valley in the rock appearing sufficient to bring to the surface these slates and schists. The lowest talus noted at the measurement of Castle Bluffs, which has here proved to have consisted of metamorphic rocks, I observed first seven or eight miles above our present camp. In going down this creek this talus gradually becomes more prominent, and forms hills and knobs that inclose the creek closely, even so that we cannot get through with the train, the higher limestone bluffs retreating farther back. The following profile of the left bank of this creek shows the relative positions of the limestone bluff and those formed by the sandstone and the mica schist. This section is general. It is broken and cut by cross ravines. There are several large masses of a coarse, pebbly conglomerate on the slope nearly opposite our camp. Whether they are from the same horizon as the conglomeratic sandstone, seen in the bluff opposite camp, I cannot here decide, as the mound on which they lie, and everything above them, is turfed over smoothly.

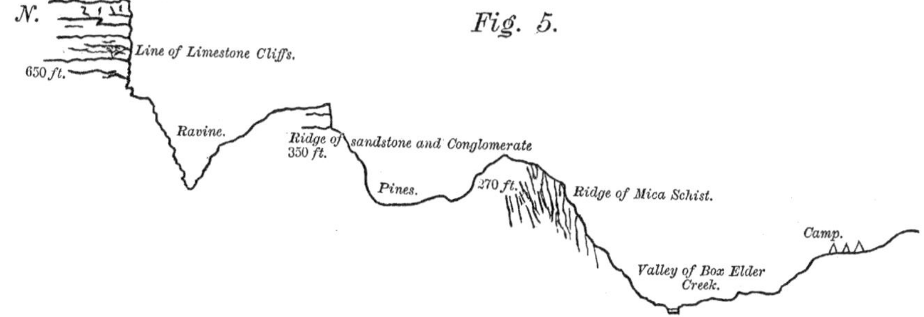

General section of the Left Bank of Box Elder Creek, at Camp, July 26.

Camp, July 27.—The same as July 26.

July 28.—In leaving camp this morning we strike nearly east, leaving the valley of Box Elder Creek, which General Custer named Castle Creek, from the rounded and high-buttressed bluffs that here inclose it, and aim to camp on the same creek, a few miles farther down, thus escaping a very narrow and deep cañon, through which the creek passes, in this mica schist. In emerging from the valley, I observe that the limestone bluffs stretch no farther south, but terminate by a line of isolated hills, that extend eastwardly, thus bringing in, in full force, the metamorphic rocks that succeed the low Silurian, that formation being involved in the bases of the limestone bluffs. Once getting away from the immediate creek valley, and so out of the effect of the principal drainage-courses, these metamorphic rocks are seen to weather down smoothly, though they would be expected on general principles to form very high and persistent hills. The whole country falls off several hundred feet toward the south on to the area of these metamorphic rocks. Here they spread out so as to form prairie-like, undulating plains, that are entirely treeless. One of these plains we pass over, and find thereon a large stack of elk-horns, whence the Indians call it Elk-Horn Valley, a name which is appropriately changed to *Elk-Horn Prairie.*

Finding it impossible to continue in this direction more than three or four miles, with the train, we turn back toward the southwest, and camp about three miles below our starting-point on the same creek.

Camp, July 28.—Three miles below the last camp on Box Elder Creek. This valley here is inclosed by rounded hills and bluffs, in the same way, that rise 50 or 100 feet, formed of the same or very similar dark rock.

July 29.—We leave camp, southeastwardly, following up another tributary valley, along which the same rock shows in similar exposures. The dip here, as in yesterday's observations, is very irregular, both in degree and direction. On our left are seen, on the tops of the hills, occasional columns, formed by jointing planes, from which the surrounding rock has been denuded, left standing 10 or 20 feet high among the pines. In this direction we find the country for two or three miles, at least, covered with pines, the most of which are but few inches in diameter. There are, however, a few scattered old trees, that are 2 to 2½ feet, and would do for timber. Some spruce is also observable. About three miles from camp we pass on our left a rocky point, or hog's-back, which at a distance appears like a trap-dyke, but which is really made up of a heavy, hard, gray, micaceous quartzite. It continues but a short distance, though one or two more can be seen rising still higher toward the southwest, about the same distance from the line of limestone cliffs. The line of limestone cliffs that marks the termination of that formation, runs northeast and southwest (nearly north and south) through here. Toward the west and north they are visible along our march for five and a half miles, about a mile away, but not to the east. At six miles from camp the view of these hills is also cut off on the west by the intervention of a high conical hill of the kind of rock last noted, which has much the outward appearance of dark trap-rock, but within is gray, with blackish glittering specks resembling mica, and consists, apparently, almost entirely of quartz—a micaceous, fine-grained quartzite, gray, hard, and homogeneous. From this point to the night's camp the general characters of the country remained much the same, though it becomes more completely wooded and more mountainous, rendering it almost impassable for our train. The valleys between the hills are frequently free from trees, beautifully grassed, and often ornamented with a great variety of flowers in bloom. In these valleys are frequent springs of cool, pure water, and small streams. Throughout the most of the day's march the mica-schist has shown a constant and high dip to the east. The rocks of the Lower Silurian are uncomformable on this schist. When they last appeared they were nearly horizontal, but the mica-schist has everywhere had a marked dip, varying from 20° to perpendicularity. In some places the mica predominates over the quartz, and then the surface is much smoother, the rock being greatly weathered down. The country then has the appearance and character of an undulating, treeless prairie, the soil of which glitters in the sun with particles of mica. In other places the quartz largely predominates, when the country becomes very rough and the rock constantly exposed. In the former case, the schist is flexible and specular. In the latter, it is hardly a schist, having more the nature of a quartzite. In both cases it is homogeneous. There is, however, a third aspect which it has, and one which is probably the most common—that of an ordinary, rather fine mica-schist, with beds and nodules of milky quartz. This quartz certainly occurs in irregular bunches, and nodular layers, following the direction of the bedding or lamination of the schist itself, though it is of course of chemical and concretionary origin, not sedimentary.

Camp, July 29.—Camp was chosen about ten miles from last night's camp, on a little ravine running east. We are surrounded by high mica-schist hills, and the little stream passes into a narrow cañon in this rock, about half a mile below our camp. The train does not reach the place selected till daylight next morning.

July 30.—Leaving camp at 7 a. m. we travel southeast, and soon strike a smooth valley running in the same direction. On the left of our march, after going about four miles, we have a rough and precipitous range of hills, one or two outliers of which (Cockscomb Peak) are on our right. The lower exposures of these hills, and also those on the right, are all of mica-schist, dipping, however, to the southwest, and finally to the south. Inclosed in lumpy masses, in a manner similar to the inclosed masses of milky quartz mentioned yesterday, in this mica-schist, are large pieces, and almost continuous layers of coarse granite, the feldspar of which is white, the quartz glassy, and mica coarse and flexible. In these large fallen pieces of granite are black crystals of what appears like tourmaline. They are prismatic and pyramidal in form, some an inch or two in diameter, and six inches long; others not more than an inch in length, and one-eighth inch in diameter at the larger end. They all seem to run to points. Passing on about three miles farther, and a little to the east, we come in full view of a range of granite hills running nearly north and south. This range of hills presents more ruggedness and bare rock than anything we have before seen. Approaching the foot of these hills I pass over one or two low parallel granite ridges that seem to lie in the mica-schist, and are now thrust 10 or 20 feet above it by reason of its being more easily and deeply eroded by surface and atmospheric agencies. These have a dip toward the west, with abrupt sides toward the east. The mica-schist becomes more and more granitic by interstratification, yet the schist itself maintains its distinct characters, and prevails up to the very base of the granite, and even appears, in thin contorted laminæ, in the granite itself. This granite is a *white* feldspathic granite, and not red, as Dr. Hayden describes that he saw in the Black Hills, and all its ingredients are coarsely crystalline.

Camp, July 30.—We traveled ten miles, nearly southeast from our last camp, and are in a wide, grassed valley, through which runs a stream. This valley here subsequently receives the name of Custer Park. The gold-seekers who accompany the expedition report the finding of gold in the gravel and sand along this valley.

Camp, July 31.—Custer Park. The expedition delays here a day or two to allow the animals to recuperate, and to afford time for reconnaissances into the hills in different directions, and to the Cheyenne Valley, south and east.

Camp, August 1.—We are four or five miles about east of our last night's camp. We had yesterday a long and tiresome trip to Harney's Peak, of which I made brief notes on the spot. We reached camp so late as twenty minutes before one o'clock this morning. The reconnoitering party consisted of General Custer, Colonel Ludlow, General Forsyth, Professor Donaldson, and myself. Colonel Ludlow's assistant, Mr. Wood, also accompanied the party, who were escorted by a company of horse under Lieutenant Barnum. The party shaped its movements according to the desire of Colonel Ludlow for topographical purposes. We set out north, and passed to the southeast of the peaks which were mentioned the day before in coming into Custer Park. We traveled about two miles in that direction, among bald knobs of granite and schist, with some grassy valleys between, when we turned more eastward and ascended a ridge of granite hills, passing it at a low point, which by aneroid was 903 feet above our camp. On ascending this ridge a most magnificent prospect burst suddenly upon us, which caused us each, on reaching the summit, to utter an exclamation of surprise and wonder. An expanse of from six to fifteen miles stretched out before us toward the east, south, and northeast, filled up with just such objects, in just such positions and proportions, as go to make up an artist's ideal mountain-landscape. This expanse consisted in the main of a valley, winding through the timber of which, toward the south, could be seen a beautiful meadow, through which ran a stream of water half concealed by the tall grass. In the east we could limit the view only by timbered hills of granite, the bare rock of which stood out in isolated peaks and buttresses. A grassed valley, but narrower, also ran off in that direction, fingering out among the mountains from which it gathered its many tributaries. To the northeast, however, was the grandest sight I ever beheld. This was a truly Alpine view. Here was Pelion on Ossa. This was toward Harney's Peak, only the top of which, as we supposed, could be seen from our position. Very near us, and cutting off our view north, was a series of spindled peaks which, though massive and imposing, proved to be mere pigmies to the giants of the same shape and character that rose in the distance. These latter hid Harney from our view, though we mistook another peak, very similar, about two miles to the southeast, for Harney, and made for it on descending. In the valley before us stood up scattered, conical, granitic "sugar-loaves," in the background of which, rising nearly as high as old Harney himself, was a perfect nest of organ-pipe peaks, whose sharp spindling tops immediately suggested the name Organ Peaks, which name they retain. There are two such nests, and they were both in view, separated not more than three-quarters of a mile. These bare rocks, presenting in the morning sun a light surface, as they rose above the almost universal pines, afforded a most striking contrast with the dark-green foliage of the forest, and very appropriately received their name.

On descending from this divide, where we had made an involuntary halt, we commenced a winding course toward the peak which we took for Harney's. Its crest presented a sharp ridge, with perpendicular sides, running about north and south, having nearly a flat top, and had been seen by Colonel Ludlow and myself from a limestone bluff in Castle Valley a few days before, and so identified as Harney's. We found it very difficult making our way toward this peak, as the country was very rough, the valleys, instead of being broad and grassed, were narrow and rocky. In them, sometimes, the trees had been thrown down by fire or tempest, often half consumed and left charred, and a thousand shrubs and small aspens, that almost everywhere in the northwest follow spontaneously a downthrow of the evergreen forest, had made a perfect netted mesh, through which no horse could pass. Avoiding these, and the places that presented nothing but bald rock surfaces, we had still a winding, inconstant, intervening belt of varying width on which grew the principal and largest trees. This was on the lower flanks of the hills, where there was sufficient soil to afford strong rooting for trees, and not enough water to make it soft—for in many of the valleys there are very deceptive, and often grassy, treacherous bogs, that caused several horses to mire—so that we finally found ourselves, about noon, at the foot of the peak at which we aimed. Here ran a beautiful stream toward the east, though it was perfectly invisible till we were on its very brink, so dense were the bushes and brush through which we filed our way. At this point I read the barometer, which stood 24.35. Ahead of us could be seen an irregularly ascending, half-timbered ridge, rising toward the summit of the hill at which we aimed. We were traveling toward the northeast, and at first took the southwestern slope of this ridge, but afterward passed over its crest to the opposite side, where we picked our way slowly along, leading our horses among fallen trees, blackened logs, and sliding masses of rock, till we finally reached a point where our horses could be led no longer. By this time the advance had dwindled to three persons, Generals Custer, Forsyth, and the writer, the topographers having delayed for taking sights to prominent points, and the escort being more slow in getting up. Here we abandoned our horses, unhitched, as we knew they were too weary to go far, and the orderlies were not far behind, and began a scramble for the top, which lay at least 250 feet above us. At first we mounted with great agility an easy slope, where large, loose masses formed a rough talus, and rose to the summit of a shoulder. Here we met a perpendicular wall that forms the blade-like portion at the very top. After breathing a few minutes, General Custer and I began an examination of this wall. It stretched to the northwest about 60 rods, and afforded not a single break or niche that could be used as a support in any attempt to scale it. At length, but before the arrival of any others of the party, we discovered a place that presented a possible ascent. This blade-like ridge, which has not more than an average width of 25 feet, has, on its southern or southeastern end, a number of eroded channels, giving it a fluted surface. These gullies, if continued farther, would constitute the vacancies that exist between the Organ Peaks, and would convert the whole ridge into another magnificent set of organ-pipes. They are simply weathered-out jointing-planes, and if crossed at a proper angle by another system, would produce, under the influence of atmospheric agencies, a columnar exterior that would give the peak the aspect of the central, conical mass seen in Heeng-ya Ka-ga. We chose what appeared to be the most practicable of these eroded channels, and he with his rifle, and I with hammer and barometer, by literally crawling closely to the rock, bracing ourselves across from side to side and seizing every available knob of projecting feldspar, reached almost simultaneously, by different routes, the top, or what appeared from below to be the top. This, however, was some distance still farther, though not much higher. Descending a short notch, where we separated again for a second scramble, I found a narrow valley, (in which grew a very fine and tempting array of red raspberries, *Rubus strigosus*,) leading, by a steady ascent, out to the very summit of the peak. Passing up this, inclosed by perpendicular walls on both sides, I emerged upon the top, and sat down, or dropped down, to rest, almost exhausted. The rest of the scaling-party soon came up. General Custer fired a salute of three shots from his rifle, we drank from our canteens to General Harney, and, after a lunch, decided to visit another peak lying toward the northwest, which rises some feet higher than that we had ascended. From the point at which we stood, 1,012 feet above the creek flowing along the base of this mountain, we commanded the most extensive field of vision that we had yet beheld in the Black Hills. We seemed to be in the center of the most rugged and forbidding tract of the Black Hills. On nearly all sides, bare rock and sharp peaks rose among the pines that partially enlivened the scene. Toward the east and south we could see beyond and over the intervening hills, and discerned the plains, and distinguished some of their main features. The location of the outcropping edge of the Red Beds was evident by the redness along a belt of country near the hills. Toward the north, (7° east of north, true meridian,) Bear Butte rose high enough to show its summit and allow its identification by its regularly rounded and massive form. The Organ Peaks are the most attractive object toward the west. They lay west 15° north, by compass,* and about a mile distant. Beyond them a distant range of mountains was dimly visible, but toward the north and northwest the view was cut off by the hills themselves. Although this is the granitic nucleus of the Black Hills, the region of the sedimentary rock, particularly of the great limestone formation farther north, is without doubt the highest above the ocean. The valley in which our camp is can be seen, especially some of its easterly ramifications, from this peak. Indeed, the view toward the south, embracing a tract of open, grassy valley, with considerable pine, and much smoother than in the opposite direction, affords a remarkable contrast with the wild ruggedness of the view toward the north.

The scaling-party having decided to visit the second peak, whose ascent appeared practicable for horses, General Forsyth and the writer descended as we came up, for the purpose of taking our horses, while the rest advance northwest toward that peak and find a place of descent toward the north. Partly riding and partly leading, we passed along the western side of the blade-like crest some hundreds of feet below it, then down into a steep and deep ravine, and ascended the other side. This ravine we passed as near its head as possible, and left on our left a cluster of small granitic peaks that stand in this valley, cut by jointing-planes and weathered down to pyramidal forms by

* The variation of the compass here was 16° east.

the operations of nature. Besides the perpendicular jointing-planes, these little peaks disclose some that are nearly horizontal, so that they are near their tops disjointed or cut off, the separated joints appearing displaced and ready to totter off. In that way how many joints above them may have fallen down since their first exposure, reducing them to their present dimensions, the ages of geology will never reveal. They probably once stood as high as the Organ peaks stand now, or as high as those peaks ever stood. They are now six or eight hundred feet lower. Up the southeastern side of Harney No. 2, I with difficulty led my horse, and took him over the very summit just as the foot party were starting on the descent again, led by General Custer; for they had no sooner reached this summit than they beheld what could not be seen from the first peak we ascended, owing to the intervention of this, a third peak in direct range northwest, rising, very evidently, several hundred feet higher. Plunging into a labyrinth of ravines, ridges, trees, bushes and rocks, they were very soon out of sight. Here I found myself, with my horse, on the summit of a mountain alone, with no certainty of being able to follow the foot party, for General Forsyth had been delayed by taking charge of the escort. Nevertheless, my horse and I got down, and on the opposite side, for this peak was very much smoother than the first one we climbed, the rock having crumbled so that in many places the surface was covered with rusted crystals of feldspar. The foot party, by a detour to the left, round a lower intervening hill, reached the foot of the difficulties of the real Harney's Peak some time later than I with my horse, by plunging into a ravine toward the right that was wooded with small pines, but afforded good footing for my horse. Dismounting to fire at a doe that was startled by my approach, and following it up unsuccessfully, General Custer encountered my horse and rode up to the same place. The ascent of this peak was very similar to that of the first. We made it together, the rest of the party being delayed for similar reasons as before. We found here a long, narrow ridge of bare rock, along which we passed, occasionally coming to broken-down spots that had to be crossed by letting each other down and helping each other up. Finally, a massive wall, the very end of a higher ridge, confronted us, barring our further progress. Turning to the right and descending, General Custer found a practicable ascent to the top of this second ridge, while I managed as before, and scaled a perpendicular ascent in a weathered-out angle between jointing-

Fig. 6.
Profile of the Summit of Harney's Peak, N. W. and S. E.
Total hight 1635 feet above its base.

planes, rising thus about 50 feet. This, however, was not the summit of the peak itself. We found it impracticable to further attempt its ascent. Another perpendicular wall confronted us, rising about 45 feet. The sun had already set, a long return-march was before us through a very rough and unknown region, and we made but a short stay. We saw from this peak very nearly the same view in all directions as already described from the first peak ascended, though it rises 623 feet higher than that, being 1,635 feet above the creek where my barometer was noted, near the base of the first peak. The outline of the summit of Harney's Peak, which we found inaccessible on the southeast, is shown in profile by the adjoined sketch. This profile runs northwest and southeast. The summit ridge itself is from 25 to 50 feet in thickness, and extends by estimate about an eighth of a mile, though there are other ridges toward the northwest, half a mile further, that greatly resemble this, and rise nearly as high. They are separated by deep ravines and notches, which were, doubtless, at first filled up with the same kind of rock.

Taking samples of the rock, and driving an emptied copper cartridge-case into a cleft in the granite, we left therein our names and the day of the month, and began what proved to be a long and tiresome night-march back to camp.

The rock which makes up these peaks is a gray or white feldspathic granite, the separate crystalline ingredients of which are coarse and contain crystals of black tourmaline. It is not intersected with dikes nor with quartz veins. It is simply a massive granite, with a tendency to a columnar fracture near the mountain peaks. There seems to have been an important system of joints running northwest and southeast, and a much less conspicuous one crossing it about at right angles, for the mountain peaks have the form of thin crests with nearly flat tops, running northwest and southeast, and only partially broken down by cross-openings from northeast to southwest. This granite, massive and unstratified as it is, still is joined to the overlying schists by a number of interstratifications of schist and granite, a fact that was noticed at two or three favorable points. It is not meant here to say that the granite was derived from a conformable underlying sedimentary rock, for there was not sufficient opportunity to gather data on that point, but there is certainly some reason for supposing that to have been the case.*

RECONNAISSANCE TO THE MOUTH OF FRENCH CREEK.

August 2.—Three days having been assigned to a reconnoitering party destined to trace out to the plains the creek on which we are camped, and to visit the Bad Lands toward the southeast, we set out from camp early, hoping to obtain before our return a collection of mammalian fossils from the Tertiary. This party is also accompanied by topographical observers and by Mr. G. B. Grinnell, of Yale College, and his assistant, Mr. North. Our escort is two companies of horse, under Colonel Hart.

About a mile and a half from camp we pass a reddish quartzite, that reminds me at once of the quartzite lying below the Saint Croix sandstone of Minnesota and Wisconsin. Its geological position is also very nearly the same as that. Between this point and our starting-place we passed over a country occupied by the usual varieties of micaceous schists and slates. High, sharp hills are formed by this schist, usually sparsely timbered. The same is true of this quartzite. Besides mica-schist there is seen near here a dark, apparently hornblendic, rock, appearing in exterior characters like trap, rising in sharp hills, from which fall down angular blocks. This I have seen in several places, and note again about three miles from camp. This is possibly eruptive. Near it are sometimes very coarsely crystalline granitic knobs, that appear to have been caused by, or to have accompanied, such disturbance. They slope away from the black hornblendic hills, and die out in the plain or valley on the further side. In these isolated granitic masses are some of the largest tourmaline crystals yet seen. They here reach 5 to 8 inches in diameter, and present the same internal characters as in the smaller crystals. They are embedded with white feldspar crystals in the granite. At eight miles from camp we come again upon the red or reddish-gray quartzite, having passed a short interval of schist and granite.

---

* By a system of triangulation by Mr. Wood, Harney's Peak is found to be 4,200 feet above our camp, which, by uniting my barometrical observations with it, makes the mouth of French Creek, which was nearly reached August 4 by a reconnoitering party, 6,200 feet below Harney, or about 9,000 feet for the height of Harney's Peak above the ocean.

About a mile further the valley becomes narrower, and wooded with pine. Along this valley erally is good pine, some of the trees being 3 feet in diameter, but rather short, rarely sufficient more than one log. Smaller trees are sometimes higher, and will make two or three logs, though t length is very rare. They are all apt to be knotty, with dry branches for some distance below spreading top.

At about eleven miles from camp we pass near a quartzite hill, with schist outcropping in rly vertical beds on its slope. This quartzite here is gray, but where weathered becomes red or h-colored. This hill rises about 200 feet. On the opposite side of the creek another similar rises 500 or 600 feet. Indeed, as we pass on we find ourselves in the midst of quartzite hills ng from 100 to 600 feet, their sides being often too steep for ascent. Among these the creek es a very tortuous course, the rock often shutting us off from its right or left bank. Pines cover whole. The exterior aspect of this quartzite is generally very rough and angular, large blocks ng occasioned by jointing-planes that intersect it. The declivities on which it occurs are so steep t many pieces have fallen into the valleys. I have not been able to make out any dip nor even bedding. I simply see large pieces of this quartzite, and also large, bare, smooth areas lying these hills, if not conforming in contour with the original form of the upheaval of the schist, at st giving contour to the hills at present. It is certainly a metamorphosed sandstone, and seems er to have been covered by any later formation.

In camp, August 2.—We have had a hard day. We became entrapped in the cañon through ich the creek runs, and had to retrace our steps a number of times, climbing hills where our ses could hardly go. My horse actually did overbalance backward and plunged headlong down hill over a man, who was only saved by a log that was above him. The man was somewhat rt, but the horse was not.

The character of the valley changes most remarkably before getting out of the granite. It omes a narrow gorge or cañon, the bottom of which is from 500 to 800 feet below the tops of inclosing hills. At first only occasional hills of that height shut us off, rising perpendicular, l by crossing to the opposite side we often could find a passage without ascending the bluffs; finally, as they became more numerous, they formed a continuous wall, with perpendicular rock both sides, rising several hundred feet above the creek. The perpendicular portion of these walls s generally near the top, comprising 50 or 100 feet, the creek-bed and a narrow talus on either e being completely filled with immense boulders and fallen masses, through which the creek rolled l plunged, often entirely invisible by reason of sinking below the visible surface and running ong the interstices below. Over these boulders we found it difficult to pass and impossible to duct a horse. We seemed to have reached the small end of a funnel-like valley, through which could not take our horses, so we had to retreat to some place where we could ascend the bluffs. ving found such a place, by returning about two miles, here we formed camp in the valley. The gravation of this defeat is not diminished by the fact that we had seen the prairie beyond from ne of the hill-tops, and the stratified rocks were visible on the tops of the cañon-walls in nearly izontal beds when we returned.

August 3.—Leaving camp at 7 a. m., we ascend the bluffs on the right.

I have noticed ever since the day of the visit to Harney's Peak a very slight tint of pink or sh-color appearing in the feldspar crystals in the granite. This has *apparently* increased in dis ctness and depth *gradually*, till here the feldspar is "red," as Dr. Hayden styles it. The granite also more crumbled, the general surface being often covered with a gravel made up of small ces of quartz and feldspar, among which the Norway pine seems to flourish.

Getting on the bluffs we see the open prairie immediately before us. We slept within three-rters of a mile of open, smooth traveling last night. Just before leaving the heavily-wooded nitic hills the cañon of the creek makes a right angle, turning to the east.

Immediately after getting out of the wooded portion of the hills, which here very nearly coin-es with the line of commencement of the Silurian rocks, I descend a little ravine running east, butary to the creek, and make the following observations on the horizon of the Lower Silurian:

I see no schist, but immediately on the granite seems to lie a reddish or gray compact quartz-that is probably the same as that seen yesterday, forming the capping to a number of hills. It shows here perhaps 30 feet, and passes upward into a conglomerate, though the features here of this conglomerate are less distinct, and it is much finer than the coarse conglomerate seen in Castle Valley.

Section on French Creek, ascending.

No. 1. Gray or reddish quartzite .... 30 feet.
No. 2. Somewhat conglomeritic quartzite .... 1 foot.
No. 3. Argillaceous sandstone, somewhat shaly; red; in heavy beds and in thin; also in small, lenticular masses or inconstant beds that crumble out and make the face of the wall appear massive .... 35 feet.
No. 4. Light red, nodular and laminated argillaceous sandstone, variegated with light spots, as if burned and partly fused and then hardened .... 5 feet.
No. 5. Red, arenaceous limestone, holding cyathophylloïds and fucoid marks; also crinoid stems; shows slickensides .... 30 feet.

[NOTE.—The last is also somewhat conglomeritic. It holds occasional quartz-pebbles three-quarters of an inch in diameter.]

No. 6. The last passes into lighter-colored conformable beds of heavy, arenaceous magnesian limestone, showing the same fossils and perhaps also brachiopods, and black markings that may be graptolites .... 4 feet.
No. 7. Softer, sometimes carious, light-colored, magnesian-limestone; bedding heavy, or massive and crumbling. Contains imprints of a brachiopod resembling *Spirifera*. This stone is vesicular, and seems to hold the fragments of many small fossils .... 6 feet.

[NOTE.—The last runs below a talus, and the section cannot be continued consecutively at this place. A rounded hill, that is probably made up of the beds seen to come above the foregoing in other portions of the Black Hills, rises just to the east of this exposure to the height of more than 100 feet higher. It is probably mainly composed of limestone, and its surface is overstrewn with fragments of a light sandstone or quartzite, referable to the light sandstone seen just above the (lower portion of the) Carboniferous limestone, after entering the Minna-Lusa Valley, July 24.]

Add for this limestone .... 100 feet.

Total exposure .... 211 feet.

These beds all dip at a high angle to the southeast. The hills die out very suddenly toward the south, the whole country becoming prairie-like, with grassed undulations, caused only by the rocky substructure. There is also a slight drift scattered over the surface for a short distance from the hills.

Following this ravine to its union with the creek, I find it passes into a deep cañon, where the inclosing rock is a brecciated limestone. This limestone presents much the appearance of the brecciated limestone of Mackinac Island, at the head of Lake Huron.

The Red Beds appear within a mile. At the place where I observe them there is an immense thickness of conglomerate and breccia, made up of red sandstone fragments and pieces of the Carboniferous limestone, with some shale. This, I think, covers the horizons of the sandstone and limestone seen in the northern part of the hills, July 24; the latter being the first under the Red Beds.

The Red Beds are not so much disturbed, being simply tilted. To have produced this breccia, there must have been a grand fracturing and grinding of the strata, with movements up and down. The red color of the fragments of sandstone involved in this breccia must be attributed to the downward infiltration of coloring matter from the Red Beds above. The part here observed was probably overlain by some of the shore-deposits of the Red Beds, the lapse of time having driven farther and farther back the outcropping edges of all the formations, so as to render the effect of such infiltration visible at the surface. The Red Beds here consist almost entirely of sandstone with a bed at the bottom of white sandstone. Thus, in descending order:

Section in the Red Beds, on French Creek.

Red sandstone; seen about	50 feet.
White sandstone	10 feet.
Red sandstone	35 feet.
White sandstone	1 foot.
Total seen	96 feet.

The Red Beds die out by two or three alternations with white sandstone, introducing the Dakota group of the Cretaceous. This sandstone, near the bottom, is white here, but above it is darker. It has a thickness of about 125 feet, judged only by passing along. The Fort Benton clays are very characteristically exposed, being dark purple, and have a thickness of about 75 feet. Over these appears the Niobrara, which, at the base, is limestone in thin beds, very much like the same along the Big Sioux River, above Sioux City, in Iowa, and show, as there, *Inoceramus problematicus*, Schlotheim, &c. Above it becomes softer and marly, weathering yellowish. The thickness of this member it is difficult to estimate with reliability, because the slopes it forms are turfed, so as to include, either above or below, some of the other members. Judging from a terrace, however, that is made by it, I place its thickness at 150 feet. Above this comes a light, ashen clay, forming "bad-lands," rising in huge mounds and in bluffs that inclose the valley. This is probably the Fort Pierre group, and has a thickness of at least 250 feet. Colonel Hart, finding it impracticable to proceed farther, we reluctantly abandon the idea of seeing the Bad-Lands on the other side of the Cheyenne, and make a camp.

Camp, August 3.—Within six miles of the mouth of "Plenty-Spring Creek," according to Louis Agard, our guide. He says the names of French and Spring Creeks, as represented on the map of Captain Raynolds and Lieutenant Maynadier, 1859–'60, are interchanged.

August 4.—Return march. In passing back up the valley, I observe that between the Fort Benton clays and the Niobrara is a coarse, pebbly sandstone, 15 feet. This seems here to be in different beds and local, one bed being 30 feet or more below the other.

We follow the valley of the creek to the hills, and then turn off to the right, passing to the north, more directly toward camp, and camp early on a stream that has very little current, thickly beset with beaver-dams.

During the day I have not been able to make any valuable observations. I have seen no gypsum in the Red Beds on this side of the Black Hills.

I cannot resist the conviction that the largest portion of the upheaval of the Black Hills took place after the deposit of the Carboniferous limestone, else there would be isolated areas of the Red Beds at higher levels, and they would show everywhere more disturbance. They seem only to occupy a regular belt, surrounding the hills on all sides, never rising so as to be seen within the hills. I have no doubt but the hills have been elevated farther subsequent to the Red Reds, but the shattered condition of the Carboniferous limestone and the underlying sandstone (July 24) is so complete, that it shows plainly that the Red Beds, if overlying, could not have escaped a similar breaking up. I have seen the former made up of limestone and sandstone in angular pieces of all sizes to 6 feet, thoroughly mixed, the whole stained red, overlain by the Red Beds, undisturbed beyond a gentle dip. All the other formations—those of the Cretaceous—are in this respect like the Red Beds. There must also have been a still earlier upheaval, throwing out the Devonian, unless that be represented in the great limestone formation.

I have said the granite shows apparently an increasing redness toward the south. That is so; but I do not feel sure that it is not entirely due to weathering and iron stains. To-day I have seen large white crystals of feldspar in the rock, the same as at points farther north, and, at the same time, near by, the ground appeared red from red feldspar-gravel from the disintegration of the rock.

Camp, August 4.—We are about six miles from the general camp, in the midst of large pines, on a small creek, which is shut in by high hills of schist.

August 5.—Reached camp after traveling about two hours, at 9.30 a. m.

The reconnaissance toward the south, accompanied by Colonel Ludlow, took one day less time, and arrived back to-day about two hours later than we.

RETURN MARCH—FROM CUSTER PARK TO BEAR BUTTE.

August 6.—We leave camp this morning on our return march to Fort A. Lincoln. In passing northwest along our old trail, I see the change in the dip of the schist again plainly exhibited about fifteen miles north of our last camp. The change is from northwest or west to east or south-east. When we reach sight again of the Lower Silurian, which is about twenty-five miles north of our starting-place of this morning, I see the beds nearly horizontal, but the schist is highly inclined to the east, though these two observations are here two or three miles apart. The lime-stone capping the high hills to the northwest is not sufficiently tilted to have been thrown up when the schist was. The line of strike of this line of limestone bluffs is north, 25° or 30° east, by compass.

During this day's march we get from the tops of some of the hills most magnificent views of the mountains in our rear; the ruggedness of the peaks, and the shading of blue from mountains at different distances, uniting to make a picture that, for boldness and variety, is seldom equaled.

Camp, August 6.—We have returned nearly on our trail, passing two of our camping-places, but made a detour to the west by which we found a better road and made the distance somewhat shorter. Our present camp is about four miles southeast of that of July 28.

August 7.—In passing again over Elk-Horn Park, we travel about a mile east of the interrupted line of limestone bluffs, and I observe everywhere the schist dips east at a high angle, such that the limestone, which is nearly horizontal, could never have been conformable with it, and as I have seen no unconformability between that limestone and the Lower Silurian, I cannot but think also that the Lower Silurian never lay conformably on the schist; and hence that the age of the upheaval of the Black Hills has been mistaken by Dr. Hayden, who, I believe, says they must have been thrown up since the Cretaceous.

After traveling about eight miles to-day, the schist becomes irony, and, although I have seen no iron comparable to the specular hematite of the Lake Superior region at Negaunee, yet the slatiness of the rock, and its specular cleavage, remind me of it.

A few miles farther northeast, after passing the first noticeable iron in this schist, I see a breccia, or brecciated conglomerate, made up of pieces of slaty schist, quartz pebbles, and argil-lite, the first-named greatly predominating. The whole is charged with an iron cement. This occurs within a mile or two of the line of limestone hills.

The country is much less mountainous in the belt of the schists and slates, as we approach the limestone region, than in that of the granite, and much smoother than in the area of the limestone. The most disturbed region is in the neighborhood of Harney's Peak, and, so far as I have seen yet, it may be regarded as the granitic center of the Black Hills. The eruptive force, whenever it occurred, was most powerfully exerted there, dying out much more gradually toward the north than toward the south.

Camp, August 7.—We are on a fine creek, running south and joining one from the northwest. Just as we reached this camping-place, before the arrival of the train, General Custer and Colonel Ludlow killed a large cinnamon-colored bear, and soon after the Indians killed another.

August 8.—In leaving camp we climb with the train the hills on the east of the creek, and find an open, undulating country stretching off northeast, and travel in that direction. The rock is not often exposed here, though sufficiently to exhibit plainly the geological structure. Fires have destroyed the trees, so that almost everywhere there is a growth of small aspens, with a few other shrubs. There are also a great many small pines and aspens, 10 to 20 feet long, lying dead on the ground, prostrated by wind from the northwest, some are half burned; but the most of them appear to have been dead when they fell. Similar low hills run along the west and northwest side of the creek we just left. They have no rock in outcrop and no live timber.

Passing along northeasterly about six miles, the line of limestone bluffs is plainly visible about five miles away toward the west, but northwest there is a single bluff or peak, capped with lime-stone, not more than four miles away.

On these barren knobs is a good deal of iron-ore, in loose small pieces. It is stratified in the rock with quartz, and as yet does not appear to amount to much, though I have seen a gradually increasing irony composition in the rock for a day or two. This iron pertains to the quartzite that has been mentioned as forming the tops of low hills in the southeastern portion of the Hills, (August 3.) The strata of this quartzite here have a strong dip to the east and south, but I am unable to determine its thickness. I see about 10 feet.

Passing on a little further, I see beds of strongly ferruginous quartz in the schist over which we are traveling. The schist here stands nearly vertical or dips to the northeast.

Again, a short distance further, I encounter large pieces of a conglomerate, and then come upon a red sandstone, lying in large blocks on the surface. This is coarse. This and the conglomerate seem to be nearly horizontal.*

After passing a smooth divide, we begin a descent toward the east. Before us lies almost a treeless, level tract, distant three or four miles, bounded beyond, east, by a range of low, wooded hills. This treeless area is underlain by a talcose slate, and the vertical beds rise sometimes above the surface in sharp and angular ridges.

In the distance before us, but on this side of the open ground, can be seen a ridge of white rock, rising some distance above the general surface and crowning an elevation of about 100 feet. This ridge seems to run north and south. On visiting it, I find an immense quartz "vein" that runs north 50° west by compass. It rises about 15 feet above the talus, and for that distance consists of bare quartz rock. The sloping talus on each side rises 100 feet or more, and fragments from the quartz are strewn over the surface toward the west as far as to the creek, about one-half mile. This white, opaque, quartz deposit is from 15 to 20 feet wide, and is split by jointing into cuboidal masses that lie in place on each other. Although it may be called white, it is somewhat blotched with tints of rose and red, and in the jointing-planes there is a persistent scale of iron-rust after the parts separate. This continues as a prominent quartz ridge only about three-quarters of a mile. It cannot properly be styled a vein, as it coincides with the bedding of the schist, and has the same nature as others seen in the southern part of the hills, where they also dip with the bedding of the schist. Very industrious "prospecting" is carried on in the neighborhood of these "veins" by gold-seekers, who accompany the expedition.

The open country mentioned is rolling, and has formerly been covered with pines, as shown by an occasional dead trunk. Its basis is talcose slate, with occasional patches of dislodged conglomerate. Just before entering this open tract, we encounter a little creek and follow it toward the east; but not far, before striking more to the north, where, after crossing two others, we camp on the third. During the rest of the day, after leaving the first creek we crossed, we traveled through the same sort of country, the slaty beds standing upright, and so wasted away that the included quartz-beds stand above the ground for several feet. We passed one very prominent ridge, apparently formed thus by protruding quartz, standing erect, similar to that already described, but black on the exterior and not so long. It was a very striking object, the jointing-planes having caused the dislodgment of some of the separated blocks, giving the crest a serrated edge. Another is about a mile below our camp, in the valley of the creek.

Camp, August 8.—The road during the day has been very rough, some of the creek-crossings having delayed the train so that it does not arrive in camp till about 10.30 p. m. We are in a beautifully grassed valley, through which runs a creek. The edges of the valley are clothed with good Norway pine, but the hills about are generally very barren and desolate. Indeed, we have passed through to-day the poorest and most repulsive part of the Black Hills we have yet seen.

August 9.—We leave the creek and go more to the north, through the same sort of country. About three miles from camp, we ascend a grassy knoll, from which can be seen ahead, a mile distant, a few hills capped with stratified limestone. This is toward the northeast. Toward the north no limestone is visible; but to the west the line of limestone bluffs can be seen about fifteen miles away.

We are very near the edge of the belt of schist and slate, some of the ferruginous sandstone of the Lower Silurian appearing on the tops of the little knolls. These knolls are at first weathered down smooth and turfed over, but the sandstone can still be detected by the occurrence of small fragments among the grass. Further still toward the east the tops of the little knolls begin to have bare, stony spots, and the sandstone, in nearly horizontal strata, appears further and further down their slopes.

*At this point we had a view of a very small area on the plains.

Camp, August 9.—We turned south again and camped early in a wide, grassy valley in the midst of the Potsdam sandstone, about six miles from our last night's camp. This is owing to the impracticability of the country east and northeast for a train. On the knolls on both sides of our camp are numerous fragments of rusty sandstone. Just below our camp, about a mile, is an outcrop of what appears like a fine-grained granite, somewhat schistose.

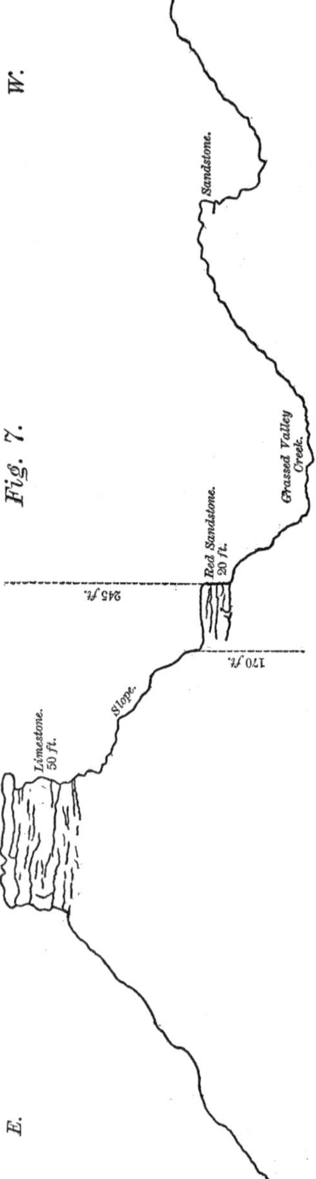

Fig. 7.

August 10.—Leaving camp we turn south and come within a mile upon hills and ridges that are capped with limestone. They show a dip to the south. There is a line of red sandstone in outcrop along the slopes of these bluffs, breaking the talus, which is otherwise turfed or wooded with small or dead trees. Hence I can get at first a view only of the limestone on the top, and of this sandstone. The limestone shows the same lithological characters as described where it was first met, in the upper portion of Floral Valley, being a firm, heavy-bedded, light-colored limestone, that is rarely vesicular or fossiliferous. The sandstone is red and in heavy layers, and shows no fossils. There are two intervals that cannot be well made out here. One is just below the limestone that caps the hills, and the other below the top of the red sandstone. About 20 feet of the sandstone can here be seen. From the bottom of the valley in which we travel to the top of the red sandstone shoulder, by aneroid is 170 feet, and thence to the top of the limestone ridge is 245 feet. The bluffs here are in the form of north and south ridges, formed by the outcropping edges of the formations. We follow down one of the grassed valleys, with the high limestone ridge on our left, and the low sandstone hills on the right. Sometimes the limestone constitutes two parallel ridges, that to the right or toward the west rising somewhat higher than the other, owing to a southeasterly dip, but generally the topography here is very simple, and regularly governed by the successive geological formations. Figure 7 is a profile across the valley down which we pass, intended to show the relative positions of the outcropping belts, and the usual form of the ridge of limestone on our left, at the point near where we first entered the valley.

After passing down this valley toward the south about two miles, another shoulder slowly rises, dimly outlined along the base of the bluff on our left, the upper shoulder rising accordingly above the level of the creek and crowding closer to the limestone so as to leave a narrow unexposed talus. Thus the wall of rock becomes more precipitous. This second shoulder at first seems to consist of a light, bedded sandstone, and reaches a thickness of about 25 feet. At a point a little below its first outcrop, and on the opposite (west) side of the valley, I meet with a more massive and conspicuous exposure of the contents of this lower shoulder. Here it is conglomeritic, with pebbles 1, 2, and 3 inches in diameter; but the most of the whole, even here, is a light-colored sandstone.

About three miles further down a black or purplish-black siliceous iron-ore occurs in short conical hills, rising from the immediate valley. This lies below the conglomerate. It is banded and in beds that dip like the schist at a nigh angle to the east. This iron does not pertain to the sandstone that lies in horizontal beds, but to a lower siliceous rock which I am disposed to regard stratigraphically the same as the red quartzite seen in the southeastern portion of the Hills. There seems to be an abundance of this iron-ore along this valley. Whether it extends any distance toward the west I have no opportunity to ascertain, but probably it continues as far as the formation of which it seems to be a metamorphic condition. About a mile further I ascend the bluff on the east and take aneroid measurements of the ascent. The formations here seen are the same as mentioned this morning on entering this valley, but the wall of the bluff is much more precipitous and affords a more constant exposure of the beds.

No. 1. From the bottom of the valley to the top of the conglomerate shoulder........ 140 feet.
[NOTE.—The greater part of this height is taken up with the siliceous iron, the conglomerate not being more than 35 feet.]

No. 2. Talus, to sandstone beds........ 185 feet.

No. 3. Perpendicular ascent of hard, massive, brick-red sandstone, with bands of oblique bedding........ 45 feet.

No. 4. Talus, of red earth and limestone fragments, about half the distance belonging to each. This extends to the foot of the perpendicular limestone cliff........ 115 feet.

No. 5. Limestone, perpendicular ascent. This limestone is hard, gray, crystalline, magnesian, with generally a close texture, and some fossils, with no apparent reason for separating it into different parts or members........ 130 feet.

Total height........ 615 feet.

The above limestone is very much one thing from top to bottom, but in some places vesicular. The few fossils obtained came from near the top of this bluff, and consist entirely of brachiopods. No corals were seen, though my examination was very hasty and incomplete. This limestone plays a very important part in the topography of the Black Hills, especially in a belt surrounding the schistose and slaty metamorphics. In the north it also forms a very large area of hills and narrow valleys, stretching from north to south about thirty miles. I see nothing here of that limestone and sandstone noted in Minne-lusa Valley, as overlying this. They have probably been denuded, and occur in outcrop farther east, as the beds here dip about 20° from the horizon in that direction. A breccia seen August 4 in the southeastern portion of the Hills represents both of those members, and it is reasonable to expect the same horizon to be represented by some rock in this portion. Off to the west from this bluff are rounded hills of iron-ore. This ore, being at so great a distance from other ore-beds, and in the midst of a timbered region, will at some day be very valuable, though it does not seem very pure, especially the surface fragments. Half a mile farther down, this ore is suddenly replaced by talcose slate, and on this the conglomerate lies unconformably. This slate is strangely variable to a granular schist of a slightly greenish color, and to a greenish quartzite. The beds below the conglomerate are in each case nearly vertical. What I here call conglomerate is white sandstone with scattered pebbles of quartzite, quartz, slate, and granite. It is 30 or 40 feet thick. I cannot observe any unconformability between it and the overlying red sandstone. The exposed surfaces, especially the upper layers of the latter, are hard, dark-red or purplish, compact and metamorphic.

Camp, August 10.—We are camped about a mile and a half below the bluff above measured. We find difficulty in getting out directly with a train, and General Custer will take to-morrow to prepare a road. The iron-ore runs out suddenly near our camp, and is replaced by a talcose slate, which varies to a greenish quartzite, and to a granitoid rock that it is difficult to characterize or name. The main features of the valley we are descending remain the same; on the right the metamorphics, and on the left a high bluff of tilted sedimentary rocks.

August 11.—Remained in camp, preparing skins.

August 12.—Make a detour to the southwest over a rolling wooded district about six miles from camp, while the train moves on down the valley. In company with Colonel Ludlow and half a dozen Santee scouts, "Jo Lawrence," one of the Santees, leads the way to three dead male elk (*Cervus Canadensis*) that he had the fortune to kill, when hunting yesterday. They were permitted by General Custer to hunt, on condition that if they killed elk they would come to camp and in-form us before skinning them, with the promise of a good reward for the unmutilated hide and skull. It is with the greatest difficulty that the Indians can be got to skin a mammal, except as they have been used to do from childhood; and as they are the best hunters, the collector for scientific purposes generally laments the loss to him of many valuable specimens. We found three fine specimens, two of which, in spite of injunctions to the contrary, they had beheaded, and all of which had been visited and gnawed by wolves during the night. The only entire skin was secured for mounting, and will be placed in the museum of the University of Minnesota. To reach this place, we passed over a succession of low metamorphic knolls and ridges clothed with very good pine. Where we skin the elks the rock is a very fine-grained, greenish chlorite slate. In returning to camp we follow down the valley of a creek toward the east and reach

Camp, August 12.—In the midst of low limestone hills and ridges, about eight miles from the camp left this morning, the sandstone and all lower having passed to the west of the line of march.

August 13.—We pass more easterly out of the valley in which we camped, and find, after ascending a difficult ravine, in which some of the wagons capsized, a more open, level country, clothed only with scattered small pines and turfed with good grass. There is still one large ridge between us and the plains. Of the latter the train-men now get the first view since entering the hills, though many of the troops and citizens, not confined to the line of march, have seen the plains from various parts of the hills since we first entered them, some having been down on to them. We have now passed the ridge caused by the Low Silurian, and that caused by the great limestone formation of the hills. Those remaining embrace the upper limestone and the Minne-lusa sandstone, as seen the first day after entering the Floral Valley, and the Lower Cretaceous.

Camp, August 13.—About two miles from our last camp, in a bend in Box Elder Creek, that being the name of the creek we have followed for a day or two, determined by parties sent to ascertain its course after leaving the hills.

August 14.—Breaking camp before sunrise, we descend an easy slope toward the east, formed by the dip of the rock, when we come, within three-fourths of a mile, facing upon a north and south ridge formed by the Minne-lusa sandstone, capped with a few feet of the Carboniferous limestone. Here we turn south to pass it. I make this sandstone to be about 75 feet. There is here, also, a thickness of about 20 feet of limestone overlying. The latter gives form and sharpness to the brow of the ridge. The dip in this part of the hills is much greater than in the north, and resembles that along French Creek. We do not go far south, but turn to the north and northeast, climbing at last over this ridge. We then strike the valley of the Red Beds and follow it north about six miles, where we cross Elk Creek and pass to the east of the ridge formed by the Dakota sandstone, reaching soon another known as the Bear Creek. Here we pass still farther east and enter on the Fort Benton, and immediately encounter another creek that comes from the northwest, mainly on the Fort Benton. This creek has a wide valley which really runs north and south, or very nearly in that direction, excavated in the Fort Benton. The upper part of this valley comes from the northwest and heads in the hills, but we continue on the Fort Benton to camp.

Camp, August 14.—We are about six miles south of Bear Butte, which is plainly visible and has been for ten or twelve miles. About three miles before reaching camp we struck the black or purplish-black slate that we had at our first crossing of the Belle Fourche, (July 18.) I am satisfied it is a metamorphic condition of the Fort Benton, though it seems very much thicker than the Fort Benton where I have seen it undisturbed. On this slate, which is cut by surface-drainage into bare knolls, are a few burr-oaks, though they are larger and more frequent in the valleys.

In the Red Beds I noticed the white gypsum to-day, that abounds in the same beds in the northern part of the hills, and which was also seen by Colonel Ludlow in the southern part. Thus it appears the gypsiferous character of these beds is nearly constant in the region of the hills. The only place they have been encountered without exhibiting abundance of gypsum was at the point where French Creek intersects them in the southeastern portion. Its not having been seen there is, however, only negative evidence. It may still exist.

August 15.—I find in the Fort Benton, near our camp, a couple of thin layers of a more calcareous composition and a lighter color. They are separated by an interval of about 10 feet. These layers part in the weather, like marly shale, into angular, conchoidal, small pieces. In these layers are fish-remains, spines and cycloid scales. In a similar bed, but thicker, was found yesterday, by one of the men, a coiled cephalopod, about four inches in diameter, that I took for *Ammonites percarinatus*, H. and M. This identification was not absolute, and I have no means to verify it.

August 15—*Visit to Bear Butte.*—With Colonel Ludlow and an escort, we go about five miles north to this celebrated butte, though I believe it has only been reported on by Dr. Hayden and the commander of the expedition with which he traveled. It is a singular conical mass, rising above the level of the plains 1,200 feet with that abruptness that makes it very difficult to climb, and such regularity of slope on all sides that from almost all directions it has, from a distance, nearly the same sugar-loaf-like outline. It stands in the midst of the Fort Benton slate, and has an elongation northwest and southeast. In ascending, Professor Donaldson and myself pass round to the northwest side, where we have the advantage of both shade and a strong northwest wind. After leaving the Fort Benton slate, we enter upon the underlying sandstone, belonging to the Dakota group. This is tilted up somewhat, but far less than the general inclination of the side of the butte. We then enter on the Red Beds, the dip of which it is difficult to ascertain, owing to their being weathered and covered with fallen pieces from above. Some of the larger of these pieces are so deeply impacted in these beds as to have a deceitful appearance of being in place. I see no gypsum. The Red Beds outcrop above a kind of terrace round the base of the butte. We come next upon the rock of which the hill itself is made, or on the shingle from it. It is the same as the rock that forms Heeng-ya Ka-ga, or at least the same as the lower outer ridge, that forms there a kind of encircling horseshoe. We pass through a gap on the west side, a short distance above the beginning of the shingle, formed by a quartzite spur, that rises perpendicular and stands out from the base of the butte. This may be from the Minne-lusa sandstone that underlies the Carboniferous limestone, or at least that portion of it which has already been mentioned as just below the Red Beds. On all sides the slopes are almost covered with shingle from the rock that forms the butte. Nothing lower can be seen than the spur of sandstone just above which we pass. The shingle lies in sliding uncertainty on slopes as nearly vertical as it will lie, but it is crossed by ascending zig-zag paths, that form all angles on the side of the butte, made by goat or other animals in climbing it. The little valleys or ravines that ascend convergently toward the summit of the butte contain the most of this loose shingle, the intervening ridges often being almost destitute of it. Following these paths mostly, we reach the top of the shingle, after a climb of about half an hour, when we find ourselves at the northwestern extremity of a ridge. Walking along this ridge, we reach in a few minutes the summit of the butte, the ridge continuing some distance to the southeast from the summit. Indeed, the remainder of the scaling-party, having ascended from the southeast, approach the summit from that direction along the same ridge. The butte is about six miles from the foot of the Black Hills, between the two being a small alkaline lake. It is thinly scattered over, about half way down, with small Norways. A few trailing cedars are also seen on the slopes. Cactus, of the usual kind seen on the plains in Dakota, grows even to the top; also sage-brush. About the summit of the butte there is also a low brush, that bears small red berries with stony pits. This rock, I believe, Dr. Hayden calls trap; but if he is right, it is different from any trap I ever saw. It is gray, and weathers white, falling to pieces in thin slabs, that, being broken, make a talus of innumerable fragments, reminding one of a slaty shale, though this is much harder and tougher. These pieces lie all about, from ¼ inch to 2 inches in thickness, and generally less than 10 inches across. It is very uniform in all its outward characters. It looks like a dirty chalk, somewhat porous, or like brown mortar set, without distinct grains of sand, sprinkled with minute scales of mica. It is hard, tough, and sonorous. In some cases it is very compact. It seems to be an igneous rock, resembling phonolite. It was probably thrust up after the deposition of the Carboniferous limestone, though I have been unable to detect any limestone about its flanks, and is older than the age of the Red Beds. As to the origin of this rock, it is undoubtedly eruptive. It appears to be such as would have resulted from a fusion, or semi-fusion, of the older rocks. It is made up of a considerable per cent. of the alkaline earths, in various chemical combinations, but with very little resulting evident crystallization. It is not entirely amorphous, since there are scattered glittering surfaces, resulting from the cleavage of crystallization. It appears as if the constituents had not opportunity to seek their affinities, and that, hardening in that incomplete stage, the rock presents, consequently, a confused external character and chemical composition.

The amount of lime and magnesia apparently present seems to point to the great limestone formation of the Black Hills as its probable origin, the carbonic acid having been expelled by the heat attending the outburst. The silica that is in composition with these bases must have come from the quartzites and sandstones below, or from the schists of the metamorphic rocks. The intermixing of some portion of the lower granitic rocks, even, with the fused mass, at the point of upheaval, or to greater depths, is not at all prohibited by the color or composition of the rock of this butte. If this hypothesis of the local origination of the rock of this butte be tenable, the limestones that have been mentioned as constituting a great portion of the sedimentary rocks of the hills, must have furnished a great proportion of the material.

Camp, August 15.—In the same place as August 14.

RETURN MARCH—FROM BEAR BUTTE TO FORT ABRAHAM LINCOLN.

August 16.—In passing Bear Butte this morning, I see there is a low rim or ridge round the east side, having a more rugged exterior than the butte itself, comparable in shape to the horseshoe rim that incloses Heeng-ya Ka-ga. It is hardly perceptible on the west side, but a low ridge of tilted sandstone, dipping south, runs from the butte to the hills. Thus Bear Butte compares again with Heeng-ya Ka-ga. On the side toward the hills, in each case, the encircling ridge is low or wanting. Ever since we left the hills there has been a noticeable drift deposit, so that the rock is much less frequently seen. It continues to Bear Butte, and also to the Belle Fourche. Where we cross the Belle Fourche it is much larger than at the place of our other crossing, and has a strong current. Its water is muddy, and like the Little Missouri. Cottonwoods grow along the bottoms, with box elder.

Camp, August 16—On a little creek in the plains directly north of Bear Butte. Throughout the whole of the day's march there has been a light drift, some of which appears to be foreign, but far the larger part originated *in situ;* hence I have not been able to determine the changes in the rock. Terraces and benches that are plainly due to the Cretaceous, as in Minnesota, cross the face of the country. These are turfed over evenly. This observation I have made a great many times, and specially in the valley of French Creek, between the Black Hills and the Cheyenne, but have not before recorded. Such appearances are universal on the plains, and make the topography that diversifies them. Along some of the valleys such terraces are very plainly marked for miles. This observation has an important bearing on the question of the existence and nature of a distinctly terrace epoch in the Post-Tertiary.

August 17.—Soon after leaving camp this morning we came on a change in the geology. The drift becomes light or wanting, and finally disappears altogether, leaving occasional pieces of the siliceous limestone that was seen on the plains in coming out from Fort A. Lincoln (July 14) scattered over the almost grassless surface. We are on a bedded clay or shale, that has all the characters of that at Castle Butte, (July 14.) It has argillo-calcareous concretions, that become rusty in the weather, and also part into small, angular pieces, with conchoidal surfaces. Sometimes these concretions contain shells, but not frequently. They are apparently the same kind as seen in the march out near the camp of July 16. They here contain an *Inoceramus* and a *Scaphites.* This clay spreads out here over an immense tract of country, and must have a great thickness. It seems to form a sterile soil, that produces only scattered weeds, and gives out dense clouds of dust as the train passes along. The surface is undulating, and has been since we left the hills. In this clay are crystals of gypsum and layers of heavy spar.

Slave Butte stands on this shale or bedded clay, which also constitutes its lower half. The rest of this butte is sandstone and arenaceous marl, the same as in Short-Pine Hills, in horizontal layers. Throughout this tract of country the rocks are horizontal, and, from appearances, this condition prevails and continues uninterruptedly to the Short-Pine Hills. We are here on the same plain and on the same formation that furnished similar concretions (July 16) a few miles farther west during our outward march.

On our left, and running almost to Slave Butte, is a line of broken hills, through some of the gaps in which we pass. These low hills are formed by the weathered-down sandstone that caps Slave Butte.

Slim Butte, as identified by Colonel Ludlow, seems rather to be a ridge, fully ten miles long, running north and south.

Camp, August 17—On this plain of clay and cactus.

August 18.—There are two series of ridges known as Short-Pine Buttes. They run north and south. They are geologically the same, but the west ridge is the higher, owing to an easterly dip in the rock. Prospect Valley runs between them. The eastern ridge consists, at its southern extremity, of a massive, friable sand, of dark-gray or bluish color, looking at the distance of a few rods like a blue clay. This occupies the bottom and supports the soil of Prospect Valley. Above this comes a series of sands and arenaceous marls, as already noted in the western ridge on the outward march, though this series is less evident as we pass along to-day in the eastern ridge. Below this sand is the clay of the bad-lands, at the northwest extremity of the western ridge, July 16, as noted.

Camp, August 18.—In Prospect Valley, about five miles north of our old camp in this valley.

Camp, August 19.—March north and then east, and camp on the North Fork of Grand River, passing some "bad-lands" and entering upon a region of bluffs capped with a rusty sandstone, distance thirty-five and a half miles. I have lost, to-day, the line of connection or superposition of the main geological features. We go too fast for anything reliable in my line of investigation; indeed have always done so, except at great extra labor.

Many fragments of the same siliceous limestone that were seen in coming out have been seen on the surface in to-day's march. They were also seen the day before. About three miles out from camp this morning, lignite was seen in the bluffs along our march.

August 20.—March northwest through a more or less drift-covered country, with frequent siliceous limestone fragments, as already mentioned, the grass having been consumed by prairie fires, and after thirty miles travel we camp on the Little Missouri, the bluffs along which are made up as below, in descending order:

No. 1. Sandstone, massive, no turf, about	25 feet.
No. 2. Clay, with lignite and globular masses of laminated sandstone	100 or 200 feet.

Making a kind of bad-lands like that at Castle Butte, the horizon of which, I think, is identical with this. There is here a slight dip to the east. No fossils seen.

August 21.—Remain most of the day in camp, preparing skins and repacking for long marches, and quick departure from Lincoln on reaching there.

August 22.—Breaking camp at the usual hour (about 4 a. m.) and passing out of the Little Missouri Valley by the same road as that by which we entered, we turn more east and come on to a region thickly strewn with large masses of siliceous limestone, or slightly calcareous quartzite, the same as those already frequently mentioned. They always lie on the surface, and I am at a loss to account for their being here. They are fossiliferous with wood. I have never yet seen a piece of this kind of silicified wood *in situ.* They seem always to lie on the surface, and I think it may be they are closely associated in origin with this siliceous limestone. Here the pieces of the latter almost cover the ground. There are no other bowlders. I can see nothing but these pieces that would indicate a foreign drift. They have about the same color as the masses of silicified wood that are frequently seen on the western plains.

After traveling about eight miles from camp we come to a creek. Before reaching this creek the toning down of the hills into low knolls, and the prairie-like aspect of the face of the country, coincide with the observation on the dip of the rock at the Little Missouri, and both bring in a loosely cemented sandstone, sometimes massive or obliquely bedded. At this creek is a very fine bed of lignite, exposed 6 feet. The lower limit cannot be seen. It is abruptly terminated upward by the above sandstone, which, in a fresh break in the bank of the creek, rises perpendicularly about 20 feet above the lignite. This is the first ravine with water that we have seen since leaving camp this morning, and this seems to have a drainage eastwardly. I have seen lignite in outcrop two or three times to-day before reaching this place, in weathered slopes, but it was in the clay below.

The rest of this day's march was through a fine region of undulating plains, strewn with buffalo bones, running north, distant from the Little Missouri eight or ten miles, with a line of red hills on the east, about three miles away.

Camp, August 22.—We are on the very edge of a district of bad-lands, which stretch off toward the north and northwest. The Little Missouri has here turned east, and is distant from our camp about two miles toward the north. To the north is an unbroken view of bad-lands looking over the river valley, while toward the south the landscape presents a beautiful undulating prairie, though now blackened by prairie-fires.

Camp, August 23.—Marched east, over much the same kind of country as yesterday, about eighteen miles, and camped in the Bad-Lands, in a fine grassy plain of small extent, through which flows a creek. About five miles before camping here we struck an old trail, said to have been made by a return party of General Stanley last year.

August 24.—Leave camp in the dusk of the morning, and travel east, passing through a district of bad-lands, and following still the old trail. Although I call these bad lands, (for so they are generally known among the men who have before crossed here,) they are not so *bad* as I had been led to expect from descriptions that I have read. There is no great difficulty in passing through them with a train. There are a great many bare clay and sand buttes, and deep perpendicular cañons, cut by streams in rainy seasons; but there are also a great many level and grassy, sometimes beautiful valleys, with occasionally a few trees and shrubs. With some care a good road can be selected by following these low and more level tracts. There is but little water in here, the most that we have found being due to recent rains. The tops of a great many of the buttes are red, and often they are overstrewn with what appears like volcanic scoria. This, I am satisfied, arises from the burning of the lignite, which occurs in nearly all these lands, there being one large bed of it, and sometimes two distinct beds, in the same slope. The lignite is ignited by fires that sometimes prevail over the plains, set by Indians; and when fanned by the strong winds that sweep across them, produces a very intense heat, fusing the over and under lying beds, and mixing their materials in a confused slag, which, although generally of a reddish color, is sometimes of various colors. The clay makes a very hard, vitreous or pottery-like slag that is sometimes green or brown. Iron stains the whole with some shade of red. There are no fossils in these bad-lands. Besides myself, Mr. G. B. Grinnell, and Mr. North, his assistant, have given as much time to searching for fossils as the rate of our progress will permit. We have not succeeded in finding any fossils that indicate the age of these beds. In that respect they are very strikingly different from the beds of the White River Tertiary, a fact which suggests their differing from those beds in geological age. Judging by topographical and lithological indications, they are formed by the same strata that constitute Castle Butte (July 14) and the arid plains that we traveled over for some distance east of it. The clay at the base of the Short-Pine Hills, making bad-lands on the west of Prospect Valley, is also, on the same evidence, of the same, or nearly the same, age. There is an immense clayey formation that extends toward the south, and toward the southwest, producing, in the vicinity of drainage-courses, a series of bad-lands, that probably causes this region of bad-lands. If this parallelization be correct, the fossiliferous concretions taken from the clay shale August 17, which contained an evident *Inoceramus*, make this clay Cretaceous. This, however, will make the whole region between here and the Belle Fourche, mapped as Tertiary by Dr. Hayden, also Cretaceous, bringing about a considerable reduction in the supposed Tertiary area. In short, the evidence seems to me to point to the Fort Benton, of the Lower Cretaceous.

During the march of the 22d of August, and also the 23d, there were evidences of a light foreign drift. They were very slight at first, and became more evident at the close of the march of the 22d.; but they die out on entering the bad-lands, (see under August 28.) A march of four or five miles takes us out of the Bad-Lands. Thence to camp we travel over a desolated, burnt plain eastward, to a small creek, making twenty-five and a half miles altogether.

August 25.—After marching about eight miles over a burnt plain, with a few small grassed patches, protected from the fire by ravines on nearly all sides, we reach a butte which, at a distance, appears like sandstone, but, on a nearer approach, I see it is but partly composed of sandstone. South of this butte, but near it, is a larger exposure of the same beds, the exposed edges facing north and east, with a dip southeast of 4° or 5°. One butte is isolated and rises about 75 feet. The layers here exposed are as follows, in descending order:

No. 1.	Clay, calcareous and concretionary, the round concretions from which lie on the top in great numbers and roll down the sides, about	15 feet.
	[NOTE—This forms the crown of a cap, the rim being formed by the next.]	
No. 2.	Bedded, marly clay, persistent and projecting	15 feet.
No. 3.	Marly sand, with pebbles	8 feet.
	[NOTE.—This passes into the next.]	
No. 4.	Massive sand, with oblique bedding containing water-worn pebbles as large as walnuts, conglomeritic and incoherent	25 feet.
No. 5.	Fine bedded clay	6 feet.
No. 6.	Carbonaceous clay and lignite	6 feet.
No. 7.	Fine bedded clay; seen	2 feet.
	Total exposed	77 feet.

In this series of beds I see no fossils, but the whole reminds me of the Niobrara.

Traveling on about six miles farther, I find exposures of a sandstone. In low knolls, or rather on them, are round or oblong concretionary pieces, some of which hold silicified wood. This wood, however, is much less compact and has a different color from that seen commonly on the surface. I do not think the well-known silicified wood which occurs in vitrified fragments in the drift and on the surface of the plains is derivable from this sandstone.

Camp, August 25.—We are on a creek, and in its bank is a lignite bed. The section downward is as follows:

No. 1.	Sandstone	10 feet.
No. 2.	Carbonaceous clay and lignite	5 feet.
No. 3.	Arenaceous clay	5 feet.
	Passing into	
No. 4.	Massive sand, seen	20 feet.
	Total	40 feet,

August 26.—On the march eastward we cross the Heart River in about fifteen miles, the country being an undulating prairie, burnt over. The banks of the Heart River are in sandstone in part at least, and terraced. After crossing the Heart we travel eastward to a weathered butte, where we find good oak wood and beautiful springs of water. Near here were seen elk when we came to camp. The butte, which is properly styled Spring Butte, is about a mile east of our place of camping. Off to the north is a wide, rough valley lying below us, which is, I think, wrought in the sandstone seen at Heart River crossing, Spring Butte being in a clay overlying. This judgment is based on appearances from our camp, there being no opportunity to carefully examine either the valley or the butte.

Camp, August 26.—We have traveled to-day thirty-two and one-half miles, the weather being hot and the grass consumed by late fires.

August 27.—Travel in a dense fog till about noon, which then clears up. We make an early

Camp, August 27, at a beautiful spring, remarkably copious, that issues from the base of a low hill. This hill is one of a series that inclose a wide, shallow valley, and are capped with sandstone. Here we have very fine grazing, this valley having escaped the late burning. Our distance to-day has been seventeen miles over a burnt plain.

August 28.—This sandstone I see dips east, and on the march we pass a number of clay buttes, likewise generally capped with a little sandstone, which seems to be rather a course of concretionary nodules. Their composition is that of common sandstone. In these buttes is a bed of Carbonaceous clay, near the base.

Camp, August 28.—On a creek with a plenty of good grass and wood. The outer banks of this creek are made up of red, burnt chips and slag for about 15 feet, probably from a bed of burnt lignite overlying, and of horizontally-bedded clays, the lowest seen part of which for about 10 feet is Carbonaceous. About midway in these outer bluffs is an interrupted bed of lignite that is different from any I have seen. It seems to be calcareous and bituminous, and weathers white, parting into thin shingle that shows impressions of twigs and roots and long slender stems of marine leaves. Silicified wood also weathers out in small pieces from the same layer.

In regard to the drift, I think that the conglomerate I saw a few days ago, (August 25,) may have furnished all the pebbles of a foreign nature that I have seen on the surface and regarded as evidences of drift. (See under August 24.) It was, however, during to-day's march, about midway, that I saw unmistakable foreign drift. It consisted of boulders of granite and metamorphic rock, distributed over the surface and especially on the little knolls mingled still with the almost universal fragments of what I have styled siliceous limestone. These fragments and boulders gradually became more abundant as we came into camp. In the valley, though, none are seen, as they are covered by alluvium. In these pieces of silicified rock I saw, a few days ago, near the Little Missouri Valley, impressions and also pieces of wood. There were in the midst of a great many large pieces of silicified limestone a good many pieces of silicified wood. There were also, in the former, cavities from which very evidently the latter had become loosened on weathering, and some pieces of the wood were not yet entirely freed from the rock. This shows the intimate connection between these two singular but common objects that the traveler sees on these plains, the same as is shown by their very similar composition and external characters.

Camp, August 29.—On the Sweetbrier, a tributary of the Heart River. The country has been drift-covered during the day's march.

August 30.—Leave camp at the usual hour, and after crossing the Heart again at about twelve miles from Fort A. Lincoln, where the expedition halts to rest and lunch, we march into Fort A. Lincoln about 4½ p. m.

RESUMÉ OF GEOLOGICAL RESULTS.

Introductory to this resumé may be quoted the following from Dr. F. V. Hayden, Fourth Annual Report of Progress of the Geological and Geographical Survey of the Territories, 1870, p. 98: "The Black Hills of Dakota will form one of the most interesting studies on this continent. There is so much regularity in the upheaval that all obscurity is removed, and all the formations known in the West are revealed in zones or belts around the granitic nucleus in their fullest development. A careful, detailed topographical and geological survey of this range would be a most valuable contribution to science. In all the western country I have never seen the Cretaceous, Jurassic, Triassic, or Red Beds, the Carboniferous and Potsdam rocks, so well exposed for study as around the Black Hills."

The geological results of the late expedition by General G. A. Custer to the Black Hills of Dakota are much less than they would have been had it been possible to allow more time for examination. In a military expedition, or one mainly military, the accompanying geologist can only be industrious in gathering facts, as they occur during the daily march. His opportunity for comparing his observations with the geology of a belt of country adjoining on either hand, or for following up a train of investigations to solve problems that arise to his mind from what he sees, is very meager. Still, when the geological observations made during the past season are compared with facts that have been similarly gathered by Dr. F. V. Hayden, and by others, they throw additional light on the character of that portion of Dakota, and serve, as far as they go, to establish the true geological age of some of the rocks about which there has been considerable uncertainty and some discussion.

THE CRETACEOUS.

The plains along our line of travel afforded but very meager fossil remains, but those that were found indicate the continuation of the Cretaceous, from the Missouri River at Fort A. Lincoln to the foot-hills of the Black Hills. Indeed the topography of the country and the lithological character of the successive members of the Cretaceous, as passed over, indicate this fact, without any appeal to the fossil contents of the rocks. This was perhaps a little more evident on the return than on the outward march. About the bases of the Black Hills, and especially near Bear Butte, the light-colored sandstones of the Dakota group of the Cretaceous are unmistakable. Overlying these sandstones is a bluish or grayish, bedded clay, which, near the hills, becomes a purplish slate. This clay stretches over a wide valley, running mainly north and south from the Little Missouri river, to and beyond the Belle Fourche, forming, along the east side of the Little Missouri, a series of Bad Lands. This is a desolate, alkaline plain, and in it stand Slave Butte, Deer's Ears Buttes, Owl Butte, and Short-Pine Hills. The formations, even as far removed from the axis of upheaval as the Little Missouri, show a slight dip to the eastward, for, although the general slope is to the east, the observer, in traveling east, finds himself rising in the rocks to higher and higher geological horizons. The first indications of an approaching change in the geology of this alkaline plain, formed by the Fort Benton clays, consist of occasional buttes and broken-down ridges that have withstood the attacks of time, rising to the height of several hundred feet above the general level, facing to the westward, and capped with more enduring rock. This enduring member consists of arenaceous marls, and marls that pass into an arenaceous limestone, and give form and existence to the Short-Pine Hills and the other ridges and buttes that bound this plain on the east. These ridges and buttes finally become so frequent and persistent as to connect in one, and the face of the country is thus raised to the top of that geological horizon, though still intersected by east and west drainage-courses. This horizon of marly rock is believed to embrace the Niobrara of the Cretaceous. Between this line and that of the Fox Hills group, which outcrops along the tops of the bluffs at Fort A. Lincoln, lies the belt of the Fort Pierre. This, also, forms a series of washed buttes and light-colored bluffs, and is overlain by a sandstone which forms the surface of the country to the Missouri River, or at least exists in the tops of the hills and buttes. If an accurate map of the areas of these formations were to be constructed, it would show a great many winding tortuosities in the outlines of the various rocks. The valleys, even in the Fox Hills area, are in the Fort Pierre, and within the Niobrara belt the Fort Benton makes very frequent and very great intrusions.

The same order of succession for the various members of the Cretaceous was observed in a reconnaissance from the Black Hills toward the Cheyenne, toward the southeast. The fossils that indicate the Cretaceous age of this alkaline plain formed by the Fort Benton, alluded to, and of the Bad-Lands along the east side of the Little Missouri, are as follows, identified by Mr. G. B. Grinnell, of New Haven, Conn. By reference to the accompanying geological map of the localities, as described in the foregoing report, and the general topographical map of the route of the expedition, the area of this Cretaceous belt may be seen and the significance of the fossils fully understood. The dates attached refer to the day of the month on which they were collected, and their localities are expressed by the general map.

JULY 17.

Scaphites Conradi, Mort.
Aturia biangulata, M. and H.
Actæon concinnus, M. and H.
Vanikoro ambigua, M. and H.
Baculites ovatus, Say.
Pteria linguiformis, Ev. and Shu.
Scaphites larvæformis, M. and H.
Amauropsis paludinæformis, M. and H.
Nucula planimarginata, M. and H.
Terebratula, (sp. undet.)
Limopsis striato-punctata, Ev. and Shu.

AUGUST 17.

Inoceramus convexus, M. and H.
Scaphites Conradi, Mort.
Scaphites nodosus, Owen.
Anchura (Drepanocheilus) Americana, M.

The writer is not familiar with the lignites of the Lower Tertiary, and cannot compare the lignites found in this Cretaceous belt with those that occur in that formation. These, however, were found to occur in the Fort Pierre and in the Fort Benton groups. Some beds were 5 or 6 feet thick, but generally when they showed that thickness some part of the bed was made up of an impure lignite or Carbonaceous earth. They appear as if they were old peats. They often have a shining conchoidal fracture, though as black as ebony. They sometimes pass into a clay, and are sometimes abruptly terminated by a bed of sand. Cretaceous lignites in Minnesota are associated with irregular deposits of ash (or what has every appearance of ash) and with charred woody fiber, and belong to the Fort Benton. Although no ashy deposits were found in the lignites in Dakota during the expedition to the Black Hills, yet some woody fiber, not charred, was taken out. It is difficult to say to what use, if any, these lignites can ever be put. They will certainly serve as an inferior kind of coal. In cases of exigency, they will furnish a fuel for any use. They lie horizontal, inclosed in non-indurated rocks. Hence, any attempt at mining them, wherever seen in Dakota, would be attended with difficulties resulting from the caving in of the superincumbent rock. Many chemical analyses of these lignites have been made from different portions of the Northwest. While they embrace a considerable per cent. of inflammable, volatile substances, they also comprise enough carbon to make a valuable fuel. It seems that the only difficulty that will attend their general utilization will arise from the cost of mining compared with the currentprices of other fuel. In the first settlement of the Territory, before the construction of railroads for the transportation of wood or coal from other parts, the various outcrops of these lignites will no doubt be eagerly sought for the fuel they will supply, since the whole country, until reaching the Black Hills, is nearly destitute of trees.

THE JURASSIC AND TRIASSIC.

The rocks that lie below the Cretaceous are characterized by a brick-red color, and hence, though they are known to cover the edges of the Jurassic and Triassic with indefinable relative limits, they are also well known as the Red-Beds. They have a thickness in the northern bases of the Black Hills of about 325 feet. They are associated near the top with a conglomerate, which is overlain by a greenish, bedded shale or clay, having a thickness of about 45 feet. No fossils were found that could be referred directly to this shale, but at some places a species of *Belemnites*, supposed to be *B. densus*, characteristic of the Jurassic, was found in considerable numbers lying on the surface of turfed slopes that must have covered this horizon. Below this greenish shale is a conglomerate of about 2 feet in thickness, containing fossils. Of these Mr. Grinnell reports only two identifications, viz, *Camptonectes bellistriatus*, Meek, and, doubtfully, *Gryphæa calceola*, Quenst., var. *Nebrascensis*, M. and H.

The value of the Jurassic, and Triassic, economically, consists in the immense quantities of gypsum that they contain. In the Redwater Valley this gypsum occurs in the tops of a great many buttes and along the crests of a great many ridges. It forms the floor of a long extent of country running north and south over which the expedition passed. It is purely white, and crystalline and massive. It is seen in beds of different thicknesses, the principal bed being about 22 feet. It could be quarried in large blocks, and occurs in the most favorable positions. It seems to be inexhaustible, since the Red-Beds were found to surround the Black Hills, and to present nearly everywhere equal opportunities for taking it out.

THE CARBONIFEROUS LIMESTONE.

The Red-Beds were found to lie unconformably on the Carboniferous limestone. There was a period of upheaval and metamorphism succeeding the Carboniferous limestone, the effects of which can be seen along a north and south belt, from New Mexico, along the eastern spurs of the Rocky Mountains, to the Black Hills. The upper surface of the limestone sometimes shows undulations, as well as sudden breaks and upthrows, the former indicating a steadier and longer continued disturbing force. This disturbance, which seems to have caused in New Mexico an argentiferous character to pervade the limestone, is equally displayed in the Black Hills, but as yet no similar metalliferous deposits have there been found. This limestone is found forming the steep slopes to a great many hills; its unbroken upper surface conforming to the contour of the hills, and sometimes exhibiting upward and downward flexures in short intervals. This upheaval added largely to the former area of the Black Hills, such addition being mainly on the north.

How much of the great limestone formation that succeeds the Red-Beds below, and forms one of the chief sedimentary formations of the Black Hills, belongs to the Carboniferous age, it will be for future observers definitely to settle.

Whatever may be the age of this limestone in the Black Hills, in whole or in part, it is separated into two portions by a white sandstone, which for the purpose of designation has herein been named the Minne-lusa sandstone, having a thickness of about 75 feet. Is is a singular circumstance that in the neighborhood of Heeng-ya Kaga Peak and Bear Butte, two characteristic outbursts of igneous rock, only the upturned beds of the upper portion of this limestone appear. It is only within the Hills themselves that the lower portion of this great limestone formation can be seen. The upper has a thickness of about 100 feet, and the lower about 225 feet, which, with the included sandstone, makes an aggregate of 400 feet. A few fossils were gathered near the top of the lower portion, and have been identified as follows, by Mr. G. B. Grinnell:

AUGUST 10.

Terebratula ?
Spirifera, (sp. undet.)
Rhynchonella, (sp. ?)
Retzia, (*Eumetria* of Hall.) ?
Euomphalus, (sp. ?)
Internal cast of a Terebratuloid shell.
Syringopora, (probably *S. mult. attenuata*.)

The following were obtained also from the lower member of the great limestone formation:

JULY 25.

Athyris, *Streptorhynchus*, and *Zaphrentis*.

The upper portion of this limestone is fine-grained, compact, and highly crystalline, rendering it a good marble. It is also sometimes of a pink or reddish color, mottled with lighter spots. It passes into a rough and somewhat arenaceous limestone, however, within the first 75 feet, and has a coarse grain, with some porous and vesicular beds. The intervening sandstone is white and homogeneous. It is sometimes broken and iron-stained. The lower limestone is also mainly a very compact and fine-grained stone, but it shows some porous and coarse-grained layers. It is of a light color, and weathers into majestic, castellated bluffs and buttresses. There is a large area in the northern central portion of the Black Hills in which this lower limestone, in a horizontal position, forms the surface-rock, the upper limestone outcropping about its outer boundary. This portion of the hills is very rough, and is cut by cañons through this limestone into a net-work of short, narrow valleys, separated by intervening rocky ridges and plateaux. These cañons are inclosed by more or less perpendicular escarpments of this limestone.

In the southern portion of the hills there is a great thickness of brecciated limestone, covering the horizon immediately below the Red Beds, such breccia also containing masses of sandstone, referable to the upper or Minne-lusa sandstone, that in other places separates the great limestone formation of the Black Hills into two distinct members.

Near the bottom of the lower member of the great limestone formation it becomes slightly red, and is more compact and firm. It is also often arenaceous. Whether this lithological change is accompanied by a corresponding change in its fossil contents, warranting the separation of this portion from the rest, and whether any important distinction should be made as to its geological age, it is impossible to determine by the meager fossil representatives that could be secured. In this red limestone, which sometimes overlies a coarse white sandstone, and sometimes a red laminated argillaceous sandstone, were observed a cyathophylloid form resembling *Zaphrentis centrallis*, Ed. and Haine, crinoid stems; a species of *Campophyllum*, (or *Amplexus*,) an undetermined *Spirifera*, and a species of *Productus*, according to the identifications of Mr. Grinnell.

THE POTSDAM SANDSTONE.

This term is intended here to cover a quartzite, a conglomerate, and a red sandstone, all of which have been by authors referred to the age of the Potsdam of New York. Those three lithological and stratigraphical distinctions that are noticeable in the Primordial sandstone in the Northwest generally, are also observable in the Black Hills. There is in the first place a red, compact, massive quartzite, that appears in the southern portion of the Hills, dipping at high angles in different directions, and rising as low hills, of which it forms at least the surface-rock, 100 to 200 feet, which seems to underlie the other portions. This has very much the appearance of the red quartzite outcrops at New Ulm in Minnesota, and near Baraboo in Wisconsin. It apparently becomes more and more ferriferous, till in some places it may properly be styled a siliceous iron-ore, and it then rises in tilted beds in the form of hills, short and conical, in very much the same manner. This condition of this quartzite was seen especially along the eastern portion of the Hills. It underlies the conglomeritic sandstone, or the conglomerate. The latter is white and massive, with scattered quartz-pebbles. That, at least, is its character in the eastern portion of the Black Hills. It has a thickness, carefully measured, of about 35 feet. There is then an unobserved interval of over 100 feet, from which have been derived fossiliferous slabs of rusty sandstone, containing *Lingulepis*, and referable to the "Lingula Beds" of the Potsdam. Above this rises, in the eastern portion of the Black Hills, an immense formation of brick-red sandstone, which seems to be largely attenuated in other portions, or wanting. In the central portion of the Black Hills, along Castle Valley, a conglomerate was seen immediately underlying the lower, reddish portion of the lower limestone, but it is not known to be the same as that seen below the massive red sandstone in the eastern part of the Hills.

SCHISTS AND SLATES.

Below the Primordial sandstones and quartzites lies a series of slates and schists, that contain intercalated beds of quartz. These beds of schist and slate, largely micaceous, often stand nearly vertical, when the inclosed beds of quartz rise often nearly 50 feet above the surrounding rock. They have a deceptive appearance of veins, but have not the banded structure of true veins. These schists, in the neighborhood of granitic areas, are found to be interstratified with beds of true granite, like that of the region generally. The belt of schists is characterized by parks, that are often approximately level, nicely turfed and arable, due to the homogeneous and erosible nature of the rock. This is especially the case when the rock is talcose.

GRANITE.

The granitic area is near the southern part of the Hills, and is much smaller than has been supposed. Harney's Peak may be taken as the center of the granitic area, but it probably is somewhat too far north. The granite is usually coarse, and contains a white feldspar. Toward the southern limit of the granite, however, much of the feldspar is reddish. This seems to be due to weathering, the iron from surface-water having left a rust that seems to permeate the whole Whether due to weathering or to an original difference of composition, it seems to clearly indicate a different history for the southern portion of the Black Hills.

SUMMARY SECTION OF THE ROCKS OF THE BLACK HILLS.

In entering the hills from the north, passing through their central portion, and leaving them toward the south, and afterward toward the east, the following general section of rocks was observed:

No. 1. Blue or purplish shale, becoming, nearer the Hills, a slate of nearly a black color, seen at the first crossing of the Belle Fourche; the Fort Benton of the Cretaceous. Thickness		300–400 feet.
No. 2. Sandstone, light-colored, sometimes rusty; the Dakota of the Cretaceous. Thickness about		500 feet.
No. 3. Green shale, 45 feet	Jurassic?	57 feet.
No. 4. Fossiliferous conglomerate, 2 feet		
No. 5. Purplish shale, toward the top arenaceous, 10 feet		
No. 6. Snowy gypsum		4-6 feet.
No. 7. Red marl, arenaceous, massive or laminated		75 feet.
No. 8. Snowy gypsum		22 feet.
No. 9. Red marl, the same as No. 7		18 feet.

No. 10. Snowy gypsum.......... 2½ feet.
No. 11. Red marl, the same as No. 7.......... 30 feet.
No. 12. Snowy gypsum.......... 2½ feet.
No. 13. Red marl, the same as No. 7, seen.......... 35 feet.
No. 14. Interval unseen, (red marl,) about.......... 135 feet.

[Nos. 6 to 14, inclusive, have been doubtfully referred to the Triassic, though Jurassic fossils have been found near the bottom of the Red Beds.*]

No. 15. Fine-grained limestone, mottled with pinkish and light-colored cloudings, containing no known fossils; below this becomes harsh, magnesian, and even arenaceous. Carboniferous (?); the Upper Limestone of the accompanying geological map.......... 100 feet.
No. 16. White sandstone; locally stained with iron, so as to have a brick-red color. Carboniferous (?); the Minne-lusa sandstone, called the Upper Sandstone on the accompanying geological map.......... 75 feet.
No. 17. An immense limestone formation, stretching over a large area in the northern part of the Hills; light-colored, often saccharoidal, variable; usually hard, crystalline, compact, sometimes vesicular. Carboniferous (?); the Lower Limestone of the accompanying geological map.......... 225 feet.
No. 18. Hard, reddish limestone, with chert; containing cyathophylloid and crinoid corals.......... 16 feet.
No. 19. White, coarse sandstone, with small, rounded quartz-pebbles, (seen in Castle Valley; wanting on French Creek).......... 25 feet.
No. 20. Red sandstone, with oblique bedding; seen in the eastern slopes of the Hills; on Castle Creek the *Lingulepis* fossils, found in rusty slabs, belong below or near the bottom of this sandstone; the Potsdam; the Lower Sandstone of the accompanying geological map; about.......... 100 feet.
No. 21. The Conglomerate, containing rounded quartz pebbles; color white.......... 35 feet.
No. 22. Metamorphic schists and slates.
No. 23. Coarse, white, feldspathic granite.

THE STRUCTURAL SYSTEM OF THE BLACK HILLS.

"The geological structure of the Black Hills may be mentioned briefly in this connection. The nucleus or central portion is composed of red, feldspathic granite, with a series of metamorphic slates and schists superimposed, and thence upon each side of the axis of elevation the various fossiliferous formations of this region follow in their order to the summits of the Cretaceous, the whole inclining against the granitoid rocks at a greater or less angle. There seems to be no unconformability in these fossiliferous rocks, from the Potsdam inclusive, to the top of the Cretaceous.

"From these facts we draw the inference that prior to the elevation of the Black Hills, which must have occurred after the deposition of the Cretaceous rocks, all these formations presented an unbroken continuity over the whole area occupied by these mountains. This is an important conclusion, and we shall hereafter see its application to other ranges, and also to the Rocky Mountain range, taken in the aggregate." (Dr. F. V. Hayden, Second Annual Report of the United States Geological Survey of the Territories.)

The foregoing description agrees, in the main, with the observations of the writer. He did not, however, see sufficient evidence of unbroken conformability in the fossiliferous formations of the Black Hills to warrant him in adopting the important conclusion above quoted concerning their age. On the contrary, there seems to be no reason to exempt the Black Hills from the general principle applicable to most of the mountain ranges of North America; that after an elevation of a granitic nucleus, the successive sedimentary formations that surround it were raised by a series of paroxysms, produced by the long-continued application of a cosmical force. The writer sees no more reason to suppose the sedimentary strata were, until a comparatively late geological

* Page 11. "*Geological Report of the Exploration of the Yellowstone and Missouri Rivers.*" By Dr. F. V. Hayden, under the direction of Capt. W. F. Reynolds, Corps of Engineers, 1859–'60.

period, entire and continuous over the region of the Black Hills, than to suppose the similar granitic and metamorphic axis of Minnesota was at first covered by the continuous strata of the Silurian and Devonian that bound it on both sides. It is by no means certain that the dates of all the successive upheavals that brought the Black Hills to their present height above the sea-level can be determined. The general elevation of vast continental areas would not produce such discordance in strata as to appear in the rocks of every mountain-chain, especially after the lapse of time sufficient to cause the denudation of the shore-deposits. They would be detected at points, sometimes far remote, where circumstances were favorable for the greatest displacement of the formations, or where minute examination may have been made. The rocks of the Black Hills show, in the opinion of the writer, the following periods of successive disturbance and upheaval, at each of which there must have been an accession both to the altitude and area of the Hills:

1st. The granitic nucleus, which forms the highest portions of the hills, has a marked boundary separating it from the schists. This granite is generally massive, though near its union with the schists it is somewhat interstratified with them. It cannot be supposed to have been originally entirely covered by the schists.

2d. The schists show evidence of great disturbance and upheaval. They dip in opposite directions and at high angles, standing sometimes vertical.

3d. In the southern portion of the Black Hills a red quartzite, later than the schists, rises in undulating hills, dipping with their slopes and forming their surfaces, and must have been thrown into those positions by elevating forces before the deposition of the later sedimentary strata.

4th. After the upper limestone was deposited there was a very profound disturbance and a large accession to the area of the Hills. This accession was mainly in the northern portion, the limestone and all the lower sedimentary rocks rising *en masse*, horizontally stratified, above the level of the ocean. It seems inevitable that some of the later formations, Cretaceous for instance, should still rest on this level plateau in some part, if they existed there when the elevation took place.

5th. After the Cretaceous, the absence of the Tertiary is sufficient evidence, although the position of the beds is undeniable.

Very respectfully, your obedient servant,

N. H. WINCHELL,

Colonel WM. LUDLOW,
Saint Paul, Minn.

APPENDIX TO THE GEOLOGICAL REPORT.

A.

BOTANY.

LIST OF TREES AND SHRUBS, BY N. H. WINCHELL.

In the march outward, the first pines met with were found growing on the tops and rocky bluffs of the sandstone at Ludlow's Cave. We found the same pine on the Short-Pine Hills more abundantly, and from there to the Black Hills most of the ridges and rocky bluffs had pine in their upper valleys. The following list comprises the trees and shrubs seen in the Black Hills:

PINUS RESINOSA, *Ait.* Norway pine. This is the only species of pine found in the Black Hills. The trees generally are small, but sometimes nearly two feet in diameter. They sometimes stand thick, but usually are very sparse. They constitute the forest entirely, except near the divide in the northwestern part of the hills, where they are mixed with spruces. There are, also, in some situations in the lower levels, a few scattered, stunted, burr-oaks.

QUERCUS MACROCARPA, *Michx.* Burr-oak. This tree is never large, and only appears round the flanks of the hills.

POPULUS TREMULOIDES, *Michx.* American aspen. Usually about wind or fire falls, and in the valleys; often seen skirting along the sides of the valley below the pines, creeping out toward its center among the underbrush and grass. Not seen larger than six inches in diameter.

JUNIPERUS COMMUNIS, *L.* Common juniper. Both the trailing and tree-like varieties.

ABIES, *(sp. ?)* There are two species of spruce, which are probably the common black and the white spruce, though they were not satisfactorily so identified. They are easily distinguishable at a distance by their habit.

PRUNUS PENNSYLVANICA, *L.* Wild red cherry. About the flanks of the hills, and especially in the neighborhood of wind and fire falls.

PRUNUS VIRGINIANA, *L.* Choke cherry. Common along the valleys.

SAMBUCUS PUBENS, *Michx.* Red-berried elder.

RIBES PROSTRATUM, *L'Her.* Fetid currant. Common on rocks.

RIBES FLORIDUM, *L.* Wild black currant.

RUBUS STRIGOSUS, *Michx.* Wild red raspberry. Abundant about Harney's Peak.

RUBUS HISPIDUS, *L.* Running swamp blackberry. Not common.

AMELANCHIER CANADENSIS, *Torr. and Gray, var. alnifolia.* The service-berry is very abundant, both in the form of low bushes in open, dry, sparse copses and as thickets in the valleys, growing about as high as a man's head. It furnished the most abundant berry met with by the expedition.

RIBES HIRTELLUM, *Michx.* Smooth gooseberry. Moist grounds and along the banks of streams.

SYMPHORICARPUS OCCIDENTALIS, *R. Br.* Wolfberry.

SALIX, (different species.) Willow.

CORNUS STOLONIFERA, *Michx.* Red osier dogwood.

CORNUS, *(sp. ?)* Cornel.

BETULA ALBA, *var. populifolia, Spach.* American white birch. Noticed first near Harney's Peak. Afterward seen sparsely generally.

POTENTILLA FRUTICOSA, *L.* Shrubby cinque-foil.

ROSA, *(sp. ?)*

ARCTOSTAPHYLOS, UVA URSI, Spreng. Bearberry.

In a reconnaissance toward the Bad Lands, the following species were noted along the lower slopes of the Black Hills, in the valley of French Creek:

PINUS RESINOSA, *Ait.* Norway pine. Some of the largest pines seen in the Hills occur in the southern portions.

QUERCUS MACROCARPA, *Michx.* Burr-oak.

ULMUS AMERICANA, *L. (pl. Clayt.) Willd.* American elm.

FRAXINUS AMERICANA, *L.* White-ash.

VITIS, *(sp. ?)* Grape.

AMPELOPSIS QUINQUEFOLIA, *Michx.* Virginia creeper.

CORYLUS AMERICANA, *Walt.* Hazel-nut.

NEGUNDO ACEROIDES, *Moench.* Box-elder. The box-elder is a most hardy tree. It is the usual tree or treelike shrub along the streams on the plains, and endures the greatest extremes of moisture and dryness.

RHUS TYPHINA, *L.* Staghorn sumach.

RHUS TOXICODENDRON, *L.* Poison ivy.

CORNUS STOLONIFERA, *Michx.* Red-osier dogwood.

BETULA ALBA, *var. populifolia, Spach.* White birch.

PRUNUS VIRGINIANA, *L.* Choke-cherry.

SPIRÆA OPULIFOLIA, *L.* Nine-bark.

ROSA, (*sp. ?*) Common everywhere.

PRUNUS AMERICANA, *Marshall.* Wild plum.

RIBES (*sp. ?*) Smooth white gooseberry.

PRUNUS PENNSYLVANICA, *L.* Wild red cherry.

During the progress of the expedition, Prof. A. B. Donaldson made a small collection of plants These were sent to Prof. John M. Coulter, of Hanover, Ind., for naming. The following is his report thereon, with notes on various species:

HANOVER, IND., *December* 3, 1874.

DEAR SIR: I send you a list of the plants you sent me as I make them out. I arrange them in the order of Gray.

RANUNCULACEÆ.

ACONITUM NASUTUM, *Fisch.*

LINACEÆ.

LINUM PERENNE, *L.*

GERANIACEÆ.

GERANIUM FREMONTII, *Torr. Plant. Fendl., p.* 26.

The specimens are covered with pilose hairs, seeds beautifully reticulated, 1 to 2 lines long, half as broad. Capsule sparingly hairy; more densely so along the dorsal ridge. At the base of each capsule, just within, after splitting, may be noticed a tuft of bright white hairs, one-half its length.

RHAMNACEÆ.

CEANOTHUS VELUTINUS, *Dougl., var. lævigatus,* T. and G.

LEGUMINOSÆ.

LUPINUS ORNATUS, *Dougl.* (*Watson's Rev.* in *Proc. Amer. Acad., v.* 8, *p.* 528.)

LUPINUS PARVIFLORUS, *Nutt.*, (*Watson's Rev., l. c., p.* 531.)

LUPINUS LEUCOPHYLLUS, *Lindl. ?*

HOSACKIA PURSHIANA, *Benth.*

PETALOSTEMON VIOLACEUS, *Mx.*

PETALOSTEMON CANDIDUS, *Mx.*

ASTRAGALUS ADSURGENS, *Pall.*

ASTRAGALUS PICTUS, *Gray.*

GLYCYRRHIZA LEPIDOTA, *Nutt.* In flower, but undoubted.

ROSACEÆ.

POTENTILLA ARGUTA, *Pursh.*

ONAGRACEÆ.

EPILOBIUM ANGUSTIFOLIUM, *L.*

ŒNOTHERA PINNATIFIDA, *Nutt.*

ŒNOTHERA CÆSPITOSA, *Nutt. Form.*, (*Watson's Rev. in Proc. Amer. Acad., vol.* 8, *pp.* 585, 605, including *Œ. montana* and *Œ. marginata*, Nutt.; also, *Œ. eximia*, Gr.) The capsules are sessile, conical, 1 inch long, tapering upward from the base, with two wing-crested ribs on each valve, (*vide Hayden's Miscell. Pub., No.* 4, *Syn. Fl. Col., p.* 45.)

ŒNOTHERA SERRULATA, *Nutt.*

GAURA COCCINIA, *Nutt.*

LOASACEÆ.

MENTZELIA NUDA, *T. and G.* Capsule 5-valved at the summit; seeds numerous, ½ to 2 lines long, ¾ line broad; flat, membranous-winged, and disposed to wrinkle in drying. Capsules very rough, with a barbed pubescence, conical or cylindrical, 1½ to 2 inches long, 6 to 8 lines wide.

CACTACEÆ.

MAMILLARIA VIVIPARA, *Haw.*

OPUNTIA MISSOURIENSIS, *D. C.?* Probably this species, but too fragmentary.

UMBELLIFERÆ.

CARUM GAIRDNERI, *Benth.* and *Hook.* Eaten by the Indians of Wyoming and Idaho, and known as "yamp." Has the flavor of carrot.

RUBIACEÆ.

GALIUM BOREALE, *L.*

COMPOSITÆ.

LIATRIS PUNCTATA, *Hook.*

LIATRIS SCARIOSA, *Willd.*

ASTER MULTIFLORUS, *Ait.*

ASTER AESTIVUS, *Ait.*

MACHÆRANTHERA CANESCENS, *Gr. Form.* Pubescence roughish; stem purple, sparingly branched; leaves lanceolate, repand, mucronate. This form seems to be between *M. canescens*, Gr., and *M. canescens* var. *latifolia*, Gr.

ERIGERON MACRANTHUM, *Nutt.*

ERIGERON GLABELLUM, *Nutt.*

ERIGERON DIVERGENS, *T. and G.*

SOLIDAGO VIRGO-AUREA, *L., var.*

SOLIDAGO RIGIDA, *L.*

SOLIDAGO NEMORALIS, *Ait., var.*

SOLIDAGO CANADENSIS, *L.*

BIGELOVIA GRAVEOLENS, *Gr.*, (*Proc. Amer. Acad., v.* 8, *p.* 644.) (LINOSYRIS GRAVEOLENS, *T. and G.*)

APLOPAPPUS SPINULOSUS, *DC.*

GRINDELIA SQUARROSA, *Dunal.*

CHRYSOPSIS VILLOSA, *Nutt.*

WYETHIA AMPLEXICAULIS, *Nutt.?* Too fragmentary.

ECHINACEA ANGUSTIFOLIA, *DC.* A variety with shorter rays than usual.

RUDBECKIA HIRTA, *L.*

LEPACHYS COLUMNARIS, *T. and G.*

LEPACHYS COLUMNARIS, *T. and G.*, var. *pulcherrima;* rays crimson, tipped with yellow.

HELIANTHUS PETIOLARIS, *Nutt.*

HELIANTHUS LENTICULARIS, *Dougl.*

HELIANTHUS LAETIFLORUS, *Pers.*
GAILLARDIA ARISTATA, *Pursh.*
ACHILLEA MILLEFOLIUM, *L.*
ARTEMISIA DRACUNCULOIDES, *Pursh.*
ARTEMISIA LUDOVICIANA, *Nutt.*
CREPIS RUNCINATA, *T. and G.* Root-leaves wanting.
MACRORRHYNCUS TROXIMOIDES, *T. and G.*
MULGEDUIM PULCHELLUM, *Nutt.*

CAMPANULACEÆ.

CAMPANULA ROTUNDIFOLIA, *L.*

ERICACEÆ.

ARCTOSTRAPHYLOS, *Uva ursi*, *Spreng.*

PRIMULACEÆ.

LYSIMACHIA CILIATA, *L.*

SCROPHULARIACEÆ.

PENSTEMON GLABER, *Pursh.*
PENSTEMON ACUMINATUS, *Dougl.*
PENSTEMON PUBESCENS, *Soland*, var. *gracilis*, Gr.

LABIATÆ.

MONARDA FISTULOSA, *L.*
LOPHANTHUS ARISTATUS, *Benth.*
STACHYS PALUSTRIS, *L.*, var. *cordata*, Gr.

POLEMONIACEÆ.

PHLOX CANESCENS, *T. and G.*
PHLOX CAESPITOSA, *Nutt.*
COLLOMIA LINEARIS, *Nutt.*

CONVOLVULACEÆ.

CUSCUTA? Too immature to determine the species.

CHENOPODIACEÆ.

OXYBAPHUS ANGUSTIFOLIUS, *DC. Form.*

POLYGONACEÆ.

ERIOGONUM MULTICEPS, *Nees.*

LILIACEÆ.

ZYGADENUS GLAUCUS, *Nutt.*
CALOCHORTUS NUTTALLII, *T. and G.*
ALLIUM? Too fragmentary.

GRAMINEÆ.

BOUTELOUA OLIGOSTACHYA, *Torr.*
TRITICUM CANINUM, *L.*

I remain, very truly, yours,

JOHN M. COULTER.

Prof. N. H. WINCHELL.

B.

LIST OF ELEVATIONS ABOVE THE SEA.

The following tabulated list of elevations above the sea has been furnished for this report by W. Milnor Roberts, chief engineer of the Northern Pacific Railroad. The level of Lake Superior is taken at 600 feet above the ocean, and the elevations are referred, through that datum, to the ocean-level.

FROM LAKE SUPERIOR TO THE MISSOURI RIVER.

Table of distances and elevations above the sea.

Locality.	Miles.	Elevation.	Remarks.
		Feet.	
Lake Superior	0	600	Surface of the lake above the ocean.
Junction	24	1,080	Junction of the Lake Superior and Mississippi River Railroad with Northern Pacific Railroad.
	104	1,300	Summit (ground) east of the Mississippi River, 10 miles east of Brainerd.
Mississippi River	115	1,204	Brainerd—ground.
Do	115	1,161	Highest water ever known, 1866.
Do	115	1,156	High-water-mark.
Do	115	1,144	Low-water.
Gull River	122	1,184	Ground.
Do	122	1,162	Surface of water.
Crow-Wing River	136	1,124	Ground.
Do	136	1,112	Surface of river; ordinary.
Do	136	1,107	Low-water.
Partridge River	151	1,323	Ground.
Do	151	1,305	Surface of water.
Wing River	156	1,328	Ground.
Do	156	1,310	Surface of water.
A small summit	173	1,442	Ground.
Otter-Tail River	183	1,344	Ground.
Otter-Tail River	183	1,328	Surface of river.
A small summit	201	1,400	Ground.
Pelican River	205	1,335	Railroad.
Do	205	1,325	Stream.
A marsh	215	1,275	Marsh.
Hay Creek	221	1,260	Ground.
Do	221	1,230	Creek.
Buffalo River	227	1,149	Ground.
Do	227	1,139	River.
Buffalo River, 6th crossing	238	940	Grade of railroad.
Do	238	923	River.
Glyndon	242	912	Ground.
South Branch Buffalo River	245	902	Ground.
Do	245	882	River.
Moorhead	252	888	Ground east side of Red River.
Red River	252	876	High-water of Red River.
Do	252	842	Low-water of Red River.
Fargo	....	....	On the west side of Red River.
Do	....	903	Grade of Northern Pacific Railroad.

Table of distances and elevations above the sea—Continued.

Locality.	Miles.	Elevation.	Remarks.
		Feet.	
Maple River	265	906	Grade of Northern Pacific Railroad.
Do	265	886	Bed of stream.
Goose Creek	272	933	Low banks.
A summit	288	1,206	Ground and railroad.
Small stream	291	1,138	Railroad.
Do	291	1,128	Small stream flowing south.
A summit	304	1,436	Railroad; ground nearly the same.
Cheyenne River	309	1,228	Railroad.
Cheyenne River	309	1,198	Cheyenne River.
Small summit	314	1,430	Railroad, and ground.
	317	1,450	
Lake Eckelson	323	1,445	Railroad grade.
Do	323	1,430	Surface of lake.
Small summit	326	1,460	Railroad grade.
Depression	326½	1,434	Grade of railroad. Ground 8 feet lower.
Small summit	334	1,477	Grade of railroad, and ground.
	336	1,412	Grade of railroad.
Spirit Wood Coulée	336	1,400	Water-way.
Small summit	341	1,493	Grade of railroad and ground.
Jamestown	344	1,406	Do.
James River	344	1,391	James River.
A summit	363	1,861	Railroad grade. Slight undulating between James River and this summit.
A depression	367	1,814	Railroad grade.
Small summit	367½	1,827	Do.
Flat and wet	379	1,727	Do.
Small summit	381	1,791	Do.
A depression	391	1,736	Railroad grade, moderate undulations.
Swale	397	1,786	Do.
	400	1,845	Do.
	408	1,793	Railroad grade, water, flat.
	413	1,869	Railroad grade.
	417	1,808	Flat region.
Summit	422	1,880	Ground 1,900 feet above the sea.
	426	1,705	
	434	1,676	
Apple Creek Valley	436	1,709	
Do	441	1,640	
Do	443	1,665	
Do	445	1,632	Old bottom of the Missouri River.
Missouri River, near Bismarck	450	1,640	Surface of the Missouri River.

Elevations between the Missouri River and the Yellowstone River, via Heart River and Glendive's Creek. (From the Northern Pacific Railroad survey of 1871.)

Locality.	Distance.	Elevation.	Remarks.
	Miles.	*Feet.*	
Missouri River	....	1,640	
West of the Missouri River	135	2,530	One hundred and thirty-five miles west of the Missouri River.
	140	2,580	
	145	2,680	
Summit, (Heart River)	146½	2,703	
Do	150	2,555	
Do	154	2,400	
First crossing of Little Missouri	160	2,270	
Mouth of Andrew's Creek	165	2,250	
Along Andrew's Creek	170	2,390	
Do	175	2,550	
Do	180	2,690	
Summit, (Andrew's Creek)	183	2,790	
	185	2,780	
	187½	2,715	
	190	2,780	
	195	2,730	
Inman's Fork	197	2,630	
Glendive's Creek divide	200½	2,815	
Down Glendive's Creek	210	2,390	
Do	215	2,265	
Do	220	2,140	
Do	225	2,050	
Yellowstone River	226	2,013	Yellowstone River.

PALEONTOLOGICAL REPORT.

By GEORGE BIRD GRINNELL.

NEW HAVEN, CONN., *January* 1, 1875.

DEAR SIR: I beg leave to hand you herewith my reports on the zoology and paleontology of the region traversed during the past summer by General Custer's reconnaissance to the Black Hills.

My preliminary report, as you know, was necessarily written very hurriedly on the cars, and without access to my note-books or collections. It was, therefore, very incomplete, and in one or two details incorrect.

The rapidity with which the command traveled admitted of but a very hasty and incomplete survey of the region. The time allowed for collections was short, and only such animals were observed as could be most readily found.

The fossils were collected by Professor Winchell and myself, our labors in that department being mutually supplementary. Hence in the report on Paleontology I have used the pronoun "we," desiring so to indicate the joint character of the collection.

For constant sympathy and assistance in the field permit me to express my sincere thanks to General Custer, General G. A. Forsyth, and yourself. To Professor O. C. Marsh and Mr. R. P. Whitfield, I am indebted for valuable assistance in the identification of my fossils.

I am, sir, with great respect, your obedient servant,

GEO. BIRD GRINNELL.

Col. WILLIAM LUDLOW,
Chief Engineer of the Department of Dakota.

REPORT.

We left Fort Lincoln July 2, and proceeded in a generally southwesterly direction over a rolling prairie, in some places covered with granite bowlders, all smoothed and polished by the sand which the almost unceasing wind blows against them. These bowlders are often of large size and are worn and rounded by the constant friction to which they have been exposed during their long journey. The whole country for many miles west of the Missouri River is covered with this drift, and no outcrop of sedimentary rocks appears for some distance. Thirty miles from Fort Lincoln the first fossils of the trip were found, high up on a lofty butte, and just beneath the layer of friable yellowish sandstone with which all the higher bluffs were capped. The fossils were a few shells, indicating a fresh-water deposit, and included a *Unio*, a *Corbula*, and *Melania* (*Goniobasis*) *nebrascensis*, Meek; one or two specimens of the last-mentioned showing an approach to var. *tenuicarinata*. The relative position of the beds to which these belong is well determined, but in the uncertainty which prevails among high authorities as to in which formation, Cretaceous or Tertiary, they should be placed, it is sufficient for our present purpose merely to indicate the exact horizon.

From this point on, no fossils were found nor were any bad lands seen, until after leaving Ludlow's Cave, July 12. Soon after this, however, the country became much more rough and barren. Washed clay bluffs were seen in great numbers, and seams of lignite, generally finely crumbling and impure, were almost invariably present. Many of these washes were visited and thoroughly explored, but all proved barren of fossils. Soon, however, the bare bluffs became so numerous that it was impossible for us to visit all of them and still keep up with the column, and we were obliged to content ourselves with examining such as seemed most promising, passing the others with merely a glance.

At Castle Butte, a lofty, square-shaped bluff, named from its resemblance to a mediæval castle, were found the first vertebrate remains. This locality is about six miles north of Prospect Valley, and is eight or ten miles distant from the Little Missouri. Here were found the crushed and flattened leg bone of some enormous animal and a few fragmentary turtle bones, all so fragile and weathered that we were unable to transport them to camp. It was impossible to determine at the time, without specimens for comparison, what the former fossil was. A hasty examination on the spot led me to conclude that it was part of a mastodon; a careful study of similar remains since made, together with the subsequent discovery of more characteristic fossils from what were evidently the same beds, renders it highly probable that it was the femur of a dinosaur.

At Short-Pine Buttes on the Little Missouri, which point we passed July 16, is an extensive range of bare, denuded bluffs, a favorite basking-ground of the Big-horn, (*O. Montana.*) These washes gave promise of considerable richness in vertebrate remains. Unfortunately, however, as we were able to devote but a very short time to their examination, little was accomplished. Two large vertebræ and the base of a skull were secured, both of which proved to be remains of gigantic dinosaurs, and would seem to be very near the genus *Hadrosaurus*, Leidy. The vertebræ are characteristic, and indicate herbivorous dinosaurs. They represent a species nearly as large as *Hadrosaurus Foulkii*, Leidy.

Later in the day a few fossiliferous concretions were found on the prairie among the sage-brush and cactus. These were all Cretaceous, and consisted principally of a new species of *Terebratula* and *Anchura biangulata*, M. and H.

On the 17th of July many more invertebrates were found. Large numbers of limestone concretions were seen lying on the prairie, as on the preceding day, and many of these, cracked and broken by exposure to the weather, had become little more than mere shell-heaps. The fossils were most of them badly weathered; but when a concretion could be found which had not broken up, the specimens from it were well preserved. Among the species found were the following, all of them marine forms: A new species of *Terebratula*, *Limopsis striato-punctata*, Ev. and Shum.; *Amauropsis paludiniformis*, H. and M.; *Vanikora (Neritopsis?) ambigua*, M. and H.; *Pteria linguiformis*, Ev. and Shum.; *Scaphites conradi*, Morton; *Nucula planimarginata*, M. and H.; *Scaphites nodosus*, Owen; *Cinulia (Avellana) concinna*, H. and M. A comparison of these fossils with specimens collected by Dr. Hayden, and now in the Yale Museum, indicates that these beds belong to the so-called Fort Pierre group.

No more fossils were seen until July 21, when, traveling through a very rough country, we noticed many fragments of *Belemnites*, and during the day secured undoubted specimens of *Belemnites densus*. In some beds of hard, yellowish clays large numbers of *Gryphæa calciola*, Quenst, var. *nebrascensis*, M. and H., were found, together with a few fine specimens of *Camptonectes bellistriata*, Meek. These characteristic fossils determine, beyond the possibility of a doubt, the formation to be Jurassic. The beds in which these fossils were found overlie the bright-red gypsiferous beds that have been referred to the Triassic. Unfortunately, although a careful search was made for them, no fossils were found in these latter strata.

For two days we traveled through a country where these deposits were constantly in view; the bright red of the rocks pleasantly relieved by the layers of pure white gypsum that everywhere intersected them. At one point which we passed there was a large mass of pure gypsum which rose from the plain 8 feet high, 8 feet wide, and about 20 long. We could see that it had once been much larger, and the Sioux scouts with us stated that the Indians had for centuries been in the habit of visiting it and carrying away fragments from which to make ornaments.

On the 25th of July a gritty, metamorphic limestone made its appearance, which proved to be Carboniferous, as indicated by the following fossils which were found in it: *Spirifera centronata*, Winchell, a coral near *Zaphrentis*, a species of *Athyris*, a *Syringopora*, much resembling *S. mult-*

attenuata, a *Streptorhynchus*, probably referable to *S. Keokuk*, Hall, (*Hemipronites crenistria*, Dav.) This limestone, which was a pinkish gray, was very thick, and covered the hills in all directions. Although it contained many fossils, it was a difficult matter to find any sufficiently well preserved to retain their specific characteristics. The next day, July 26, we observed a limestone much resembling that of the 25th, but light purple in color. It was, however, evidently of the same age with the preceding. All these beds dipped sharply away from the hills. The purple limestone contained crinoidal columns, a *Spirifera*, a *Productus*, and a finely radiated species of coral resembling *Zaphrentis*, but not sufficiently perfect for identification.

July 27th, along Castle Creek several outcrops of a coarse granite, containing large crystals of white feldspar, were noticed, and this soon became the only rock to be seen. Here, however, it was overlaid by a hard, fine-grained mica-slate, and over this, horizontally, was a deposit of brown sandstone, somewhat laminated, apparently the Potsdam. This contained a new *Obolus*, associated with *Lingulepis primæformis*, M. and H., and *Obolella nana*, Billings. These forms were so abundant as to give the stone a speckled appearance, the shells being crowded closely together and evenly distributed through the rock. There were no other fossils found in these beds.

On the 1st of August, while the command was lying in camp near Harney's Peak, General Custer, who on this occasion, as on all others, manifested the most kindly interest in our work, informed us that he was about to send two companies of cavalry to the Big Cheyenne, and inquired if we would like to accompany the party. It was originally intended that they should be gone only two days, but General Custer afterward consented to extend the time to three days, in order to give us an opportunity to make collections. We started the following morning, but were unsuccessful in our attempt to reach the river. The country proved even worse for traveling than had been anticipated, and on the evening of the second day we found ourselves on Spring Creek, still twelve or fifteen miles from the point where the river was supposed to run. To the southeast of us the high, white bluffs that indicated the Tertiary *Mauvaises Terres* could be seen stretching away for many miles, apparently without a trace of vegetation; but we were obliged to turn back without an opportunity of visiting them. In leaving the Black Hills we passed over the granite, the mica slate, the purplish carboniferous limestone, which here contained a coral resembling *Zaphrentis centralis*, Ev. and Shum, an *Athyris*, and *Spirifera centronata*, Winchell. Above the limestone we found the Red Beds, (Jurassic or Triassic,) but we were unable, during our hasty march, to find any characteristic Jurassic fossils. Immediately above the Red Beds were 40 or 50 feet of hard, yellow, arenaceous clays, containing *Inoceramus problematicus* in great numbers, but no other fossils. Later in the day we saw, on a little washed place, a few fragments of bone. These were parts of the rib of a large mammal, which must have nearly equaled an elephant in bulk. Judging from the nature of the specimen, as well as from the surrounding clays, this animal was probably *Brontotherium*, Marsh, and if so, would indicate Lower Miocene, or the older of the great lake-basins that once covered this region.

The Miocene lake, as Professor Marsh, of Yale College, has shown, had the Black Hills as its northwestern boundary, the Rocky Mountains as its western border, and extended southward only to near the northern line of Kansas; the Pliocene lake above it being much larger, reaching southward even to Texas. Our own observations during the past summer have defined the northern limits of these basins, and show that they probably did not extend much beyond the Big Cheyenne. The animals of both of these lakes were mainly tropical species, and those of each lake quite distinct from those of the other, and all widely different from any now living. In contrast of our lack of success in obtaining collections from this section of the country, it may be well to mention that Professor Marsh, during a short expedition that he recently made to these beds, secured about two tons of vertebrate fossils.

We reached the main camp again on the morning of August 5, and the next day commenced our return march to Fort Lincoln. Nothing of interest was observed until August 10, when we passed over a Carboniferous limestone similar to that mentioned as having been seen July 25, but containing a few additional fossils. Most of these, unfortunately, are but poorly preserved, and cannot be specifically identified. The genera, however, can be made out. One or two specimens were found in these beds, resembling in their form and in their evenly plicated surface, the genus *Retzia*, (*Eumetria*, Hall.) There were also many specimens of *Rhynchonella*, and a single *Euomphalus*, all too imperfect for specific identification.

On the 15th we passed over a buff shale, apparently Cretaceous, which contained cycloidal fish-scales and a few vertebræ and spines, or rather the impressions of all these, for none were preserved.

August 17th we came again to the black and purple shales, Fort Pierre group, that we first saw near the Belle Fourche, and which border the Black Hills on the north and east. In these, a short distance north of Slave Butte, we found many large limestone concretions lying in position in the shale. These, on being broken up, were found to consist wholly of marine Cretaceous shells, principally *Inoceramus convexus*, H. and M.; *Anchura biangulata*, M. and H.; *Limopsis striato-punctata*,; Ev. and Shum.; *Vanikora* (*Neritopsis?*) *ambigua*, M. and H.; *Scaphites conradi*, Morton.; *S. nodosus*, Owen.; *Anchura* (*Drepanocheilus*) *americana*, M.; and *Baculites avatus*, Say.

We reached the Little Missouri August 20, striking the river a few miles south of the Bad Lands. I had been informed that this locality was very rich in fossils, and all the time spent near the river was employed in searching for them. We were unable, however, to discover any trace of animal remains. Beds of lignite were very numerous, and though much of it was impure and shaley, still occasionally a seam occurred where it closely resembled cannel-coal in the massive compactness of its texture and its smooth even fracture. We saw many examples of the baking and fusing of the superincumbent rocks by the burning out of the lignite beds, as mentioned in Dr. Hayden's Report,* and more recently by Professor J. A. Allen, to whose very interesting and exhaustive article on the subject I would especially refer.† A part of the beds explored by us on the Little Missouri may, perhaps, be referred to what Dr. Hayden calls "beds of transition,"‡ but in many cases they contained seams of lignite. But one day was spent upon the Little Missouri, and then, directing our course eastward, we set out for Fort Lincoln.

On the 28th of August, in a ravine near the Sweetbriar, I noticed a large number of silicified stumps of trees. They were about 30 feet below the surface of the ground, and all were standing upright, in the natural position. The trees were large, the smallest being about 2½ feet in diameter and ranging from that up to 4 feet. All through the trip we found silicified wood very abundant scattered over the prairie, but this was the only instance in which we found it apparently in position. The absence, however, of any characteristic fossils rendered the age of this formation doubtful.

---

* Dr. Hines, in Hayden's Geological Report of the Exploration of the Yellowstone and Missouri Rivers. Chap. II. p. 96.

† Proc. Bost. Soc. Nat. Hist., Vol. XVI, part III, p. 246. Metamorphoses produced by the burning of lignite beds in Dakota and Montana. By J. A. Allen.

‡ Geological Report of the Exploration of the Yellowstone and Missouri Rivers, by Dr. F. V. Hayden, assistant. Chap. V, pp. 45–46.

ZOOLOGICAL REPORT.

CHAPTER I.

MAMMALS.

FELIDÆ.

1. FELIS CONCOLOR, *Linn.*

Cougar; American Panther.

I saw but a single panther while we were in the Black Hills, and that one, as far as I can discover, was the only one observed by any member of the expedition. I believe, however, that they are quite numerous in this locality, as on several occasions I saw indications of their recent presence, and once found the partially devoured remains of a deer that had just been left by one of these animals.

2. LYNX RUFUS, *Raf.*

Bay Lynx; Wildcat.

Neither this nor the next species were seen by any one connected with the expedition. Nevertheless, the descriptions given by Charles Reynolds, the hunter, of two small cats, not uncommon about Fort Lincoln and to the west of that post, were such as to satisfy me of the existence of *L. rufus* and *L. canadensis* in considerable numbers along the larger rivers that we passed, and they are doubtless common in the Black Hills as well.

3. LYNX CANADENSIS, *Raf.*

Canada Lynx.

Probably common in Black Hills.

CANIDÆ.

4. CANIS OCCIDENTALIS var. GRISEO-ALBUS, *Rich.*

Gray Wolf; Timber Wolf.

I found the gray wolf one of the most common animals in the Black Hills, and hardly a day passed without my seeing several individuals of this species. They were generally observed singly or by twos and threes, sneaking along the mountain sides or crossing the narrow valleys. They were quite shy, and lost no time in plunging into the dense woods as soon as they perceived us. Their howlings were often heard at night; and on one occasion I heard the doleful sound at midday—a bad omen, if we may trust the Indians.

5. CANIS LATRANS, *Say.*

Prairie Wolf; Coyoté.

The coyoté was found in considerable numbers on the plains, and was especially abundant among the elevated table-lands that were crossed just before reaching the Black Hills. After penetrating into the hills proper, however, I did not see a single specimen until I left them for the Big Cheyenne, when I again noticed coyotés in numbers. In the Black Hills this species would seem to be replaced by the preceding. Among the *Mauvaises Terres* of the Little Missouri I saw a few of both species.

6. VULPES MACROURUS, *Baird.*

Prairie Fox.

Only three individuals of this species were seen by me—an old female and two young. They had established themselves in a commodious burrow on the edge of a prairie-dog town, where they could obtain an abundant supply of food with very little exertion.

7. VULPES VELOX, *Aud. & Bach.*

Kit-Fox; Swift.

This pretty little fox is abundant everywhere on the plains, though not often seen, on account of its small size and its disposition to hide when it can, in preference to running. An exaggerated idea of this animal's fleetness prevails among hunters and plains-men, probably induced by the extreme evenness and regularity with which it runs. The animal seems fairly to glide along the earth, and its movements resemble the flight of a bird rather than the gait of a quadruped. The Swift undoubtedly runs very fast, but not as fast as the jackass-rabbit, (*L. callotis.*) I saw General Custer's hounds catch one after a chase of not more than half a mile, while the capture of a full-grown hare often necessitated a run of fully two miles.

MUSTELIDÆ.

8. PUTORIUS LONGICAUDA, *Rich.*

Weasel.

A single weasel of this species was taken August 24 on the headwaters of Heart River.

9. PUTORIUS VISON, *Rich.*

Mink.

This species is abundant on the larger streams flowing into the Missouri River. I saw no living specimens while in the Black Hills, but observed frequent signs of their presence along the streams, and saw a skin which the owner told me he had taken while there.

10. LUTRA CANADENSIS, *Sab.*

Otter.

Abundant on Heart and Cannon-Ball Rivers, and probably in the Black Hills.

11. MEPHITIS MEPHITICA, *Baird.*

Skunk.

Common about the Missouri and Heart Rivers and in the Black Hills.

12. TAXIDEA AMERICANA, *Baird.*

American Badger.

I found the badger very abundant from Fort Lincoln to the edge of the Black Hils, but saw none after leaving the plain country. They are generally to be seen prowling about through the settlements of the prairie-dogs, (*Cynomys ludovicianus*,) which animals constitute a considerable portion of their food.

URSIDÆ.

13. URSUS HORRIBILIS, *Ord.*

Grizzly Bear.

Although we saw indications of the presence of large numbers of grizzlies during our march through the Black Hills, only a few were killed, chiefly from lack of time to devote to their capture. The first one killed was secured by General Custer and Colonel Ludlow. It was a very old male, the canine teeth being mere broken stumps, many of the incisors gone, and the molars worn down almost to the gums. In color it was everywhere a deep, glossy black, except on the head and on the lower parts of the shoulders and thighs, where there was a slight sprinkling of dark-gray hairs. The old veteran bore on his body the marks of many a conflict. On his back, just behind the shoulders, was a rugged scar 10 inches long and 2 wide; his face was marked in several places, and his sides and thighs were disfigured in the same manner. These scars, I am led to believe, were the result of battles with some rival during the rutting season.

Very different in appearance were an old female and two cubs that were killed later in the trip, and much farther to the eastward, by two of our Indian scouts. The cubs were about half grown, and, with the mother, were of a yellowish clay color. The inner half of each hair was deep black, but the outer extremity was a bright reddish-yellow. This gave them a curious mottled appearance and induced many of those who saw them to consider them a different species from the one killed by General Custer. I saw no evidences of any great ferocity in any of the specimens killed by the party. None made any attempt at defense unless so badly wounded as to be unable to escape by flight; even the old female just referred to continued to run after both her cubs had been disabled.

The swiftness of the grizzly is considerable, and in a rough country it can easily run away from a slow horse. Even on the prairie it requires a pretty good animal to catch them, and it took several hours' hard riding to overtake the three last mentioned. The most easterly point at which I noticed this species was on the headwaters of the Heart River, about thirty miles east of the Little Missouri.

SCIURIDÆ.

14. SCIURUS HUDSONIUS, *Pallas.*

Red Squirrel.

Specimens of this squirrel collected in the Black Hills are in all respects similar to those from the Eastern States.

15. (?) PTEROMYS ALPINUS, *Rich.*

Flying Squirrel.

A single Pteromys, believed to be of this species, was seen in the Black Hills.

16. TAMIAS QUADRIVITTATUS.

Missouri Ground Squirrel.

This interesting little squirrel is common throughout all the country traversed by the expedition. Wherever there was timber or washed bad lands, there we heard the sharp note and saw the active form of this little burrower. It was especially numerous in the pine forests of the Black Hills and in the *Mauvaises Terres* along the Little Missouri; in which latter locality it, with the rock-wren and horned toad, was almost the only animal to be seen. This species was by no means shy, and seemed not at all to regard the near presence of an observer.

17. (?) SPERMOPHILUS RICHARDSONII, *Cuv.*

Richardson's Ground Squirrel.

A Spermophile, probably of this species, was seen near the headwaters of the Heart River, on our return march, but I was unable to secure any specimens.

18. SPERMOPHILUS TRIDECEM-LINEATUS, *Aud. & Bach.*

Striped Prairie Squirrel.

This squirrel was found in large numbers on the plains, but was not seen after crossing the Belle Fourche, until we left the Hills on our return march.

19. CYNOMYS LUDOVICIANUS, *Baird.*

Prairie Dog.

Abundant everywhere on the plains.

20. ARCTOMYS FLAVIVENTER, *Bach.*

Western Woodchuck.

A single specimen was killed in the Hills.

21. CASTOR CANADENSIS, *Kuhl.*

Beaver.

This species was common on all the large streams which we crossed on our way to the Black Hills, in many places having by means of their dams retained a plentiful supply of water when the creek both above and below was dry. They were also numerous in the Hills, as their dams and houses in many of the streams bore witness.

SACCOMYIDÆ.

22. GEOMYS BURSARIUS, *Rich.*

Pouched Gopher.

One specimen observed on the headwaters of Heart River.

23. THOMOMYS RUFESCENS, *Maxim.*

Fort Union Gopher.

This species was seen on Heart River, near Fort Lincoln; a miner caught one in his naked hand. It was very gentle, and made no attempt at resistance.

24. FIBER ZIBETHICUS, *Cuv.*

Muskrat.

The muskrat is very abundant on all flowing streams in that part of Dakota which we traversed, and still more so farther to the north. Especially is this true of the Mouse River, where, as I am informed, these animals may be seen swimming about by hundreds in the spring when the river has overflowed its banks and forced them to leave their holes.

HYSTRICIDÆ.

25. ERITHIZON EPIXANTHUS, *Brandt.*

Yellow-haired Porcupine.

Several individuals of this species were captured on the headwaters of Heart River, and brought into the post alive.

LEPORIDÆ.

26. Lepus callotis, *Wagler*. (?)

Jackass Rabbit.

Abundant on the plains. Several young ones were captured and brought in alive.

27. Lepus artemisia, *Bach*.

Sage Rabbit.

Common near the Missouri River, and observed also on the Little Missouri.

CERVIDÆ.

28. Cervus canadensis, *Erxleben*.

Elk; Wapiti.

Although but few elk were seen during the trip, we found in the Black Hills every indication of their recent presence in large numbers. During a single day's march eleven pairs of horns, attached to the skull, were picked up by members of the expedition. Horns that had been shed were very abundant, and it was by no means an unusual thing to see fifteen or twenty single antlers in a morning's ride.

On Elkhorn Prairie we came upon a collection of horns gathered together by the Indians. Three lodge-poles had been set up in the ground so as to form a tripod, and supported by these was a pile of horns 8 or 10 feet high. The horns had all been shed, and had apparently been collected from the surrounding prairie and heaped up here by the Indians. There is much variation in the horns of this species, most of which I imagine to be due to injuries to the horns while young and soft. Many of the specimens examined this summer were much flattened near the extremities, so much so in one or two cases as to be from 6 to 7 inches wide. In two instances the basal prong of the horn, instead of projecting forward and downward in the usual manner, turned outward and downward, and then, curving inward and up again, brought the point of the snag immediately under the animal's throat.

29. Cervus virginianus, *Boddaert*.

Virginia Deer; Red Deer.

A few of these deer were seen near the Missouri River, and on the Cannon Ball. In the Black Hills, however, this species is replaced by the following.

30. Cervus leucurus, *Douglas*.

White-tailed Deer; Cotton-tail.

The difference in size between this and the preceding species is so great, that there exists even among hunters a very general opinion that the red deer of the mountains is different from the red deer of the Missouri River and the Eastern States. This species was very abundant in the Black Hills, and especially so in the vicinity of Castle Creek and Elkhorn Prairie. I imagine that near this point there are some salt "licks;" at least members of the Sioux hunting party which we encountered spoke of places where the deer "eat the ground," and said that they watched for them there. They were also very numerous about the head of Elk Creek, and, indeed, all through the northeastern portion of the hills. It was said that one hundred deer, principally of this species, were killed by the command August 9.

31. Cervus macrotis, *Say.*

Mule Deer.

This deer was observed in considerable numbers in the Black Hills, in the neighborhood of Elkhorn Prairie, but they were by no means so abundant there as in the rough, broken country through which we passed just before reaching the Hills.

Near our first crossing of the Belle Fourche, and for a day or two while we were skirting the Hills, this was the only species seen. In the *Mauvaises Terres* of the Little Missouri, and on the headwaters of the Heart River, they were quite numerous. We saw but few bucks during the trip, most of the individuals noticed being does, and each one followed by two pretty little fawns.

CAVICORNIA.

32. Antilocapra americana, *Ord.*

Prong-horned Antelope.

Until within a short time, antelope were very common about Fort Lincoln, but the Arickaree Indians that are now maintained at that post as scouts have hunted them so persistently that the few that still remain in the vicinity are exceedingly wild, and one may ride ten or fifteen miles from the fort without seeing more than five or six. As we proceed, however, the antelope become more numerous, until finally there is no hour of the day when they are not to be seen either running gracefully off over the prairie or curiously watching the command from the top of some distant bluff.

The antelope is regarded by hunters as the most difficult to kill of any animal found on the prairie or in the mountains. In proportion to its size, it is more tenacious of life than the grizzly bear, and from its astonishing speed it is often enabled to escape even after having received a wound that would have brought a deer or an elk immediately to the ground. A specimen, shot by Charles Reynolds, had one fore leg broken at the knee and one hind leg broken just below the knee. Notwithstanding these wounds, it ran much faster than a horse could gallop for over two miles and a half, when, becoming exhausted, it lay down and awaited the approach of the hunter, who gave it the *coup de grace.* I have seen several specimens wounded in such a manner that their entrails dragged along the ground as they ran, but even under such conditions they can outstrip a horse, until exhausted by loss of blood.

33. Ovis montana, *Cuv.*

Bighorn; Mountain Sheep.

A female of this species was seen near the Little Missouri August 23. The first "signs" seen were at Short Pine Buttes, near the Little Missouri, and all along this stream they seemed to be very numerous. So wary were they, however, that it was impossible under the circumstances to secure any specimens.

34. Bos americanus, *Gmelin.*

Buffalo.

No buffalo were seen during the trip, nor do I know that any exist at present in the region traversed; but one or two circumstances lead me to infer that there may still be found a few individuals in this section of the country.

In Prospect Valley I found the skull of an old bull, with part of the hide still clinging to it. Also, on French Creek, not far from the Big Cheyenne, I noticed the lower jaw of a cow, with the priosteum still on it.

It is but a few years since the country through which we passed was the favorite feeding-ground of the buffalo, and their white skulls dot the prairie in all directions. Sometimes these are collected by the Indians, and arranged on the ground in fantastic patterns. In one of these collections which I noticed, the skulls had been painted red and blue in stripes and circles, and were arranged in five parallel rows of twelve each, all the skulls facing the east.

CHAPTER II

BIRDS.

TURDIDÆ.

1. TURDUS SWAINSONI, *Cabanis.*

Olive-backed Thrush.

This thrush is abundant in the thick timber on the Missouri River bottom, near Fort Lincoln, where I heard many of them singing each morning and evening.

2. TURDUS MIGRATORIUS, *Linn.*

Robin.

I found the robin abundant about Fort Lincoln early in June. They had just brought their first brood from the nest, and were building again. Late in July and early in August I saw them in flocks in the Black Hills. They were feeding in company with *Colaptes mexicanus* on the red raspberries that grew in the greatest profusion on the rocky slopes of the mountains.

3. HARPORHYNCHUS RUFUS, *Cabanis.*

Brown Thrasher; Red Thrush.

This species was common along the Missouri, on the Heart River, and on the elevated wooded buttes which we passed at short intervals. They were quite shy, and seemed desirous of avoiding observation, scuttling into the thickets when approached.

4. GALEOSCOPTES CAROLINENSIS, *Cabanis.*

Cat-Bird.

Breeding in considerable numbers along the Missouri and Heart Rivers.

CINCLIDÆ.

5. (?) CINCLUS MEXICANUS, *Swains.*

American Dipper.

A single specimen was observed on Elk Creek, but I was unable to secure it.

SAXICOLIDÆ.

6. SIALIA ARCTICA, *Swains.*

Rocky Mountain Blue-bird.

This interesting and beautiful bird was very abundant in the Black Hills. I first noticed it near Short Pine Buttes, where I saw a family of full-grown young. Afterward I saw it in the open woodlands near the Belle Fourche, and on French Creek, not far from Harney's Peak. In the latter locality it was especially common, and each little opening in the woods was occupied by a family. In their habits of feeding they closely resemble the eastern blue-bird, (*S. Sialis.*) There is, however, a noticeable difference in their notes; the call of *arctica* being shorter than, and not nearly so mellow as, that of its eastern congener.

PARIDÆ.

7. PARUS ATRICAPILLUS var. SEPTENTRIONALIS, *Harris.*

Long-tailed Chickadee.

This busy and familiar little bird was rather common in the Black Hills. They were always seen in small parties, apparently members of one family, and were constantly engaged in searching for food in the pines.

SITTIDÆ.

8. SITTA CAROLINENSIS var. ACULEATA, *Cass.*

Slender-billed Nut-hatch.

This nut-hatch I saw for the first time in the heavy pine timber near Elk Creek, August 12 The birds were in small parties, and were feeding along the branches and trunks of the trees in the ordinary manner. They were industrious, and withal noisy, their notes differing somewhat from those of the eastern form. There were a few specimens of *Parus atricapillus* var. *septentrionalis* associated with them.

9. SITTA CANADENSIS, *Linn.*

Red-bellied Nut-hatch.

A single family of this species, of which one individual was secured, was observed among heavy pine timber near Elk Creek, August 12.

TROGLODYTIDÆ.

10. SALPINCTES OBSOLETUS, *Cabanis.*

Rock Wren.

About a high sandstone butte, thirty miles southwest of Fort Lincoln, I first saw this species. The birds were numerous, running about over the detached blocks of the sandstone, and darting in and out of the weather-worn holes in the rock. I again saw them in numbers among the *Mauvaises Terres* on the Little Missouri. They are active, vivacious little birds, now flying up the face of a perpendicular bank with the dancing movements of a butterfly, now darting into some hole in the bluff, and unexpectedly reappearing at the mouth of another. At short intervals they utter a grating, querulous cry.

11. TROGLODYTES AEDON, *Vieillot.*

House Wren.

This familiar little wren was quite abundant about Fort Lincoln, where it was breeding in all the little wooded ravines near the river. I saw none after leaving the post.

SYLVICOLIDÆ.

12. DENDROICA ÆSTIVA, *Baird.*

Summer Yellow-bird.

Observed in numbers on Heart River and on the head of Knife River.

13. DENDROICA AUDUBONII, *Baird.*

Audubon's Warbler.

A single bird of this species was taken August 1, near Harney's Peak.

14. Icteria virens, *Baird.*

Yellow-breasted Chat.

I heard the familiar notes of this bird several times, both on the Missouri and on Heart River, but was unable to catch a glimpse of the bird itself.

HIRUNDINIDÆ.

15. Progne subis, *Baird.*

Purple Martin.

This species was very abundant in the Black Hills. Early in August I observed them in families, resting on the highest branches of the tall dead pines, whence they made short excursions. They were quite tame; one little group in the top of a high tree, out of reach of fine shot, remaining until three of their number had been killed by Mr. North with his rifle. Such birds as were brought to the ground only wounded screamed and bit with much spirit.

16. Petrochelidon lunifrons, *Baird.*

Cliff Swallow.

Early in July I found a colony of these birds breeding on some low sandstone buttes near White Cedar Creek. The buttes were capped with a layer of harder rock, and beneath a projecting shelf of this the nests were built. They all contained young about two-thirds grown.

The parent birds displayed much uneasiness while I remained near the spot, circling about my head in a dense flock, and constantly uttering loud cries of anxiety.

17. Hirundo horreorum, *Barton.*

Barn Swallow.

The barn swallow is common about Fort Lincoln, but I saw none on the plains after leaving the Missouri River. In the Black Hills, however, they were numerous, and were often seen flying about over the valleys in search of food.

18. Hirundo thalassina, *Swains.*

Violet-green Swallow.

I observed a single family of these beautiful birds in the Black Hills. They were resting on one of the lower limbs of a dead pine, whence they took short flights every few minutes.

VIREONIDÆ.

19. Lanivireo solitarius *var.* plumbeus, *Coues.*

Lead-colored Vireo.

This species was observed in considerable numbers near Harney's Peak. They are active, industrious little birds, all that I saw being busily engaged in seeking for food among the topmost branches of the pines. They uttered constantly a peevish, whining note, somewhat like that of the black-capped titmouse.

20. Vireosylva gilvus *var.* swainsoni, *Baird.*

Western Warbling Vireo.

A single specimen was taken, August 15, near Bear Butte.

AMPELIDÆ.

21. Ampelis cedrorum, *Sclat.*

Cedar Bird; Wax Wing.

A few pairs of cedar birds were seen about Fort Lincoln. At that time, June 17, they had not yet commenced to build.

LANIIDÆ.

22. Collurio ludovicianus *var.* excubitoroides, *Baird.*

Western Shrike; White-rumped Shrike.

The western shrike is one of the most common birds of the region traversed by the expedition. It was abundant near Fort Lincoln, and from there southwest, wherever we encountered timber in any quantity we saw this species. Thus, it was abundant on Heart River, on the Cannon Ball, and on the Little Missouri; also, on the Belle Fourche and all along the *edge* of the Black Hills. I saw none, however, among the dense woods of the mountains.

TANAGRIDÆ.

23. Pyranga ludoviciana, *Bonap.*

Louisiana Tanager.

This beautiful tanager was abundant in the Black Hills. I saw the first specimen among the low pines near the Belle Fourche, and from that time until we left the Hills, hardly a day passed without my seeing several of these interesting birds. They were rather shy, and spent most of the time seeking for food in the topmost branches of the tallest pines. Occasionally I saw them nearer the ground, but in such cases the birds seemed restless and uneasy, flying from limb to limb and from tree to tree, thus making it quite difficult to secure them.

In the early morning I frequently heard them utter a pleasant song, something like that of the scarlet tanager, (*P. rubra.*) Their brilliant colors make them a conspicuous and beautiful object when seen amid the dark green foliage of the pines.

I secured males in three stages of plumage. First, full-grown young of the year, which resemble the female in all respects. Second, young male, probably in the second year, the wings and tail brownish-black—much darker than the same parts in the female, yet not glossy like the full-plumaged male. In this specimen the back is brownish-black, the yellow of the breast brighter than in the female, and the throat and chin show faint traces of crimson. Third, full-plumaged males, in the most brilliant of which the crimson feathers of the head mingle with the yellow of the hind neck, and almost reach the black of the back. The breast is strongly tinged with red as far as the abdomen, which is pure, rich yellow. The upper and under tail-coverts have touches of crimson. Very young birds have a band of brownish-yellow across the breast, and are streaked somewhat like the young cedar bird (*Ampelis cedrorum*) on the breast and sides.

FRINGILLIDÆ.

24. Chrysomitris tristis, *Bon.*

Yellow Bird; Thistle Bird.

I observed this little bird at Fort Lincoln, and again on the plains just after leaving the Black Hills.

25. Plectrophanes ornatus, *Townsend.*

Chesnut-collared Longspur; Black-shouldered Longspur.

This interesting species is most abundant from Fort Lincoln to the Black Hills. In company with *P. maccownii* and *Eremophila alpestris*, it was breeding on the high desert plains over which we passed, and I found many nests in these localities. They breed early, and by July 10 the eggs f the second laying are deposited. The nest is always placed on the ground at the foot of a small ʼeed or a bunch of grass. It is formed externally of coarse grasses, and is generally lined with ner, though in two instances I found a neatly woven lining of antelope hair. The eggs differ con-iderably in their markings, and somewhat in size. The largest of twelve before me measures .79 y .60 inch, the smallest .75 by .55 inch. The ground-color is dull white, profusely dotted and plashed with black, brown, and purple of varying shade and intensity. Generally the markings re most numerous at the larger end, forming a ring about that part, and sometimes entirely con-ealing the ground-color. One egg is marked with light-brown blotches, and has no black or purple narks; another has no brown markings, and only a few black and purple dots. One or two closely esemble in their markings the eggs of *P. gramineus*. When startled from the nest, the female vould fly off to a convenient perch beyond the reach of shot, and from that point would watch my roceedings. If I remained long by the nest, she would fly past me within fifteen or twenty yards, ttering a sharp chirp. The male sings sweetly on the wing, much in the manner of *P. maccownii* nd *C. bicolor.*

The observations of Professor Allen and Doctor Coues having settled the question of the iden-ity of this species with *P. melanomus*, Baird, (Birds N. Am., 1858, p. 436,) anything more on that ubject is perhaps superfluous. I may mention, however, that my observations during the past ummer led me to the same conclusion which they arrived at.

26. PLECTROPHANES MACCOWNII, *Lawrence.*

Chesnut-shouldered Longspur; Maccown's Bunting.

I first noticed this bird near Dog-Teeth Creek, about thirty-five miles southwest of Fort Lin-oln. It was rather abundant, though not so much so as the preceding species, which, in many of s habits, it greatly resembles. Like it, this bird frequents the high dry plains, where it breeds, nd where it is by far the most melodious songster. It rises briskly from the ground, after the nanner of *C. bicolor*, until it attains a height of 20 or 30 feet, and then, with outstretched wings nd expanded tail, glides slowly to the earth, all the time singing with the utmost vigor. The male nd female manifest an unusual degree of attachment for one another. While watching them when eding in the early morning, for they were very unsuspicious and would allow me to approach ithin a few yards of them, I noticed that they kept close to one another, generally *walking* side by ide. If one ran a few steps from the other to secure an insect or a seed, it returned to the side of s mate almost immediately.

On one occasion, a pair were startled from the ground while thus occupied, and I shot the emale. As she fell, the male, which was a few feet in advance, turned about, and flew to the spot here she lay, and, alighting, called to her in emphatic tones, evidently urging her to follow him. Ie remained by her side until I shot him.

I did not see these birds hop at all. Their mode of progression was a walk, rather hurried, and ot nearly so dignified as that of the cow-bunting, (*M. pecoris.*) The nest of this species resembles, oth in position and construction, that of *P. ornatus*, but the eggs are quite different, those of *. maccownii* being larger and much rounder than those of the preceding species. Thus an aver-ge egg of the former measures .80 by .65 inch, while the largest of twelve eggs of the latter neasures but .79 by .60 inch. The color is a livid white, irregularly blotched and dotted with rown and black. There are many faint, dark markings on the eggs, which look as though they ad been overlaid with white, and only just show through. A breeding female, taken July 5, has he chesnut shoulders, but the color is not so bright nor so well defined as in the male.

27. POOCÆTES GRAMINEUS var. CONFINIS, *Baird.*

Grass Finch; Bay-winged Bunting.

This species was common everywhere on the plains. It seems especially to delight in the bar-en deserts, where nothing grows except cactus and sage-bush, and it was most abundant in these ocalities. I found many nests with fresh eggs in July. The manner of nesting does not differ aterially from that of the two preceding species, though this bird seems to prefer the side of a luff, rather than the level prairie, for the location of its nest.

28. Coturniculus passerinus var. perpallidus, *Ridgway.*

Western Yellow-winged Sparrow.

I secured a single bird of this species near Dog-Teeth Buttes, and several others in a little creek-bottom near Bear Butte. They were not easy to find, and kept among the high grass, running quite swiftly.

29. Chondestes grammaca, *Bonap.*

Lark Finch.

The lark finch is one of the most common as well as one of the most interesting birds observed about Fort Lincoln. It may be seen all day long either singing most sweetly in the dead tops of the scrub-oaks in the small ravines, or hopping about the prairie in search of food. It often visits the corrals, where, in company with the doves, (*Z. carolinensis*,) it picks up insects, grain, and seeds. When alarmed or uneasy at the presence of man, it throws back its head, erects its crest, and hops about, jerking its tail and chirping complainingly. This species seems quite tenacious of life; several that, upon examination, proved to have been shot through and through, flew sixty yards or more before falling. After leaving Fort Lincoln, I did not see this species again until we reached Short-Pine Buttes, near the Little Missouri. From this point on we found them abundant about wooded buttes.

30. Junco hyemalis var. aikeni, *Ridgway.*

White-winged Snow-bird.

I found this species very numerous in the Black Hills near Harney's Peak. They had bred in the vicinity, and I saw many broods of young, hardly fledged, on the 1st of August. On one occasion I came upon a family, the young of which had but just left the nest. They could fly but a short distance, and were, of course, still under the care of their parents. On being approached, they flew a few yards and then concealed themselves behind logs, stubs, and stones, while the female, alighting on a branch near my head, uttered a quick, rolling cry, something like the sound that would be made by striking two large stones together in quick succession, but the notes duller and more prolonged. I think that this is the most common bird in the more elevated portions of the Black Hills.

Young birds, though everywhere profusely streaked, show faint traces of white on their wing-coverts.

31. Spizella socialis var. arizonæ, *Coues.*

Western Chippy.

I saw a few of these birds in the Black Hills, but they were nowhere abundant. In habits they closely resemble the eastern variety.

32. Spizella pallida, *Bonap.*

Clay-colored Sparrow.

This species is abundant in the Black Hills. It seems to delight in the open woodlands, where it feeds in company with *Junco hyemalis* var. *aikeni*, and the preceding species. I saw the old birds feeding full-grown young, August 1, and have no doubt that they breed in numbers. It spends much of its time on the ground, and is very unsuspicious.

33. Calamospiza bicolor, *Bonap.*

Lark Bunting; White-winged Blackbird.

A few individuals of this interesting species were noticed before reaching the Missouri River, and it becomes very numerous soon after leaving that stream, and continues to be found in large numbers until we reach the Black Hills. It seems to prefer broken country to the level prairie, and was most abundant near low buttes, on the borders of streams, and along ravines and *coulés.* They are sociable little birds, and were generally seen in small companies, several pairs breeding within a short distance of each other. The males, conspicuous by their colors, are sprightly and powerful songsters, and it is by no means unusual to see several individuals in the air at the same time, each striving to outdo the others in the length and beauty of his lay. When uttering his song, the male springs from the ground, and mounts 30 or 40 feet into the air, with rapid beats of the wings, singing all the time most melodiously, and then, with outspread wings, glides slowly toward the earth, uttering the last note of his song just as he reaches the ground. The song is sweet and ringing, and somewhat resembles the notes of the Bob-o-link, (*D. oryzivorus,*) with a few trills of the canary interspersed through it. The female manifests a greater attachment for her nest and eggs than any other small bird that I have met with in the West. On being startled from the nest, she flies but a short distance, and is uneasy and complaining while it is being examined, and as soon as the intruder has retired a few steps, she returns to investigate the extent of her loss. I found this species sitting on fresh eggs July 9 and 10, no doubt a second brood; and in every nest that I found there was a cow-bunting's egg. The nest is placed on the ground, generally on the side of a low bluff, though in one instance I found one in the midst of a little valley, and is built with great care. The only one that I saw in a position where it might have been inundated in case of a heavy rain, was raised an inch and a half from the ground on a frame-work of coarse weeds, each one as thick as a lead-pencil. Externally the nest is composed of coarse grass and weeds, and has a lining of softer grass and a few fine roots. It is placed at the foot of a clump of weeds or sage-brush, and is well concealed. The eggs, which vary slightly in color and much in size, are four in number, and are pale-blue, sometimes with a few scattered spots of golden brown at the larger end. One nest, containing four eggs, had three thus spotted and one uniform in color; another contained three, none of which were spotted. I saw a few of these birds in the broader valleys and parks in the Black Hills. They were generally seen among the low bushes along the borders of streams, but were by no means common in such localities.

34. Cyanospiza amœna, *Baird.*

Lazuli Finch.

This beautiful finch was very abundant about Fort Lincoln, where it was breeding in all the little wooded ravines. They had probably already raised one brood, (June 25,) for I saw the gorgeous little male ardently pursuing his quaker-colored mate, and this not only once but in many instances. They are no doubt as pugnacious as their eastern relatives. At all events, only one pair were to be seen in each of the little patches of timber which they particularly affect. The male all through the morning sits perched on the top-most limb of some dead tree, and at short intervals utters a screaming little song, much resembling that of *C. ciris.*

35. Pipilo maculatus var. arcticus, *Swains.*

Arctic Towhee.

This bird, which in many respects so closely resembles the eastern species, was very abundant about Fort Lincoln; and from that point west to the Black Hills was seen on every wooded butte. It was breeding about Fort Lincoln, but I was not so fortunate as to find any nests. The cry of this species, when alarmed, closely resembles that of the cat-bird in similar circumstances. The song is a mere monotonous trill, scarcely deserving the name.

ALAUDIDÆ.

36. Eremophila alpestris var. leucolæma, *Coues.*

Shore Lark; Horned Lark.

This bird, one of the most characteristic of the species inhabiting the high dry plains of Dakota, was found in the greatest abundance all the way from Fort Lincoln to the Black Hills.

Early in July I found their nests with well-advanced eggs, and on the return march the prairies, which had been burned since we passed over them before, were fairly alive with flocks of old and young birds. When alarmed, they would crouch for an instant, and then, springing from the ground, would move off with an easy gliding flight, uttering at the same time a clear, mellow whistle.

ICTERIDÆ.

37. MOLOTHRUS PECORIS, *Swainson.*

Cow Bunting; Buffalo-bird.

This species was abundant everywhere on the trip. A large number of them would often accompany the column for the greater part of the day, alighting almost under the horses' hoofs, and displaying the utmost indifference as to the presence of man. I found the eggs of this species only in the nests of *C. bicolor.*

38. AGELAIUS PHŒNICEUS, *Bonap.*

Red-winged Blackbird.

Abundant along the Missouri River, and a few observed on the Little Missouri.

39. XANTHOCEPHALUS ICTEROCEPHALUS, *Baird.*

Yellow-headed Blackbird.

I noticed a single male of this species in Prospect Valley, and on our return march saw a few young birds near the Little Missouri.

40. STURNELLA MAGNA, *Swains.*

Meadow Lark.

This species was observed near the Missouri River, but was not seen after leaving that stream.

41. STURNELLA MAGNA var. NEGLECTA, *Aud.*

Western Meadow-lark.

This bird was very abundant not only on the plains, but also in some of the more extensive parks and valleys of the Black Hills. Its loud, sweet song was heard almost constantly throughout the day.

42. ICTERUS BULLOCKII, *Bonap.*

Bullock's Oriole.

A single bird of this species was seen among the low pines near our first crossing of the Belle Fourche.

43. SCOLECOPHAGUS CYANOCEPHALUS, *Cab.*

Brewer's Blackbird.

This species is very abundant about Fort Lincoln, breeding in the dense woods at the mouth of the Heart River. It was also observed in considerable numbers along the edge of the Black Hills, and by the 1st of August flocks of two or three hundred individuals were seen. I saw two of these birds, male and female, pursue a *Buteo borealis* var. *calurus* for several hundred yards, the hawk meanwhile making every effort to escape from his merciless tormentors.

CORVIDÆ.

44. CORVUS CORAX var. CARNIVORUS, *Bartram.*

Raven.

Ravens were seen almost every day on the way to the Black Hills, but never more than one pair at a time, except on one or two occasions, when we saw a pair of old ones with their newly-fledged young. They had bred on many of the lofty buttes that we passed. They were also observed in the Black Hills.

45. Corvus americanus, *Aud.*

Crow.

Observed occasionally in small flocks on the Little Missouri.

46. Pica caudata var. hudsonica, *Bonap.*

Magpie.

The magpie is rather common all through the country traversed by the expedition. At the season when I first saw them, late in July and early in August, they were generally to be seen in companies of ten or a dozen, and were very noisy, hopping about through the trees, and screaming like a flock of excited jays. At other times they were more silent, and would walk up to within a few yards of me as I sat watching them, and apparently converse about me in low tones. They carry the tail much elevated when on the ground.

47. Perisoreus canadensis var. capitalis, *Baird.*

Canada Jay; Gray Jay.

Four specimens of this species were observed on Elk Creek, August 12, the day before we left the Black Hills. They were evidently members of one family, and were quite shy. Three of them were secured, one of which, being only wounded, made a vigorous resistance when caught. They were active and restless, flying about constantly among the tall pine trees, and moving uneasily through the branches; but without uttering any note.

TYRRANIDÆ.

48. Tyrannus carolinensis, *Baird.*

Kingbird.

Very numerous along creeks and wooded ravines from the Missouri River to the Black Hills.

49. Tyrannus verticalis, *Say.*

Arkansas Flycatcher.

A pair of these birds were observed at Short-Pine Buttes, on the Little Missouri, and the female was secured. From this point, to and through the Black Hills and all along the Little Missouri, they were quite abundant, one or more pairs being seen on every wooded ravine. They were fearless and noisy when their nest was approached, though rather shy under other circumstances.

50. Sayornis sayus, *Baird.*

Say's Flycatcher.

I first observed this species in the river-bottom of the Belle Fourche. It was perched on a low bush, and in its actions reminded me much of *S. fuscus.* Later in the trip I saw it on the Little Missouri, but never more than a single specimen at a time.

51. Contopus borealis, *Baird.*

Olive-sided Flycatcher.

A female of this species was taken August 16 on the northeastern edge of the Black Hills, near Bear Butte. It was found in a dense pine forest.

52. Contopus virens var. richardsonii, *Baird.*

Western Wood Pewee.

This was one of the most common flycatchers seen during the trip. I did not observe it until we had reached the Black Hills, and had penetrated some little distance into the heavy pine woods, with which their sides are clothed. When it did appear, however, it was in such numbers that it seemed that every tree had one or two occupants of this species, and the woods fairly resounded with their loud, harsh cries. In their habits they closely resemble the eastern variety, but differ considerably from it in their note. Specimens of this bird, obtained late in July and early in August, were in fine plumage, while all the other birds taken at that time were moulting and very ragged.

ALCEDINIDÆ.

53. Ceryle alcyon, *Boie.*

Kingfisher.

Observed on the Little Missouri.

CAPRIMULGIDÆ.

54. Chordeiles popetue var. henryi, *Cassin.*

Western Night-hawk.

This species is abundant everywhere on the plains and in the broken country bordering the Black Hills. They were very unsuspicious, and would permit a near approach. I saw a pair sit undisturbed on the bare prairie while two companies of cavalry passed by within three feet of them.

CYPSELIDÆ.

55. (?) Chætura pelagica, *Baird.*

Swift.

A Chætura, probably this species, was observed in small numbers in the Black Hills. I was unable to secure specimens, as they were only seen twice, and on both occasions were flying high in the air.

CUCULIDÆ.

56. Coccygus erythrophthalmus, *Bonap.*

Black-billed Cuckoo.

This species was abundant about Fort Lincoln late in June, and was no doubt breeding in the wooded ravines near the river. The females were probably incubating, as none but males were taken.

PICIDÆ.

57. Picus pubescens, *Linn.*

Downy Woodpecker.

A single specimen, probably of this species, was seen in the Black Hills, but unfortunately I was unable to secure it.

58. Melanerpes torquatus, *Bonap.*

Lewis's Woodpecker.

This woodpecker was by no means common in the Black Hills, and I saw but few specimens while there. They were quite shy, and I was not often able to approach within gunshot of them. Although my opportunities for observation were very limited, there seemed to me a striking difference in habits between this species and the other members of the group. While at rest, these birds clung, supported by the tail, to an upright limb or stump, never alighting on a horizontal branch in the usual manner. They seemed lazy and indifferent in their search for food, and only occasionally made short excursions from their perches to secure passing insects. On the wing, their easy, gliding movements and the dark-greenish hue of their dorsal aspect made them conspicuous objects when flying over the clearings on the edge of which they were generally found. They were tough and muscular, and were hard to kill.

59. MELANERPES ERYTHROCEHALUS, *Swain.*

Red-headed Woodpecker.

All through Dakota, wherever there was timber, I saw the red-headed woodpecker, and in the Black Hills it was especially abundant. It seemed to me the most common species there, and its harsh cries resounded through the forest from morning till night. When the nest is approached, the parent birds give themselves little concern about the result. At first they would give a few sharp cries, expressive of displeasure, and then, flying off into the woods, would not be seen again.

60. COLAPTES AURATUS, *Swain.*

Golden-winged Woodpecker; Flicker.

This species was abundant on the Missouri River as well as on Heart and Knife Rivers. West of these streams it was not seen.

61. COLAPTES MEXICANUS, *Swain.*

Red-shafted Woodpecker.

I first saw this species among the scrub-oaks near our first crossing of the Belle Fourche. They were rather common all through the Black Hills. I could distinguish no difference between their habits and those of the preceding species.

STRIGIDÆ.

62. OTUS VULGARIS var. WILSONIANUS, *Less.*

Long-eared Owl.

Common in the Black Hills.

63. OTUS BRACHYOTUS, *Steph.*

Short-eared owl.

This owl was found in considerable numbers on the Little Missouri and on the headwaters of Knife and Heart Rivers. It was generally started from among the thick grass in the bottoms, and, after flying a short distance, would alight and conceal itself again.

64. BUBO VIRGINIANUS, *Bonap.*

Great-horned Owl.

Although none of these birds were seen while in the Black Hills, they were said by the Indians to be quite abundant there. I saw many dresses of the Sioux that were ornamented with their feathers.

65. NYCTEA SCANDIACA var. ARCTICA, *Gray.*

Snowy Owl; White Owl.

I am informed that this species is very abundant about Fort Lincoln in winter.

66. SPHEOTYTO CUNICULARIA var. HYPOGEA, *Bonap.*

Burrowing Owl.

This species was abundant in the prairie-dog towns through which we passed.

FALCONIDÆ.

67. FALCO LANARIUS var. POLYAGRUS, *Cassin.*

Lanner falcon.

This fine hawk was abundant everywhere on the plains, but was not seen in the Black Hills. Its breeding-places were found on almost every high butte that we passed, but all that I saw contained young generally about two-thirds grown, late in July. In no case did I see the least attempt at the construction of a nest, the young resting simply on the bare rock. In every instance when I approached the nest of this bird, I was attacked in the boldest way by the female. She would generally fly back and forth over my head at a height of 50 or 60 feet, all the while uttering shrill screams of rage, and, from time to time, would dart almost vertically downward, passing within 2 or 3 feet of my face. This species is, indeed, unusually courageous. Several times I have seen them swoop down on their prey within 20 feet of a company of cavalry, and on one occasion the bird commenced to devour the animal that it had captured within thirty yards of the column. A shot fired at it by a soldier made it rise and fly a few yards without its prey, but it immediately returned, and, seizing it, moved off a short distance farther, where it finished its meal. The feathers of this hawk are used by the Indians to ornament their head-dresses.

68. FALCO COMMUNIS var. ANATUM, *Bonap.*

Peregrine Falcon; Duck-hawk.

The peregrine falcon was not seen until late in August. At that time we were returning to Fort Lincoln, and were near the end of our journey. The prairies, the river-bottoms, and the streams swarmed with birds of various species, all moving southward, while, following and preying upon the various flocks, was this splendid falcon. The following extract from my note-book will give some idea of the power and daring of this bird:

"*August* 28.—About 6.30 a. m., while we were halting for a short time on a little knoll, a most interesting and exciting chase came under my observation. The ground was wet from the rain that had but just ceased to fall, and the men were, most of them, standing by their horses, instead of lying asleep on the ground, as is usually the case when a halt is made. I was looking out over the plain, when I observed two birds in rapid flight, approaching the hill where we were standing. They flew with astonishing velocity, and it was but a short time before they were quite near us. From the manner of their flight, I at first thought they were two falcons engaged in play, but a nearer view showed me that the foremost bird was much the smallest, and that it was making most strenuous efforts to escape from its pursuer by darting and twisting from one side to the other, up or down, or by straightforward flight. In one of its turnings it came quite close to the column, and, forgetting in its intense fear its natural shyness, it darted in among the men and horses. The larger bird, a peregrine falcon, as I could now see, hesitated not an instant, but dashed after, following the object of its pursuit in every cut and twist that it made, now passing under the horses, now low over their backs or close to the men's heads. After, perhaps, a minute of rapid pursuit, the smaller bird by a quick double put a group of men and horses between itself and the falcon, and then darted swiftly along the ground to where I was standing, an interested observer. Here, almost exhausted, it alighted on the saddle of a horse standing within arm's length of me, and I was able to distinguish that it was a passenger pigeon, (*Ectopistes migratoria.*) Meanwhile, the falcon, baffled for a moment, had risen 30 feet in the air, and was hovering over the group, looking for his prey. Hardly ten seconds had elapsed since the pigeon alighted, when he saw his pursuer above him, and, terror-stricken by the sight, the luckless bird darted away again over the open prairie. The falcon followed, and the doubling and twisting recommenced before they had gone a quarter of a mile. The pigeon once tried to regain the shelter of the command, but his relentless pursuer cut him off and drove him toward the plain, and, in a few seconds, by a tremendous burst of speed, caught up to his victim, and, throwing out his powerful feet, seized him, and, without checking his flight, bore him off to a neighboring butte, there to devour him. It was a splendid sight, and I can compare it to nothing unless it be a scene of ancient falconry, the only difference being that the birds were so much more evenly matched than in the old-time sports. It would, I think, be difficult to name a harder bird to catch than the pigeon, and, perhaps, the only bird that can do it in a straight-away chase is the peregrine falcon. I should mention that the soldiers made efforts to frighten the hawk away by shouting and throwing their hats at it, but it paid no attention to their demonstrations, except once to stretch out its feet as if to grasp a hat that sailed close by it."

69. FALCO LITHOFALCO var. COLUMBARIUS, *Linn.*

Pigeon-hawk.

A few birds of this species were seen on Heart River.

70. TINNUNCULUS SPARVERIUS, *Linn.*

Sparrow-hawk.

This beautiful and graceful little hawk was abundant throughout the region traversed by the expedition. Where there is timber, it seems to prefer to build its nest in trees, but a cleft in the rock or a hole in the side of a clay bluff will serve it, if nothing better is at hand. They raise two or three broods in a season, for I took young, not yet fully fledged, August 30.

71. CIRCUS CYANEUS var. HUDSONIUS, *Linn.*

Marsh-hawk.

This species is quite numerous on the plains. Its nests were seen several times, all containing well-grown young.

72. BUTEO SWAINSONI, *Bonap.*

Swainson's Hawk.

This hawk was only seen occasionally during the trip. A nest was found July 5, containing three unspotted eggs, a little larger than a hen's egg. The nest was in a small cottonwood-tree, about 12 feet from the ground, and was carelessly built of sticks and coarse weeds. One of these birds was seen on the ground. It was catching grasshoppers, and displayed considerable activity, running along quite nimbly.

73. BUTEO BOREALIS var. KRIDERI, *Hoopes.*

White-bellied Red-tail.

Two birds of this variety were observed near the headwaters of Knife River.

74. BUTEO BOREALIS var. CALURUS, *Cassin.*

Western Red-tail.

This was the most common hawk seen on the trip. It is equally abundant on the plains and in the Black Hills, breeding sometimes in trees, and, when these are wanting, in the clefts and hollows of the sandstone buttes that occur at short intervals everywhere on the plains of Dakota. I imagine that they breed rather late in this section, for I found a nest with a newly-hatched young one and an egg just chipped, July 3.

75. ARCHIBUTEO FERRUGINEUS, *Licht.*

Ferruginous hawk.

This handsome bird is abundant on the plains, and its nests were frequently found on the buttes which we passed. We were too late to secure eggs, and early in July found the young birds two-thirds grown.

76. AQUILA CHRYSAETOS var. CANADENSIS, *Linn.*

Golden eagle; War eagle.

A single individual of this species was killed by a Ree scout at Short Pine Buttes. This bird is said to occur all through the country between the Missouri River and the Rocky Mountains, though it is nowhere common. It is highly prized by the Indians, who use the tail-feathers to adorn their war head-dresses. So much is this the case that two of these birds are worth a horse, *i. e.*, \$40 to \$60, among the Sioux.

77. Haliætus leucocephalus, *Linn.*

White-headed Eagle.

I saw none of these birds myself, but am informed that they are by no means uncommon about Fort Lincoln, and that they breed in considerable numbers on Mouse River, about ninety miles north of that post.

CATHARTIDÆ.

78. Rhinogryphus aura, *Linn.*

Turkey-buzzard.

Very abundant on the plains.

COLUMBIDÆ.

79. Ectopistes migratoria, *Swains.*

Passenger Pigeon.

A single bird of this species was seen near the head of Heart River. They are said to occur occasionally on the Missouri, near Fort Lincoln.

80. Zenaidura carolinensis, *Bonap.*

Common Dove; Turtle Dove.

This species was abundant about Fort Lincoln, and on the plains, and their nests were frequently found. My attention was generally drawn to them by the bustle and hurry of the female as she darted away almost from beneath my horse's feet, for they sat very close. The nest was always on the ground, at the foot of a bunch of weeds, and was of the simplest possible character. A few blades of dried grass, just enough to keep the eggs off the ground, was all that was employed in its construction, and there was no depression in the nest—nothing to keep the eggs from rolling out, had they been subjected to a slight push.

TETRAONIDÆ.

81. Canace obscurus, *Say.*

Dusky Grouse.

A single bird of this species was seen among the dense pine forests of the higher portions of the Black Hills.

82. Centrocercus urophasianus, *Bonap.*

Sage Grouse.

Two or three families of these birds were seen on the Little Missouri, and several were taken. The young birds were only two or three weeks old when I saw them, July 17, but could fly well even at this age.

83. Pediœcetes phasianellus var. columbianus, *Baird.*

Sharp-tailed Grouse.

This species was found in all the river-bottoms that we crossed, and it was also abundant in the Black Hills. In the latter locality it seems to prefer the steep hill-sides that have been burned over, and are now overgrown with quaking-aspen brush. No nests were observed, but several broods of young were seen early in July. When a brood was approached, the mother, after manifesting her uneasiness by clucking and opening and closing her wings, would utter a short, sharp cry, and immediately all the young would rise, and, flying a few yards in different directions, would re-alight, concealing themselves so closely in the long grass that it was impossible to find them. On one occasion, late in August, I came on a mother with a brood of well-grown young, and, as usual, the family scattered and hid in the grass. The mother flew, perhaps, two hundred yards. Being in no haste, I determined to wait and see them come together again. Hardly five minutes after their dispersion, the old bird commenced to call, and one by one the young answered her until I could hear them calling on all sides. The call-note was entirely new to me. It was a rough, gutteral croak, repeated two or three times, and bore a close resemblance to the cry of the raven. In order to satisfy myself beyond the possibility of a doubt as to the origin of the cry, the call of one of the young was followed up and the bird shot. The note in question answers very well to the description given of the call of the ptarmigan.

84. BONASA UMBELLUS var. UMBELLOIDES, *Douglas.*

Mountain Grouse; Western Ruffed Grouse.

This grouse was abundant in the Black Hills, and in all its habits, so far as observed by me, resembles the eastern variety. Several broods were seen, about half grown, late in July, and in every instance the mother had recourse to the usual devices to entice the observer away from her young.

CHARADRIDÆ.

85. ÆGIALITIS VOCIFERUS, *Cassin.*

Killdeer Plover.

This species was abundant near Fort Lincoln, and was breeding in considerable numbers on the plains near the Heart River. In their efforts to draw me away from their nests, they employed the usual artifices, together with some that were new to me. They would fly close to me, screaming loudly, and, having attracted my attention, would alight at a distance of thirty or forty yards, and, looking back to see if I was watching them, would run off through the grass, and, when they reached some little clump of weeds, would squat down and apparently settle themselves on a nest. If followed, they would wait until I had approached to within a short distance, and then, running a few yards through the grass, would fly up again apparently in great distress, and in a short time would repeat the maneuver.

RECURVIROSTRIDÆ.

86. RECURVIROSTRA AMERICANA, *Gm.*

Avocet.

A few were observed about some alkaline pools near the Missouri River.

PHALAROPODIDÆ.

87. LOBIPES HYPERBOREUS, *Cuv.*

Northern phalarope.

A single bird of this species was observed on a little slough near Sweetbriar Creek. It was very gentle, and swam gracefully about more like a rail or a coot than like a duck. It was feeding on small insects, that it gathered from the reeds on the borders of the slough.

SCOLOPACIDÆ.

88. TRINGA MINUTILLA, *Vieillot.*

Least Sandpiper.

One specimen observed on the Little Missouri River.

89. TOTANUS MELANOLEUCUS, *Vieillot.*

Greater Yellow-legs; Tell-tale.

A few of these birds were taken on the return march. They were found along the edges of the small streams near Heart River, and were apparently migrating by twos and threes.

90. Totanus solitarius, *Aud.*

Solitary Sandpiper.

A few seen near the Little Missouri.

91. Actiturus bartramius, *Bonap.*

Upland Plover.

This bird was found everywhere on the plains in the greatest abundance. Newly-hatched birds were seen July 1, and for two weeks after that time nests with eggs were found almost every day. When the nest is approached, the female retreats but a short distance, and remains on the ground crying mournfully.

92. Numenius longirostris, *Wilson.*

Long-billed Curlew.

This species is numerous on the plains between the Missouri and the Little Missouri. On the first of July I saw young birds two-thirds grown and fully feathered. The quills of the wing, however, were soft, and the birds being unable to fly, the Indians caught many of them by running them down. With wings raised and half spread, the birds ran very fast, and could only be caught by the Indians when on horseback. I came on several places where I was confident that there were nests of this species, but I was unsuccessful in my attempts to discover them. From what I saw, I inferred that they bred in small companies, or at least several pairs near to one another. As soon as the first pair commence to cry, all the birds within hearing hasten to the spot, until eighteen or twenty individuals are flying about overhead, all screaming dolefully.

ARDEIDÆ.

93. Ardea herodias, *Linnæus.*

Great Blue Heron.

A few of these birds were seen on the head of Heart River and on the Sweetbrier.

94. Ardea egretta, *Gmel.*

White Heron.

A bird of this species was observed on an alkaline lake, near Bismarck, Dakota.

GRUIDÆ.

95. Grus canadensis, *Temm.*

Sand-hill Crane.

This species was occasionally seen on the plains, but it was not until we reached the Black Hills that it became at all abundant. There, however, it was numerous, breeding, the young being about two-thirds grown late in July. A nest, which contained one young one, was found about this time. It was in a tall pine tree. The female parent was not seen, but the male manifested much attachment for his young, and remained on the ground not far from the nest, croaking and displaying much anxiety. He was finally shot by General Custer. The young bird was brought into camp, and kept alive for two days, but died, probably from want of proper food. Although quite large, it could hardly stand, but it was very quick with its bill, driving off the dogs when they approached too near.

Its head and neck were wholly covered with reddish-brown down; its back well feathered, and of a deeper rusty red. The primaries and secondaries were bluish-gray, as in the adult, and were broadly edged with ferruginous. Bill and feet, a dirty orange; iris, gray.

RALLIDÆ.

96. RALLUS VIRGINIANUS, *Linn.*

Virginia Rail.

One specimen seen among the reeds near the mouth of Heart River.

ANATIDÆ.

97. BERNICLA CANADENSIS, *Boie.*

Canada Goose.

This species was abundant on the small streams between the Missouri and the Little Missouri, and was in families of from ten to fourteen individuals.

98. ANAS BOSCHAS, *Linn.*

Mallard.

Very numerous in the same localities and under the same conditions as *B. canadensis.*

99. DAFILA ACUTA, *Jenyns.*

Pin-tail.

Numerous on the Sweetbriar, late in August.

100. CHAULELASMUS STREPERUS, *Gray.*

Gadwall.

Seen in pairs on the alkaline lakes near Bismarck, Dak.

101. MARECA AMERICANA, *Stephens.*

American Widgeon.

Observed late in August on the headwaters of Heart River and on the Sweetbriar. At this time they were still in families; some of the young being scarcely able to fly.

102. QUERQUEDULA CAROLINENSIS, *Steph.*

Green-winged Teal.

Migrating in considerable numbers on small streams near the head of Heart River late in August.

103. QUERQUEDULA DISCORS, *Steph.*

Blue-winged Teal.

Same as last species.

104. SPATULA CLYPEATA, *Boie.*

Shoveller.

Observed on alkaline lakes near Bismarck.

105. MERGUS MERGANSER, *Wilson.*

Goosander.

A female, with a brood about a week old, was seen on Castle Creek, in the Black Hills.

106. Mergus serrator, *Linn.*

Red-breasted Merganser.

One specimen was taken on the Sweetbriar.

107. Mergus cucullatus, *Linn.*

Hooded Merganser.

Two specimens seen on Heart River.

LARIDÆ.

108. Larus delawarensis, *Ord.*

Ring-billed Gull.

One specimen observed on the Little Missouri.

COLYMBIDÆ.

109. Colymbus torquatus, *Brünnich.*

Loon; Great Northern Diver.

Observed on alkaline lakes near Bismarck.

PODICIPIDÆ.

110. Podiceps cornutus, *Lath.*

Horned Grebe.

Seen on alkaline lakes near Bismarck.

DESCRIPTIONS OF NEW FOSSILS.

By R. P. Whitfield.

Genus OBOLUS.

Obolus pectenoides, *n. sp.*

Shell rather small, transversely oval or very broadly ovate, the length and breadth being sub-equal; apex of the larger valve very obtusely pointed; cardinal margins sloping from the beak, and inclosing an angle of from 110° to 120°, somewhat straightened in the upper part, but gradually rounding into the lateral margins; sides and base rather regularly rounded, the latter more broadly than the former. Dorsal valve proportionally shorter than the ventral, giving a more transversely oval outline to the valve, principally arising from the shortening of the beak. Exterior surface of the shell roughly lamellose.

The substance of the shell appears to be composed of two distinct layers; the outer imbricatingly lamellose, the lamellæ readily separating from each other, and also from the inner layer; thus revealing not only the thickness of the outer layer, but exposing the surface of the inner layers to view. The inner layer is more nacreous than the outer, and the lamellæ of which it is composed extends over the entire inner surface of the shell, and, as seen when exposed by the exfoliation of the outer layer, is marked by more or less distant, flattened, radiating costæ, in the more coarsely marked individuals closely resembling those of a Pecten.

The muscular imprints have not been fully determined, but many of the specimens show evidence of the deep-curved scars placed just within the cardinal margin, seen in other species of the genus, and resembling those in *Tremerella*, termed *crescents* by Messrs. Davidson and King.

The species differs from any other described in the presence of the radiating costæ of the inner layers of shell, and as they occur in a rather coarse quartz sandstone, which adheres firmly to the shell, they generally show this feature. The larger individuals are about three-eighths of an inch in transverse diameter, the longitudinal diameter of the ventral being somewhat greater, and that of the dorsal rather less. They are found associated with *Obolella nana*, M. and H., and also with a species of *Lingulepis*, referred by those authors to *L. primæformis*, Owen, the shorter valves of which might readily be confounded with this species. The structure of the shell is, however, entirely different. A figure of a valve of this species is given for comparison.

Formation and locality.—Collected by Prof. N. H. Winchell from beds referred to the age of the Potsdam sandstone, on French Creek, in Dakota Territory. (Black Hills.)

Genus TEREBRATULA.

Terebratula helena, *n. sp.*

Shell attaining a large size, elongate-oval or ovate in outline, the point of greatest width varying from a little above to a little below the middle of the length. Valves ventricose, becoming somewhat gibbous in specimens of larger growth, especially the ventral, and also obscurely subangular along the middle of the upper portion. Ventral valve somewhat regularly arcuate longitudinally, the curvature being a little less abrupt toward the front part of the shell and somewhat flattened transversely; beak strong, moderately incurved, and obscurely subangular on the lateral portion, where the shell is inflected to form the rather broad cardinal margin; apex broadly truncated by the foramen, which, although not entirely perfect in any of the examples seen, bears evidence of having been of large size. Dorsal valve less deep than the ventral, but more angular in the upper part when not exfoliated, becoming flattened in the middle anteriorly, and abruptly bent downward or sinuate at the sides, forming an elevated flattened fold toward the front of the shell, which occupies more than one-third of the entire width of the valve, beyond which the sides abruptly decline to the lateral margins. This feature, although quite marked in large specimens, is but slightly developed in those of medium size, and not at all perceptible in young shells.

General surface of the shell smooth, or marked only by concentric lines of growth, which often become frequent and rather strong toward the front of old shells. Minute shell-structure very finely and closely punctate, the puncta having a strong tendency to form lines, owing to the regularity of their arrangement.

The species in its large size resembles *T. Harlani*, Morton, from the cretaceous sands of New Jersey, but differs materially in the greater curvature of the ventral valve and in the general form of the shell, and also in the flattened, elevated mesial portion of the dorsal valve and corresponding prolongation of the ventral, while it shows no tendency to assume a trilobate character in front, so common in that species.

Locality and formation.—The specimens are found common in the concretionary beds of the cretaceous, No. 4 of Meek and Hayden, associated with characteristic fossils of that formation. They were collected on the northeast side of the Black Hills, a few miles north of the Belle Fourche.

EXPLANATION OF PLATES.

OBOLUS PECTENOIDES.*

Fig. 1. View of a partially exfoliated dorsal (?) valve, showing fine radii, and the crescentiform markings representing muscular imprints.
Figs. 2, 3. Ventral (?) valve partially exfoliated, showing a variation in the strength of the radii.

LINGULEPIS PRIMÆFORMIS (?).

Fig. 4. View of a valve (ventral ?) associated with the above. Introduced for comparison.

TEREBRATULA HELENA.

Figs. 5, 6. Dorsal and profile views of a small specimen.
Fig. 7. Dorsal view of a larger specimen of almost symmetrically oval form.
Figs. 8–10. Dorsal profile and front views of an adult specimen, showing the characters of the species.

* The figures of this and the next species are each enlarged to two diameters.

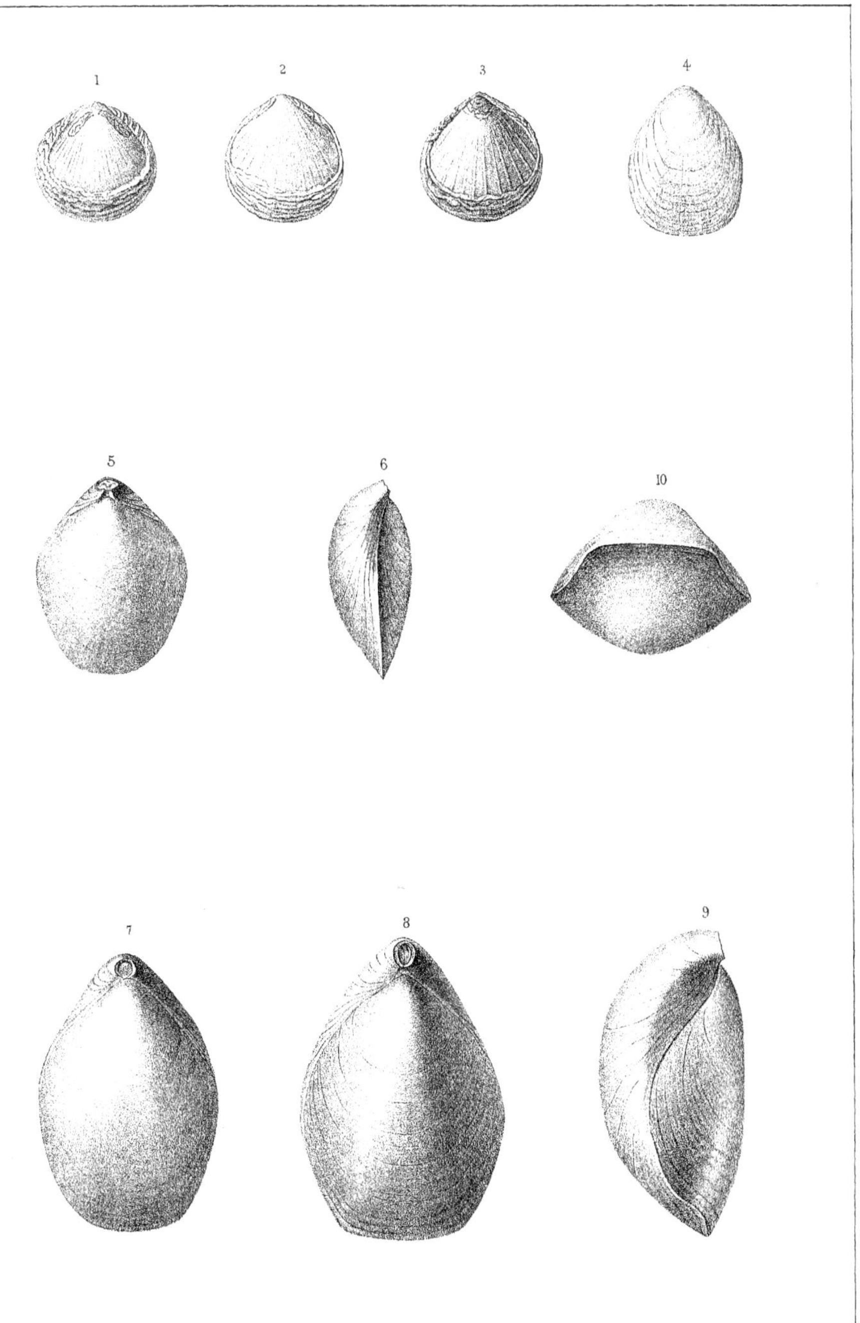

M. Martin, del. Thos Sinclair & Son. lith, Phila.

DRAWINGS OF NEW FOSSILS FOUND ON A RECONNOISSANCE OF THE BLACK HILLS OF DAKOTA, JULY AND AUGUST 1874.

To accompany a report from Mr. George Bird Grinnell.

TABLES OF OBSERVATIONS FOR TIME AND LATITUDE.

Determination of the time by observed equal altitudes of the sun's limb.

TO CORRECT THE CHRONOMETER AT NOON.

on, Prospect Valley.—Date, July 15, 1874.—Sextant, Spencer, Browning & Co., 6536.—Chronometer, Arnold & Dent, 1362.—Observer, Ludlow.—Computer, Wood.

Observed double altitudes.			Corresponding times.						$t - t'$ = elapsed time.		Equation of equal altitudes=x	Chron. fast of mean time at appt. noon by each pair of equal altitudes.	
			A. M. = t			P. M. = t'							
°	′	″	*h.*	*m.*	*s.*	*h.*	*m.*	*s.*	*h.*	*m.*		*m.*	*s.*
80	30	00	9	10	30. 0	16	24	27. 2	7	14	+ 5. 57	41	54. 63
80	35	00	9	10	43. 3	16	24	14. 0	7	13. 5	....	41	54. 68
80	40	00	9	10	58. 0	16	23	59. 3	7	13	....	41	54. 67
80	45	00	9	11	12. 5	16	23	45. 5	7	12. 5	+ 5. 56	41	55. 02
80	50	00	9	11	27. 7	16	23	30. 2	7	12	....	41	54. 97
80	55	00	9	11	42. 0	16	23	16. 0	7	11. 5	....	41	55. 01
81	00	00	9	11	56. 7	16	23	01. 7	7	11	+ 5. 545	41	55. 20
81	05	00	9	12	12. 0	16	22	47. 0	7	10. 5	....	41	55. 50
81	10	00	9	12	25. 3	16	22	32. 5	7	10	....	41	54. 90
81	15	00	9	12	39. 7	16	22	18. 3	7	09. 5	+ 5. 535	41	54. 99
81	20	00	9	12	54. 5	16	22	05. 0	7	09	....	41	55. 74
81	25	00	9	13	08. 3	16	21	49. 5	7	08. 5	....	41	54. 88
81	30	00	9	13	23. 7	16	21	34. 2	7	08	+ 5. 52	41	54. 93
Mean			....			....			....		....	41	55. 01

T	= 7^h 11^m		log A, (page 164)	= − 9. 4719	log B	=	9. 2425
δ	= − 23″. 84		log δ	= − 1. 3773	log δ	=	— 1. 3773
L	= 45° 29′		log tang	= 0. 0073	21° 29′ 21″		
1st term		= + 7. 19			log tang D	=	9. 5952
2d term		= − 1. 64		= + 0. 8565			
						=	— 0. 2150
x	=	5. 55	Equation of equal altitudes.				

h.	*m.*	*s.*	
9	10	30. 0	= t
16	24	27. 2	= t'
25	34	57. 2	= $t + t'$
12	47	28. 6	= T
	+	5. 57	= x
12	47	34. 17	= chronometer time of apparent noon.
10	05	39. 54	= true mean time of apparent noon.
	41	54. 63	= chronometer fast.

Observation for time.

on, Prospect Valley.—Sextant, Spencer, Browning & Co., 6536.—Observer, Ludlow.—Date, July 15, 1874.—Chronometer, Bond & Sons, 202.—Computer, Wood.—Object observed, Altair.—Index error, — 40″, Ex. + 40″.

le altitudes observed.			Corresponding times.		
°	′	″	*h.*	*m.*	*s.*
82	00	00	17	57	42. 5
				58	17. 5
				58	55. 0
				59	30. 5
			18	00	07. 5
				00	45. 0
				01	20. 5
				01	58. 0
				02	34. 5
83	30	00	18	03	12. 0
82	45	00	18	00	26. 3

Latitude = L	=	45	29	00
N. polar dist. = Δ	=	81	27	46
Time altitude = A	=	41	21	26
2 m = L + Δ + A	=	168	18	12
m	=	84	09	06
m − A	=	42	47	40
log cos m	=	9. 0081551		
log sin (m − A)	=	9. 8321065		
log cos m sin (m − A)	=	18. 8402616		
log cos L sin Δ	=	9. 8409513		
log $\sin^2 \frac{1}{2} p$	=	18. 9993103		
log sin $\frac{1}{2} p$	=	9. 4996551		
		°	′	″
$\frac{1}{2} p$	=	18	25	11
p in arc	=	36	50	22
p in time	=	2	27	21. 47
* Æ		19	44	40. 53
* hour-angle		17	17	19. 06

		°	′	″
Equation of time	=			
True time sid.	=	17	17	19. 06
Time by chron.	=	18	00	26. 3
Chron. fast	=		43	07. 24
		°	′	″
Refraction = R	=		− 1	04
Parallax = P	=			
Semi-diam. = S. d.	=			
R. P. & S. d.	=			
Observed 2 alt.	=	82	45	00
Index error	=			0
2 alt. corrected	=	82	45	00
Altitude	=	41	22	30
R. P. & S. d.	=		1	04
True alt. = A	=	41	21	26
log cos L	=	9. 8457903		
log sin Δ	=	9. 9951610		
log cos L sin Δ	=	9. 8409513		

Observation for time.

Station, Prospect Valley.—Sextant, Spencer, Browning & Co., 6536.—Observer, Ludlow.—Date, July 15, 1874.—Chronometer, Bond & Sons, 202.—Computer, Wood.—Object observed, Arcturus.—Index error, − 40″, Ex. + 40″.

Double altitudes observed.			Corresponding times.		
°	′	″	*h.*	*m.*	*s.*
85	00	00	18	08	45.0
				09	15.0
				09	44.0
				10	14.0
				10	41.5
				11	14.5
84	00	00	18	11	45.0
84	30	00	18	10	14.14

		°	′	″
Latitude = L	=	45	29	00
N. polar dist. = Δ	=	70	09	39
Time altitude = A	=	42	13	57
2 *m* = L + Δ + A	=	157	52	36
m	=	78	56	18
m − A	=	36	42	21
log cos *m*	=	9.2829966		
log sin (*m* − A)	=	9.7764882		
log cos *m* sin (*m* − A)	=	19.0594848		
log cos L sin Δ	=	9.8192179		
log sin² ½ *p*	=	19.2402669		
log sin ½ *p*	=	9.6201334		
		°	′	″
½ *p*	=	24	38	43
p in arc	=	49	17	26
p in time	=	3	17	09.73
∗ Æ	=	14	09	56.33

		°	′	″
Equation of time	=			
True time sid.	=	17	27	06.06
Time by chron.	=	18	10	14.14
Chron. fast	=		43	08.08
Refraction = R	=			
Parallax = P	=			
Semi-diam. = S. d.	=			
R. P. & S. d.	=			
Obs'd 2 alt.	=			
Index error	=			
2 alt. corrected	=			
Altitude	=			
R. P. & S. d.	=			
True alt. = A	=			
log cos L	=	9.8457903		
log sin Δ	=	9.9734276		
log cos L sin Δ	=	9.8192179		

Determination of the latitude by observed double altitudes of Polaris off the meridian.

Station, Prospect Valley.—Sextant, Spencer, Browning & Co., 6536.—Observer, Wood.—Date, July 15, 1874.—Index error, −40″, Ex. + 40″.—Chronometer, Bond & Sons, 202.—Computer, Wood.

Observed double altitudes.			Corresponding times.		
°	′	″	*h.*	*m.*	*s.*
89	19	30	17	26	29.7
	19	40		27	31.5
	20	10		28	21.8
	20	30		28	56.5
	20	55		29	26.2
	21	00		29	54.1
	21	15		30	27.0
	21	45		31	06.9
	22	20		31	49.2
89	22	20	17	32	25.5
89	20	56.5	17	29	38.84
44	40	28.25			
		50.6			
44	39	37.65			

log cos *p*	=	9.7743620
log Δ	=	3.6915765
log Δ cos *p*	=	3.4659385
	=	2923″.75
1st term	= +	48′ 43″.75
Alt. = A	=	44° 39′ 37″.65
2d term	= +	37″.4
Latitude	=	45° 28′ 58″.8

log sin *p*	9.90519
log Δ	3.69158
log Δ sin *p*	3.59677
log $\overline{\Delta \sin p}^2$	7.19354
log *a*	4.38454
log tang A	9.99482
log 2d term	1.57290
2d term	37″.4

Refraction	−50″.6	Bar. 26.6
Chron. correction	−43ᵐ 07ˢ.64	Ther. 67°
Dec	88° 38′ 04″.4 Δ 49′ 15″.6	

	h.	*m.*	*s.*
Æ Polaris	1	12	30.6
Sid. time at mean noon at this station			
Sid. interval from mean time of culmination			
Retardation of mean on sidereal time			
Mean time of culmination of star			
Error of chron. at time of observation	+	43	07.64
Time by chron. of culmination	1	55	38.24
Sid. time of observation	17	29	38.84
Hour-angle *p*, in sid. time	8	25	59.4
Sidereal equivalents in arc.			
p in arc	126° 29′ 51″		

Determination of the latitude by observed double altitudes of Polaris off the meridian.

Station, Prospect Valley.—Sextant, Spencer, Browning & Co., 6536.—Observer, Ludlow.—Date, July 14, 1874.—Index error, −40″, Ex. + 40″.—Chronometer, Bond & Sons, 202.—Computer, Wood.

Observed double altitudes.	Corresponding times.
° ′ ″	*h. m. s.*
90 03 45	18 37 46.0
04 00	38 46.5
04 15	39 25.5
04 25	40 15.0
06 00	41 26.5
07 10	42 13.0
07 30	43 15.0
08 05	43 54.5
08 40	44 42.5
09 00	45 34.0
10 10	46 38.0
10 30	47 23.5
11 10	48 15.0
11 25	49 02.5
90 12 25	18 49 52.5
90 07 54	18 43 54.3
45 03 57	
52	
45 03 05	

log cos p	=	9.4882939
log Δ	=	3.6916119
log Δ cos p	=	3.1799058
	=	1513″.2
1st term	= +	25′ 13″.2
Alt. = A	=	45° 03′ 05″.0
2d term	= +	53″.1
Latitude	=	45° 29′ 11″.3

log sin p	9.97838
log Δ	3.69161
log Δ sin p	3.66999
log $\overline{\Delta \sin p^2}$	7.33998
log a	4.38454
log tang A	0.00078
log 2d term	1.72530
2d term	+ 53.1

Refraction	−52″	Bar. 26.7
Chron. correction	43ᵐ 06ˢ.8	Ther. 50°
Dec	88° 38′ 04″ Δ 49′ 16″.0	

	h. m. s.
Æ Polaris	1 12 30.2
Sid. time at mean noon at this station	
Sid. interval from mean time of culmination	
Retardation of mean on sidereal time	
Mean time of culmination of star	
Error of chron. at time of observation	43 06.8
Time by chron. of culmination	1 55 37.0
Time of observation	18 43 54.3
Hour angle p, in sid. time	7 11 42.7
Sidereal equivalents in arc.	
p in arc	107° 55′ 40″

Determination of latitude by circum-meridian altitudes.

Station, Prospect Valley.—Sextant, Spencer, Browning & Co., 6536.—Observer, Ludlow.—Date, July 15, 1874.—Index error, (— 40″, Ex. + 20″=) — 20″.—Object observed, Antares.—Chronometer, Bond & Sons, 202.—Computer, Wood.

Times of obs'r by chron.	Mer. dist. = p	$\frac{2 \sin^2 \frac{1}{2} p}{\sin 1''} = k$	$\frac{\text{Cos } l \text{ cos D}}{\text{cos } a}$	Red. to mer. in arc = x	Obs'd 2 circum meridian altitudes.	Obs'd altitudes, corrected for index error.	True altitudes = a	True mer. alt's deduced = $a + x$ = A	Lat. deduced = 90° + D − A
h. m. s.	′ ″				° ′ ″	° ′ ″	° ′ ″	° ′ ″	° ′ ″
17 02 31.0	2 20	10.7	Constant multiplier, .66.	7	36 48 50	18 24 15	18 21 46	18 21 53	45 28 53
03 17.0	1 34	4.8		3	49 10	24 25	21 56	21 59	28 47
04 02.0	49	1.3		1	49 15	24 27	21 58	21 59	28 47
04 38.5	12.5	....		....	49 20	24 30	22 01	22 01	28 45
05 08.5	17.5	....		....	49 20	24 30	22 01	22 01	28 45
05 34.0	43	1.0		1	49 25	24 32	22 03	22 05	28 41
06 05.0	1 14	3.0		2	49 20	24 30	22 01	22 03	28 43
06 33.0	1 42	5.7		4	49 20	24 30	22 01	22 05	28 41
07 10.0	2 19	10.5		7	49 10	24 25	21 56	22 03	28 43
07 50.0	2 59	17.5		11	49 00	24 20	21 51	22 04	28 42
17 08 26.5	3 35.5	25.3		17	36 48 50	18 24 15	18 21 46	18 22 03	45 28 43
Mean..	....	....	....	....	....	....	....	....	45 28 45.5

		° ′ ″		
App. lat. = l	=	45 29	cos	9.84579
Dec.	=	26 09 13.7	cos	9.95309
a	=	18 22	cos	0.02282 A. C.
x	=	66		
				9.82170

	h. m. s.
Chron. correction	43 07.64
Equation of time	
Æ of sta	16 21 43.4
	17 04 51.0

Sémi-diam ..		Bar. 26.6
Refraction ..	2′ 29″	Ther. 67°
Parallax		

Determination of latitude by circum-meridian altitudes.

Station, Prospect Valley.—Sextant, Spencer, Browning & Co., 4536.—Observer, Wood.—Date, July 14, 1874.—Index error, (−40″, Ex. + 20″ =) − 20.—Object observed, Antares.—Chronometer, Bond & Sons, 202.—Computer, Wood.

Times of obs'r by chron.	Mer. dist. $= p$	$\frac{2 \sin^2 \frac{1}{2} p}{\sin 1''} = k$	$\frac{\cos l \cos D}{\cos a}$	Red. to Mer. in arc $= x$	Obs'd 2 circum-meridian altitudes.	Obs'd altitudes corrected for index error.	True altitudes $= a$	True mer. alt's deduced $= a + x =$ A	Lat. deduced $= 90° +$ D − A
h. m. s.					° ′ ″	° ′ ″	° ′ ″	° ′ ″	° ′ ″
16 58 03.5	6 47	90.3	Constant multiplier, .66.	1 00	36 47 30	18 23 35	18 21 00	18 22 00	45 28 46
58 48.7	6 02	71.5		48	47 40	23 40	21 05	21 53	28 53
59 22.2	5 28	58.7		39	47 45	23 42	21 07	21 46	28 60
17 00 23.1	4 27	38.9		26	48 20	24 00	21 25	21 51	28 55
00 48.4	4 02	31.9		21	49 00	24 20	21 45	22 06	28 40
01 34.9	3 15	20.7		14	49 00	24 20	21 45	21 59	28 47
02 16.8	2 33	12.8		8	49 15	24 27	21 52	22 00	28 46
02 47.0	2 03	8.2		6	49 20	24 30	21 55	22 01	28 45
03 20.4	1 30	4.4		3	49 10	24 25	21 50	21 53	28 53
04 08.7	41	0.9		1	49 40	24 40	22 05	22 06	28 40
04 31.5	19	....		....	49 45	24 42	22 07	22 07	28 39
05 13.4	23	....		....	49 20	24 30	21 55	21 55	28 51
05 57.0	1 07	2.4		2	49 40	24 40	22 05	22 07	28 39
06 25.5	1 35	4.9		3	49 15	24 27	21 52	21 55	28 51
06 54.9	2 05	8.5		6	49 10	24 25	21 50	21 56	28 50
07 23.0	2 33	12.8		8	49 05	24 22	21 47	21 55	28 51
08 01.4	3 11	19.9		13	48 55	24 17	21 42	21 55	28 51
08 56.4	4 06	33.0		22	48 40	24 10	21 35	21 57	28 49
09 24.5	4 34	40.9		27	48 30	24 05	21 30	21 57	28 48
09 53.4	5 03	50.1		33	48 10	23 55	21 20	21 53	28 53
10 24.0	5 34	60.8		41	48 00	23 50	21 24	22 05	28 41
10 49.0	5 59	70.3		47	47 50	23 45	21 10	21 57	28 49
17 11 17.8	6 28	82.1		55	36 47 30	18 23 35	18 21 00	18 21 55	45 28 51
Mean....	....	....	....	....	....	....	....	....	45 28 48

		° ′ ″	
App. lat. $= l$	=	45 29 00	cos 9.84579
Dec.	= −	26 09 13.7	cos 9.95309
a	=	18 22	cos 0.02271 A. C.
		.66	9.82159

	h. m. s.
Chron. correction	43 06.8
Ʀ of star	16 21 43.4
	17 04 50.2

Semi-diam.
Refraction 2′ 35″
Parallax.

Bar. 26.7
Ther. 50°

Determination of the time by observed equal altitudes of the sun's limb.

TO CORRECT THE CHRONOMETER AT NOON.

on, Permanent Camp.—Date, August 1, 1874.—Sextant, Spencer, Browning & Co., 6536.—Chronometer, Arnold & Dent, 1362.—Observer, Wood.—Computer, Wood.

Observed double altitudes.	Corresponding times.		$t-t'=$ elapsed time.	Equation of equal altitudes $=x$	Chron. fast of mean time at appt. noon by each pair of equal altitudes.
	A. M. $=t$	P. M. $=t'$			
° ′ ″	*h. m. s.*	*h. m. s.*	*h. m.*		*m. s.*
116 00 00	11 19 28.7	2 14 58.5	2 55.5	6.51	41 18.56
	11 19 49	2 14 38	2 55	....	41 18.46
	11 20 10	2 14 17	54	6.50	41 18.45
	11 20 31	2 13 56	2 53.5	....	41 18.45
	11 20 51	2 13 35	2 53	6.49	41 17.94
	11 21 12.5	2 13 14	2 52	....	41 18.19
116 30 00	11 21 33	2 12 53	2 51.5	6.48	41 17.93
	11 21 54	2 12 33.5	2 50.5	....	41 18.68
	11 22 14.5	2 12 13	2 50	....	41 18.68
	11 22 35.5	2 11 52	2 49	6.47	41 18.67
	11 22 57	2 11 31	2 48.5	....	41 18.92
	11 23 17.6	2 11 09.5	2 48	....	41 18.47
117 00 00	11 23 39.2	2 10 48.5	2 47	6.46	41 18.76
Mean......	....	....	....	....	41 18.55

T = 2ʰ 51ᵐ.5
δ = 37″.90
L = 43° 46′ 15″

log A, (page 164) = − 9.4161
log δ = − 1.5786
log tang = 9.9814
= + 0.9761

log B = 9.3850
log δ = − 1.5786
17° 56′ 49″
log tang D = 9.5104
= 0.4740

1st term = + 9.46
2d term = − 2.98

x [illegible] = + 6.48 Equation of equal altitudes.

Eq. of time, 6 01.55

11 19 28.7
14 14 58.5
25 34 27.2

25 34 27

12 47 13.6	12 47 13.5	12 47 13.5	12 47 13.5
6.51	6.51	6.50	6.50
12 47 20.11	12 47 20.01	12 47 20.00	12 47 20.00
12 06 01.55	12 06 01.55	12 06 01.55	12 06 01.55
41 18.56	41 18.46	41 18.45	41 18.45
12 47 13	12 47 13.25	12 47 13	12 47 13.75
6.49	6.49	0 06.48	6.48
12 47 19.49	12 47 19.74	12 47 19.48	12 47 20.23
12 06 01.55	12 06 01.55	12 06 01.55	12 06 01.55
41 17.94	18.19	41 17.93	41 18.68
12 47 14	12 47 13.55	12 47 13.85	
6.47	6.47	6.46	
12 47 20.47	12 47 20.02	12 47 20.31	
12 06 01.55	12 06 01.55	12 06 01.55	
18.92	41 18.47	41 18.76	

Determination of latitude by circum-meridian altitudes.

Station, Permanent Camp.—Sextant, Spencer, Browning & Co., 6536.—Observer, Wood.—Date, August 1, 1874.—Index error, (—42″, Ex. +52″= + 10″.—Object observed, ⨀.—Chronometer, Arnold & Dent, 1362.—Computer, Wood.

Times of obs'r by chron.	Mer. dist. $= p$	$\frac{2 \sin^2 \frac{1}{2} p}{\sin 1''} = k$	$\frac{\text{Cos } l \cos D}{\cos a}$	Red. to mer. in arc $= x$	Obs'd 2 circum-meridian altitudes.	Obs'd altitudes, corrected for index error.	True altitudes $= a$.	True mer. alt's deduced $= a + x = A$	Lat. deduced $= 90° + D - A$
h. m. s.					° ′ ″	° ′ ″	° ′ ″	° ′ ″	° ′ ″
12 40 20.5	7 00	96.2	Constant multiplier, 1.576.	2 32	127 45 10	63 52 40	64 08 10	64 10 42	43 46 07
41 14.5	6 05.5	72.9		1 55	128 49 30	64 24 50	08 44	10 39	46 10
41 51.5	5 28.5	58.9		1 33	127 47 10	63 53 40	09 10	10 43	46 06
42 30.0	4 50.0	45.9		1 12	128 51 00	64 25 35	09 30	10 42	46 07
43 12.0	4 08.0	33.5		50	127 49 10	63 54 40	10 10	10 60	45 49
43 47.0	3 33.0	24.7		37	128 52 30	64 26 20	10 14	10 51	45 58
44 43.0	2 37.0	13.4		20	127 50 00	63 55 05	10 35	10 55	45 54
45 16.5	2 03.5	8 3		13	128 53 10	64 26 40	10 35	10 48	46 01
45 58.5	1 21.5	3.6		5	127 50 05	63 55 07	10 37	10 42	46 07
46 45.0	35.0	0.7		1	128 53 30	64 26 50	10 44	10 45	46 04
47 17.5	2.5	....		....	127 50 10	63 55 10	10 40	10 40	46 09
47 57.0	37.0	0.7		1	128 53 20	64 26 45	10 40	10 41	46 08
48 35.5	1 15.5	3.1		5	127 50 00	63 55 05	10 35	10 40	46 09
49 03.5	1 43.5	5.8		9	128 52 50	64 26 30	10 24	10 33	46 16
49 37.0	2 17.0	10.2		15	127 49 40	63 54 55	10 25	10 40	46 09
50 34.5	3 14.5	20.6		32	128 52 20	64 26 15	10 10	10 42	46 07
51 18.5	3 58.5	31.0		48	127 48 40	63 54 25	09 55	10 43	46 06
51 56.0	4 36.0	41.5		1 05	128 51 20	64 25 45	09 39	10 44	46 05
52 51.0	5 31.0	59.8		1 34	127 47 00	63 53 35	09 05	10 39	46 10
53 41.0	6 21.0	79.2		2 04	128 49 30	64 24 50	08 45	10 49	46 00
54 13.5	6 53.5	93.3		2 27	127 45 30	63 52 52	08 20	10 47	46 02
12 54 51.0	7 31.0	1 10.9		2 55	128 47 30	64 23 50	64 07 44	64 10 39	43 46 10
Mean..	....	....	....	....	....	....	....	....	43 46 05.2

	° ′ ″			′ ″			Bar. 24.6
App. lat. $= l$	= 43 46 15	cos 9.85860	Chron. correction	41 18.55	⨀ Semi-diam.	+ 15 48.1 — 15 48.1	Ther. 90°
Dec.	= 17 56 49	cos 9.97834	Equation of time	6 01.55	Refraction	— 21.7 — 21.2	
a	= 64 10	cos 0.36076 A. C.		47 20.1		+ 3.8 + 3.8	
	1.576	0.19770			Parallax	+ 15 30.2 — 16 05.5	

Observation for time.

Station, Permanent Camp.—Sextant, Spencer, Browning & Co., 6536.—Observer, Wood.—Date, August 2, 1874.—Chronometer, Bond & Son 202.—Computer, Wood.—Object observed, Arcturus.—Index error, —40″, Ex. + 40″.

Double altitudes observed.	Corresponding times.
° ′ ″	h. m. s.
98 20 00	17 32 20.5
	32 33.5
	32 48.4
	33 04.4
	33 19.5
	33 33.5
	33 49.1
	34 05.0
	34 20.4
	34 34.2
	34 48.8
	35 04.0
97 20 00	17 35 20.0
97 50 00	17 33 49.29

	° ′ ″
Latitude = L	= 43 46 15
N. polar dist. = Δ	= 70 09 38
Time altitude = A	= 48 54 10
2 m = L + Δ + A	= 162 50 03
m	= 81 25 01.5
m — A	= 32 30 51.5
log cos m	= 9.1738868
log sin (m — A)	= 9.7303867
log cos m sin (m — A)	= 18.9042735
log cos L sin Δ	= 9.8320317
log sin² ½ p	= 19.0722418
log sin ½ p	= 9.5361209
½ p	= 20 05 59
p in arc	= 40° 11′ 58″
p in time	= 2ʰ 40ᵐ 47ˢ.87
✱ Æ	= 14 09 56.10

	h. m. s.
Equation of time	=
True time	= 16 50 43.3
Time by chron.	= 17 33 49.2
Chron. fast	= 43 05.3
Refraction = R	= — 50
Parallax = P	=
Semi-diam. = S. d.	=
R P. & S. d.	=
Obs'd 2 alt.	= 97° 50′ 00
Index error	=
2 alt. corrected	= 97 50 00
Altitude	= 48 55 00
R. P. & S. d.	= — 50
True alt. = A	= 48 54 10
log cos L	= 9.8586048
log sin Δ	= 9.9734269
log cos L sin Δ	= 9.8320317

Observation for time.

Station, Permanent Camp.—Sextant, Spencer, Browning & Co., 6536.—Observer, Wood. Date, August 2, 1874.—Chronometer, Bond & Sons, 202.—Computer, Wood.—Object observed, *a* Cygni.—Index error, — 40″, Ex. + 40″.

Double altitudes observed.			Corresponding times.		
°	′	″	*h.*	*m.*	*s.*
101	40	00	17	36	51. 4
				37	07. 0
				37	21. 1
				37	37. 5
				37	50. 5
				38	05. 5
				38	20. 4
				38	36. 5
				38	50. 9
				39	05. 5
				39	20. 0
				39	35. 3
102	40	00	17	39	49. 5
102	10	00	17	38	20.85

	° ′ ″
Latitude = L	= 43 46 15
N. polar dist. = Δ	= 45 10 05
Time altitude = A	= 51 04 14
2 m = L + Δ + A	= 140 00 34
m	= 70 00 17
m — A	= 18 56 03
log cos m	= 9. 5339533
log sin (m — A)	= 9. 5111900
log cos m sin (m — A)	= 19. 0451433
log cos L sin Δ	= 9. 7093599
log sin² ½ p	= 19. 3357834
log sin ½ p	= 9. 6678917
½ p	= 27 44 26
p in arc	= 55° 28′ 52″
p in time	= 3ʰ 41ᵐ 55ˢ. 47
✱ Æ	= 20 37 10. 62

	h. m. s.
Equation of time	=
True time	= 16 55 15. 15
Time by chron.	= 17 38 20. 85
Chron. fast	= 43 05. 70
Refraction = R	= — 46″
Parallax = P	=
Semi-diam. = S. d.	=
R. P. & S. d.	=
Obs'd 2 alt.	= 102° 10′ 00″
Index error	=
2 alt. corrected	= 102 10 00
Altitude	= 51 05 00
R. P. & S. d.	= — 46
True alt. = A	= 51 04 14
log cos L	= 9. 8586048
log sin Δ	= 9. 8507551
log cos L sin Δ	= 9. 7093599

Determination of the latitude by observed double altitudes of Polaris off the meridian.

Station, Permanent Camp.—Sextant, Spencer, Browning & Co., 6536.—Observer, Wood.—Date, August 2, 1874.—Index error, —40″, Ex. + 40″.—Chronometer, Bond & Sons, 202.—Computer, Wood.

Observed double altitudes.			Corresponding times.		
°	′	″	*h.*	*m*	*s.*
86	03	00	17	43	03. 5
	03	40		43	46. 3
	04	00		44	17. 5
	04	10		44	45. 0
	04	30		45	27. 6
	04	45		46	01. 0
	05	05		46	31. 1
	05	10		46	53. 2
	05	30		47	29. 5
86	05	40	17	48	09. 2
86	04	33	17	45	38. 39
43	02	16. 5			
		47. 5			
43	01	29			

log cos p	= 9. 7308867
log Δ	= 3. 6913291
log Δ cos p	= 3. 4222158
	= 2643″.72
1st term	= 44′ 03″.72
Alt. = A	= 43° 01′ 29″
2d term	= 38″.79
Latitude	= 43° 46′ 11″.5

log sin p	9. 92576
log Δ	3. 69133
log Δ sin p	3. 61709
log Δ sin p^2	7. 23418
log a	4. 38454
log tang A	9. 96997
log 2d term	1. 58869
2d term	38″.79

Refraction	—47″.5	Bar. 24.6
Chron. correction	43ᵐ 05ˢ.51	Ther. 60°
Dec	88° 38′ 07″.2 Δ 49′ 12″.8	

	h.	*m.*	*s.*
Æ Polaris	1	12	46. 4
Sid. time at mean noon at this station			
Sid. interval from mean time of culmination			
Retardation of mean on sidereal time			
Mean time of culmination of star			
Error of chron. at time of observation		43	05. 51
Time by chron. of culmination	1	55	51. 91
Time of observation	17	45	38. 39
Hour-angle p, in sid. time	8	10	13. 5
Sidearal equivalents in arc.			
p in arc	122°	33′	23″

Determination of the time by observed equal altitudes of the sun's limb.

TO CORRECT THE CHRONOMETER AT NOON.

Station, Permanent Camp.—Date, August 3, 1874.—Sextant, Spencer, Browning & Co., 6536.—Chronometer, Arnold & Dent, 1362.—Observer, Wood.—Computer, Wood.

Observed double altitudes.	Corresponding times. A. M. $= t$	Corresponding times. P. M. $= t'$	$t - t' =$ elapsed time.	Equation of equal altitudes $= x$	Chron. fast of mean time at appt. noon by each pair of equal altitudes.
102 30 00	10 33 35	3 00 30	4 27	+ 7.39	41 17.40
102 40 00	10 34 07.5	3 00 00	4 26	7.38	41 18.64
102 50 00	10 34 40.5	2 59 25	4 25	7.37	41 17.63
103 00 00	10 35 13	2 58 54	4 23.5	7.36	41 18.37
103 10 00	10 35 46	2 58 20	4 22.5	7.36	41 17.87
103 20 00	10 36 19	2 57 47	4 21.5	7.35	41 17.86
103 30 00	10 36 52	2 57 14	4 20.5	+ 7.34	41 17.85
Mean......	....	....	....	....	41 17.95

NOTE.—Very cloudy in afternoon.

T	= 4h 27m	log A, (page 164)	= − 9.4308	log B	= 9.3525
δ	= 39″.36	log δ	= − 1.59505	log δ	= 1.5951
L	= 43 46 15	log tang	= 9.98136	17 25 48.8	
1st term	= + 10.17			log tang D	= 9.4969
2d term	= − 2.78		= + 1.0072		= − 0.4445
x	= + 7.39	Equation of equal altitudes.		Equation of time 5 52.49	

T = 4 20.5	9.4296	9.3553
+ 10.14	1.5950	1.5951
− 2.80	9.9814	9.4969
+ 7.34	+ 1.0060	− 0.4473

10 33 35	10 34 07.5	10 34 40.5	10 35 13	10 35 46	10 36 19	10 36 52
15 00 30	15 00 00	14 59 25	14 58 54	14 58 20	14 57 47	14 57 14
25 34 05	25 34 07.5	25 34 05.5	25 34 07	25 34 06	25 34 06	25 34 06
12 47 02.5	12 47 03.75	12 47 02.75	12 47 03.5	12 47 03	12 47 03	12 47 03
+ 7.39	7.38	7.37	7.36	7.36	7.35	7.34
12 47 09.89	12 47 11.13	12 47 10.12	12 47 10.86	12 47 10.36	12 47 10.35	12 47 10.34
12 05 52.49	12 05 52.49	12 05 52.49	12 05 52.49	12 04 52.49	12 05 52.49	12 05 52.49
41 17.40	41 18.64	41 17.63	41 18.37	41 17.87	41 17.86	41 17.85

Determination of latitude by circum-meridian altitudes.

Station, Permanent Camp.—Sextant, Spencer, Browning & Co., 6536.—Observer, Wood.—Date, August 3, 1874.—Index error, − 52″, Ex. + 52″.—Object observed, ☉.—Chronometer, Arnold & Dent, 1362.—Computer, Wood.

Times of obs'r by chron.	Mer. dist. $= p$	$\frac{2 \sin^2 \frac{1}{2} p}{\sin 1''} = k$	$\frac{\cos l \cos D}{\cos a}$	Red. to Mer. in arc $= x$	Obs'd 2 circum-meridian altitudes.	Obs'd altitudes corrected for index error.	True altitudes $= a$	True mer. alt's deduced $= a + x =$ A	Lat. deduced $= 90° +$ D − A
h. m. s.	′ ″				° ′ ″	° ′ ″	° ′ ″	° ′ ″	° ′ ″
12 41 46.0	5 24.5	57.5	Constant multiplier, 1.55.	129	126 45 30	63 22 45	63 38 15	63 39 44	43 46 05
42 41.0	4 29.5	39.6		101	127 50 00	55 00	38 53	39 54	45 55
43 52.0	3 18.5	21.5		33	126 47 00	23 30	39 00	39 33	46 16
44 42.5	2 28.0	11.9		18	127 51 10	55 35	39 28	39 46	46 03
45 14.5	1 56.0	7.3		11	126 47 50	23 55	39 25	39 36	46 13
45 47.5	1 23.0	3.8		6	127 51 35	55 47	39 40	39 46	46 03
46 26.5	44.0	1.1		2	126 48 25	24 12	39 42	39 44	46 05
47 04.0	6.5	....		....	127 51 50	55 55	39 48	39 48	46 01
47 50.0	39.5	.8		1	126 48 30	24 15	39 45	39 46	46 03
48 33.0	1 22.5	3.7		6	127 51 35	55 48	39 41	39 47	46 02
49 20.0	2 09.5	9.1		14	126 48 10	24 05	39 35	39 49	46 00
50 00.5	2 50.0	15.8		25	127 50 40	55 20	39 13	39 38	46 11
50 35.5	3 25.0	22.9		35	126 47 15	23 37	39 07	39 42	46 07
51 12.5	4 02.0	31.9		49	127 50 10	55 05	38 58	39 47	46 02
51 49.5	4 39.0	42.5		106	126 46 10	23 05	38 35	39 41	46 08
52 31.0	5 20.5	56.0		127	127 49 05	54 32	38 25	39 52	45 57
12 53 12.5	6 02.0	71.5		151	126 44 30	63 22 15	63 37 45	63 39 36	43 46 13
Mean....	....	....	....	....	....	....	....	....	43 46 03

	° ′ ″		Chron. correction 41 17.95	☉ Semi-diam. − 15 48.4 ☉ + 15 48.4	Bar. 24.6
App. lat. $= l$	= 43 46 15	cos 9.85860	Equation of time 5 52.49	Refraction − 21.7 − 22.2	Ther. 90°
Dec.	= 17 25 49	cos 9.97959	47 10.44	+ 3.6 + 3.0	
a	= 63 39	cos 0.35270 A. C.		Parallax − 16 06.5 + 15 29.8	
	1.55	0.19089			

Determination of the latitude by observed double altitudes of Polaris off the meridian.

Station, Permanent Camp.—Sextant, Spencer, Browning & Co., 6536.—Observer, Wood.—Date, August 3, 1874.—Index error, (−55″, Ex. + 40″=) − 15″.—Chronometer, Bond & Sons, 202.—Computer, Wood.

Observed double altitudes.	Corresponding times.
° ′ ″	h. m. s.
86 20 30	18 09 42.5
20 50	10 27.5
21 30	11 25.5
21 50	12 13.5
22 20	12 51.5
22 40	13 32.5
23 15	14 13.0
23 40	14 59.0
24 00	15 39.0
86 24 25	18 16 15.5
86 22 30	18 13 07.95
15	
86 22 15	
43 11 07.5	
47.0	
43 10 20.5	

log cos p	=	9.6369559
log Δ	=	3.6913114
log Δ cos p	=	3.3282673
	=	2129″.45
1st term	=	35′ 29″.45
Alt. = A	=	43° 10′ 20″.5
2d term	=	44″.56
Latitude	=	43° 46′ 34″.51

log sin p	9.9548065
log Δ	3.6913114
log Δ sin p	3.6461179
log $\overline{\Delta \sin p^2}$	7.29223
log a	4.38454
log tang A	9.97221
log 2d term	1.64898
2d term	+ 44″.56

Refraction.............................. −47″   Bar. 24.6
Chron. correction...................... 43m 06s.16   Ther. 60°
Dec .... 88° 38′ 07″.4 Δ 49′ 12″.6

	h. m. s.
Æ Polaris..	1 12 46.87
Sid. time at mean noon at this station	
Sid. interval from mean time of culmination..........................	
Retardation of mean on sidereal time...............................	
Mean time of culmination of star	
Error of chron. at time of observation	43 06.16
Time by chron. of culmination...	1 55 53.03
Time of observation	18 13 07.95
Hour angle p in mean time..........	7 42 45.1
Sidereal equivalents in arc.	
p in arc..	115° 41′ 16″

Determination of latitude by circum-meridian altitudes.

Station, Bear Butte.—Sextant, Spencer, Browning & Co., 6536.—Observer, Wood.—Date, August 14, 1874.—Index error, (− 30″, Ex. + 25″=)—5″.—Object observed., δ Aquilæ.—Chronometer, Bond & Sons, 202.—Computer, Wood.

Times of obs'r by chron.	Mer. dist. $=p$	$\frac{2 \sin^2 \frac{1}{2} p}{\sin 1''} = k$	$\frac{\cos l \cos D}{\cos a}$	Red. to Mer. in arc $= x$	Obs'd 2 circum-meridian altitudes.	Obs'd altitudes, corrected for index error.	True altitudes $= a$	True mer. alt's deduced $= a + x =$ A	Lat. deduced $= 90° +$ D − A
h. m. s.	′ ″				° ′ ″	° ′ ″	° ′ ″	° ′ ″	° ′ ″
19 54 01.0	7 48	1 19.5	Constant multiplier, 1.076.	2 09	96 54 50	48 27 23	48 26 40	48 28 49	44 23 10
56 06.0	5 43	64.2		1 09	56 00	27 57	27 14	28 23	23 36
56 45.0	5 04	50.4		54	56 10	28 03	27 20	28 14	23 45
57 29.0	4 20	36.9		39	57 00	28 27	27 44	28 23	23 36
58 11.0	3 38	25.9		28	57 20	28 37	27 54	28 22	23 37
58 56.0	2 53	16.3		17	57 25	28 39	27 56	28 13	23 46
59 39.0	2 10	9.2		10	57 50	28 53	28 10	28 20	23 39
20 00 36.5	1 12.5	2.8		3	58 10	29 02	28 19	28 22	23 37
01 23.5	25.5	....		....	58 00	28 58	28 13	28 13	23 46
02 40.5	25.5	....		....	58 00	28 57	28 14	28 14	23 45
04 40.5	2 25.5	11.5		12	57 40	28 48	28 05	28 17	23 42
04 59.5	3 10.5	19.8		21	57 25	28 39	27 56	28 17	23 42
05 45.0	3 56.0	30.4		33	57 05	28 30	27 47	28 20	23 39
06 26.0	4 37.0	41.8		45	56 35	28 14	27 31	28 16	23 43
07 17.5	5 28.5	58.9		1 03	56 20	28 08	27 25	28 28	23 31
07 55.0	6 06.0	73.1		1 19	56 00	27 57	27 14	28 33	23 26
20 09 39.5	7 50.5	1 20.7		2 10	96 54 20	48 27 08	48 26 25	48 28 35	44 23 24
Mean....	....	....	....	....	....	....	....	....	44 23 36.7

App. lat. $= l$ = 44° 23′ 45″   cos 9.85402
Dec.= 2° 51′ 59″   cos 9.99946
a = 48 28   cos 0.17845 A. C.

1.076   0.03193

	h. m. s.
Chron. correction	42 37.7
Æ of star	19 19 11 2
Equation of time	20 01 48.9

Semi-diam.
Refraction, 43″
Parallax.

Bar. 26.3
Ther. 70°

Determination of the latitude by observed double altitudes of Polaris off the meridian.

Station, Bear Butte.—Sextant, Spencer, Browning & Co., 6536.—Observer, Wood.—Date, August 14, 1874.—Index error, (−30″, Ex. +40″=)+10″. Chronometer, Bond & Sons, 202.—Computer, Wood.

Observed double altitudes.			Corresponding times.		
°	′	″	h.	m.	s.
89	16	40	20	36	55
	17	20		37	45
	18	00		38	17
	18	00		38	48.5
	18	40		39	35.0
	19	20		40	15.5
	19	20		40	44.5
	20	00		41	11.5
	20	50		42	07.5
89	21	20	20	42	39.0
89	18	57	20	39	49.85
		10			
89	19	07			
44	39	33.5			
		50.0			
44	38	43.5			

log cos p	=	9.2831905
log Δ	=	3.6910815
log Δ cos p	=	2.9742720
	=	942.48
1st term	=	15′ 42″.48
Alt. = A	=	44° 38′ 43″.5
		44° 23′ 01″.02
2d term	=	55″.59
Latitude	=	44° 23′ 56″.61

log sin p	9.9918480
log Δ	3.6910815
log Δ sin p	3.68293
log Δ sin p^2	7.36586
log a	4.38454
log tang A	9.99460
log 2d term	1.74500
2d term	55.59

Refraction............................	−50″.0	Bar. 26.3
Chron. correction....................	42ᵐ 37ˢ.7	Ther. 70°
Dec	88° 38′ 10″ Δ 49″.10	

	h.	m.	s.
Æ Polaris..	1	12	56.3
Sid. time at mean noon at this station			
Sid. interval from mean time of culmination			
Retardation of mean on sidereal time			
Mean time of culmination of star...................			
Error of chron. at time of observation		42	37.7
Time by chron. of culmination......................	1	55	34.0
Time of observation................................	20	39	50
Hour angle p, in mean time	5	15	44
Sidereal equivalents in arc.			
p in arc..	78°	56′	00″

Observation for time.

Station Bear Butte Camp.—Sextant, Spencer, Browning & Co., 6536.—Observer, Wood.—Date, August 15, 1874.—Chronometer, Bond & Sons, 202.—Computer, Wood.—Object observed, "*a*" Cygni.—Index error, (−30″, Ex. +50″=) +20″.

Double altitudes observed.			Corresponding times.		
°	′	″	h.	m.	s.
119	30	00	18	27	46.5
				28	13.5
				28	42.5
				29	11.5
				29	41.0
				30	10.0
120	30	00	18	30	40.0
120	00	00	18	29	12.14

		°	′	″
Latitude = L	=	44	23	45
N. polar dist. = Δ	=	45	10	01
Time altitude = A	=	59	59	38
2 m = L + Δ + A	=	149	33	24
m	=	74	46	42
m − A	=	14	47	04
log cos m	=	9.4192188		
log sin (m − A)	=	9.4068522		
log cos m sin (m − A)	=	18.8260710		
log cos L sin Δ	=	9.7047632		
log sin² ½ p	=	19.1213078		
log sin ½ p	=	9.5606539		
		h.	m.	s.
½ p	=	21	19	23
p in arc	=	42	38	46
p in time	=	2	50	35.07
✱ Æ	=	20	37	10.61

		h.	m.	s.
Equation of time	=			
True time	=	17	46	35.54
Time by chron.	=	18	29	12.14
Chron.	=		42	36.60
Refraction = R	=			− 32″
Parallax = P	=			
Semi-diam. = S. d.	=			
R. P. & S. d	=			
Obs'd 2 alt.	=	120	00	00
Index error and ex.	=			+20
2 alt. corrected	=	120	00	20
Altitude	=	60	00	10
R. P. & S. d	=			32
True alt. = A	=	59	59	38
log cos L	=	9.8540165		
log sin Δ	=	9.8507467		
log cos L sin Δ	=	9.7047632		

Observation for time.

ation, Bear Butte. Sextant, Spencer, Browning & Co., 6536.—Observer, Wood.—Date, August 15, 1874.—Chronometer, Bond & Sons, 202.—Computer, Wood.—Object observed, Arcturus.—Index error, — 30″, Ex. + 30″.

uble altitudes observed.	Corresponding times.
° ′ ″	*h. m. s.*
76 40 00	18 33 49.0
	34 18.0
	34 47.5
	35 14.5
	35 43.5
	36 11.5
75 40 00	18 36 39.5
76 10 00	18 35 14.8

		° ′ ″
Latitude = L	=	44 23 45
P. polar dist. = Δ	=	70 09 38
Time altitude = A	=	38 03 49
2 *m* = L + Δ + A	=	152 37 12
m	=	76 18 36
m — A	=	38 14 47
log cos *m*	=	9.3741406
log sin (*m* — A)	=	9.7917218
log cos *m* sin (*m* — A)	=	19.1658624
log cos L sin Δ	=	9.8274434
log sin² ½ *p*	=	19.3384190
log sin ½ *p*	=	9.6692095
½ *p*	=	27 49 56
p in arc	=	55° 39′ 52″
p in time	=	3ʰ 42ᵐ 39ˢ.47
✱ Æ	=	14 09 55.91

		h. m. s.
Equation of time	=	
True time	=	17 52 35.38
Time by chron.	=	18 35 14.80
Chron.	=	42 39.42
Refraction = R	=	— 1′ 11″
Parallax = P	=	
Semi-diam. = S. d.	=	
R. P. & S. d.	=	
Obs'd 2 alt.	=	76° 10′ 00″
Index error	=	
2 alt. corrected	=	76 10 00
Altitude	=	38 05 00
R. P. & S. d.	=	1 11
True alt. = A	=	38 03 49
log cos L	=	9.8540165
log sin Δ	=	9.9734269
log cos L sin Δ	=	9.8274434

Determination of latitude by circum-meridian altitudes.

ation, Bear Butte.—Sextant, Spencer, Browning & Co., 6536.—Observer, Wood.—Date, August 15, 1874.—Index error, (— 30″, Ex. + 24″ =) — 6″.—Object observed, η Serpentis.—Chronometer, Bond & Sons, 202.—Computer, Wood.

Times of obs'r by chron.	Mer. dist. = *p*	$\frac{2 \sin^2 \frac{1}{2} p}{\sin 1''} = k$	$\frac{\cos l \cos D}{\cos a}$	Red. to Mer. in arc = *x*	Obs'd 2 circum-meridian altitudes.	Obs'd altitudes, corrected for index error.	True altitudes = *a*	True mer. alt's deduced = *a* + *x* = A	Lat. deduced = 90° + D — A
h. m. s.					° ′ ″	° ′ ″	° ′ ″	° ′ ″	° ′ ″
18 48 05.0	9 22.5	172.5		2 47	85 18 05	42 38 59	42 38 06	42 40 53	44 23 20
49 01.5	8 26.0	139.6		2 16	19 15	39 34	38 41	40 57	23 16
49 39.0	7 48.5	119.7		1 56	19 30	39 42	38 49	40 45	23 28
50 11.5	7 16.0	103.7		1 41	20 05	40 00	39 07	40 48	23 25
50 51.0	6 36.5	85.8		1 23	20 40	40 17	39 24	40 47	23 26
51 45.0	5 42.5	64.0		1 02	21 20	40 37	39 44	40 46	23 27
52 16.5	5 11.0	52.7		51	21 30	40 42	39 49	40 40	23 33
52 50.0	4 37.5	42.0		41	22 00	40 57	40 04	40 45	23 28
53 24.0	4 03.5	32.3		31	22 30	41 12	40 19	40 50	23 23
53 56.0	3 31.5	24.4		24	22 30	41 12	40 19	40 43	23 30
54 36.5	2 51.0	15.9		16	22 40	41 17	40 24	40 40	23 33
55 08.5	2 19.0	10.5		10	22 55	41 24	40 31	40 41	23 32
55 45.5	1 42.0	5.7		6	23 10	41 32	40 39	40 45	23 28
56 25.5	1 02.0	2.1		2	23 20	41 37	40 44	40 46	23 27
57 01.5	26.0	0.4	Constant multiplier, .97.	....	23 20	41 37	40 44	40 44	23 29
58 04.5	37.0	0.7		1	23 30	41 42	40 49	40 50	23 23
58 43.5	1 16.0	3.1		3	23 20	41 37	40 44	40 47	23 26
59 16.0	1 48.5	6.4		6	23 15	41 35	40 42	40 48	23 25
59 41.5	2 14.0	9.8		10	23 10	41 32	40 39	40 49	23 24
19 00 11.5	2 44.0	14.7		14	22 45	41 19	40 26	40 40	23 23
00 54.5	3 27.0	23.4		23	22 40	41 17	40 24	40 47	23 26
01 35.0	4 07.5	33.4		32	22 10	41 02	40 09	40 41	23 32
02 13.5	4 46.0	44.6		43	21 45	40 50	39 57	40 40	23 33
02 54.0	5 26.5	58.1		56	21 20	40 37	39 44	40 40	23 33
03 34.5	6 07.0	73.5		1 11	20 50	40 22	39 29	40 40	23 33
04 24.5	6 57.0	94.8		1 32	20 10	40 02	39 09	40 41	23 32
05 01.0	7 33.5	112.1		1 49	19 50	39 52	38 59	40 48	23 25
05 40.5	8 13.0	132.6		2 09	19 10	39 32	38 39	40 48	23 25
19 06 11.5	8 44.0	149.7		2 25	85 18 40	42 39 17	42 38 24	42 40 49	44 23 24
Mean ..	....	....	....	....	....	....	....	....	44 23 27.5

		° ′ ″		
App. lat. = *l*	=	44 23 45	cos	9.85402
Dec.	= —	2 55 47	cos	9.99943
a	=	42 40	cos	0.13353 A. C.
		97		9.98698

	h. m. s.
Chron. correction	42 38.0
Æ of star	18 14 49.7
	18 57 27.7

Semi-diam.
Refraction 53″
Parallax

Bar., 26°.3
Ther., 70°

Determination of the latitude by observed double altitudes of Polaris off the meridian.

Station Bear Butte.—Sextant, Spencer, Browning & Co., 6536.—Observer, Wood.—Date, August 15, 1874.—Index error, (—30″, Ex. + 40″=) + 10″.—Chronometer, Bond & Sons, 202.—Computer, Wood.

Observed double altitudes.			Corresponding times.		
°	′	″	h.	m.	s.
7	55	20	18	40	34.5
	55	40		41	13.5
	56	05		41	47.0
	56	30		42	15.5
	56	40		42	43.0
	57	10		43	19.0
	57	25		43	50.0
	57	50		44	38.0
	58	10		45	06.5
87	58	35	18	45	39.0
87	56	56.5	18	43	06.6
		10			
87	57	06.5			
43	58	33			
		57			
43	57	42			

log cos p	= 9.4926946	log sin p	9.99792
log Δ	= 3.6910815	log Δ	3.69108
log Δ cos p	= 3.1837761	log Δ sin p	3.68900
	= 1526″.78	log Δ sin p^2	7.37800
1st term	= 25′ 26″.78	log a	4.38454
Alt. = A	= 43° 57′ 42″	log tang A	9.98425
2d term	= 55″.82	log 2d term	1.74679
Latitude	= 44° 24′ 04″.6	2d term	+ 55.82

Refraction	— 51″	Bar.	26.3
Chron. correction	42m 38s.00	Ther.	70°
Dec	88° 38′ 10 Δ 49′ 10″.0		

	h.	m.	s.
Æ Polaris	1	12	56.6
Sid. time at mean noon at this station			
Sid. interval from mean time of culmination			
Retardation of mean on sidereal time			
Mean time of culmination of star			
Error of chron. at time of observation		42	38.0
Time by chron. of culmination	1	55	34.6
Time of observation	18	43	06.6
Hour angle p, in sid. time	7	12	28
Sidereal equivalents in arc.			
p in arc	108° 07′ 00″		

Observation for time.

Station, near Little Missouri.—Sextant, Spencer, Browning & Co., 6536.—Observer, Wood.—Date, August 22, 1874.—Chronometer, Bond & Sons, 202.—Computer, Wood.—Object observed, Altair.—Index error, — 30″, Ex. + 30″.

Double altitudes observed.			Corresponding times.		
°	′	″	h.	m.	s.
88	50	00	18	29	54.0
				30	17.0
				30	38.5
				30	59.5
				31	20.0
				31	42.5
				32	03.5
				32	25.0
89	30	00	18	32	46.5
89	10	00	18	31	20.7

	° ′ ″		h. m. s.
Latitude = L	= 46 27 20	Equation of time	=
N. polar dist. = Δ	= 81 27 40	True time	= 17 47 28.73
Time altitude = A	= 44 34 04	Time by chron.	= 18 31 20.7
2 m = L + Δ + A	= 172 29 04	Chron.	= 43 52
m	= 86 14 32	Refraction = R	= — 56″
m — A	= 41 40 28	Parallax = P	=
		Semi-diam. = S. d.	=
		R. P. & S. d.	=
log cos m	= 8.8164971	Obs'd 2 alt.	= 89° 10′ 00″
log sin (m — A)	= 9.8227546	Index error	=
log cos m sin (m — A)	= 18.6392517	2 alt. corrected	= 89 10 00
log cos L sin Δ	= 9.8333260	Altitude	= 44 35 00
log sin² ½ p	= 18.8059257	R. P. & S. d.	= 56
log sin ½ p	= 9.4029628	True alt. = A	= 44 34 04
½ p	= 14 38 59	log cos L	= 9.8381669
p in arc	= 29° 17′ 58″	log sin Δ	= 9.9951591
p in time	= 1h 57m 11s.87		
✱ Æ	= 19 44 40.6	log cos L sin Δ	= 9.8333260

Observation for time.

Station, near Little Missouri.—Sextant, Spencer, Browning & Co., 6536.—Observer, Wood.—Date, August 22, 1874.—Chronometer, Bond & Sons, 202.—Computer, Wood.—Object observed, Arcturus.—Index error, —30″, Ex. + 30″.

Double altitudes observed.	Corresponding times.
° ″ ″	*h. m. s.*
79 00 00	18 25 53.0
	26 23.0
	26 53.5
	27 23.0
78 20 00	18 27 53.0
78 40 00	18 26 53.1

		° ′ ″
Latitude = L	=	46 27 20
N. polar dist. = △	=	70 09 39
Time altitude = A	=	39 18 51
2 *m* = L + △ + A	=	155 55 50
m	=	77 57 55
m — A	=	38 39 04
log cos *m*	=	9. 3191153
log sin (*m* — A)	=	9. 7955856
log cos *m* sin (*m* — A)	=	19. 1147009
log cos L sin △	=	9. 8115945
log sin² ½ *p*	=	19. 3031064
log sin ½ *p*	=	9. 6515532
		h. m. s.
½ *p*	=	26 38 01
p in arc	=	53 16 02
p in time	=	3 33 04. 13
✱ Æ	=	14 09 55. 82

		h. m. s.
Equation of time	=	
True time	=	17 . 42 59. 95
Time by chron.	=	18 26 53. 1
Chron.	=	43 53. 15
Refraction = R	=	— 1′ 09″
Parallax = P	=	
Semi-diam. = S. d.	=	
R. P. & S. d.	=	
Obs'd 2 alt.	=	78 40 00
Index error	=	—
2 alt. corrected	=	78 40 00
Altitude	=	39 20 00
R. P. & S. d.	=	1 09
True alt. = A	=	39 18 51
log cos L	=	9. 8381669
log sin △	=	9. 9734276
log cos L sin △	=	9. 8115945

Determination of latitude by circum-meridian altitudes.

Station, near Little Missouri.—Sextant, Spencer, Browning & Co., 6536 —Observer, Ludlow.—Date, August 22, 1874.—Index error, (— 25″, Ex. + 40″ =) + 15.—Object observed, η Serpentis.—Chronometer, Bond & Sons, 202.—Computer, Wood.

Times of obs'r by chron.	Mer. dist. = p	$\frac{2 \sin^2 \frac{1}{2} p}{\sin 1''} = k$	$\frac{\cos l \cos D}{\cos a}$	Red. to Mer. in arc = x	Obs'd 2 circum-meridian altitudes.	Obs'd altitudes, corrected for index error.	True altitudes = a	True mer. alt's deduced = $a + x$ = A	Lat. deduced = 90° + D—A
h. m. s.	′ ″				° ′ ″	° ′ ″	° ′ ″	° ′ ″	° ′ ″
18 49 35. 0	9 07	163. 2	Constant multiplier, .906.	2 28	81 10 30	40 35 22	40 34 22	40 36 50	46 27 23
50 33. 5	8 09	130. 4		1 58	12 20	36 17	35 17	37 15	26 58
51 26. 0	7 16	103. 7		1 34	13 00	36 37	35 37	37 11	27 02
52 27. 0	6 15	76. 7		1 10	13 30	36 52	35 52	37 02	27 11
52 58. 5	5 44	64. 5		58	14 05	37 10	36 10	37 08	27 05
53 38. 0	5 04	50. 4		45	14 40	37 27	36 27	37 12	27 01
54 11. 0	4 31	40. 1		36	15 00	37 37	36 37	37 13	27 00
54 36. 5	4 06	33. 9		30	15 00	37 37	36 37	37 07	27 06
55 12. 0	3 30	24. 0		22	15 00	37 37	36 37	36 59	27 14
55 46. 0	2 56	16. 9		16	15 10	37 42	36 42	36 58	27 15
56 31. 0	2 11	9. 4		9	15 30	37 52	36 52	37 01	27 12
57 05. 5	1 37	5. 1		5	15 20	37 47	36 47	36 52	27 21
57 40. 0	1 02	2. 1		2	15 30	37 52	36 52	36 54	27 19
58 13. 5	29	0. 5		....	15 50	38 02	37 02	37 02	27 11
58 44. 5	2	....		....	15 30	37 52	36 52	36 52	27 21
59 23. 5	41	0. 9		1	15 20	37 47	36 47	36 48	27 25
59 55. 5	1 13	2. 9		3	15 20	37 47	36 47	36 50	27 23
19 00 33. 0	1 51	6. 7		6	15 30	37 52	36 52	36 58	27 15
01 05. 0	2 23	11. 2		10	15 20	37 47	36 47	36 57	27 16
01 31. 0	2 49	15. 6		15	15 25	37 50	36 50	37 05	27 08
02 01. 0	3 19	21. 6		20	15 20	37 47	36 47	37 07	27 06
02 29. 5	3 47	28. 1		25	14 45	37 30	36 30	36 55	27 18
03 00. 5	4 18	36. 3		33	14 20	37 18	36 18	36 51	27 22
03 22. 0	4 40	42. 8		38	14 30	37 22	36 22	37 00	27 13
03 47. 0	5 05	50. 7		45	14 10	37 12	36 12	36 57	27 16
04 34. 0	5 52	67. 6		1 00	13 30	36 52	35 52	36 52	27 21
05 05. 5	6 23	80. 0		1 12	13 10	36 42	35 42	36 54	27 19
05 34. 0	6 52	92. 6		1 23	13 00	36 37	35 37	37 00	27 13
19 06 15. 0	7 33	111. 9		1 40	81 12 10	40 36 12	40 35 12	40 36 52	46 27 21
Mean....	....	....	....	....	....	....	....	....	46 27 13. 6

App. lat. = l = 46° 27′ 30″	cos 9. 838145	
S.dec = — 2° 55′ 47″	cos 9. 999432	
a = 40′ 37″	cos 0. 119711 A. C.	
.906	9. 957289	

	h. m. s.
Chron. correction	43 52. 6
Æ of star	18 14 49. 6
	18 58 42. 2

Semi-diam.
Refraction, — 60″
Parallax.

Bar. 26.6
Ther. 76°

Determination of the latitude by observed double altitudes of Polaris off the meridian.

Station, camp near Little Missouri.—Sextant, Spencer, Browning & Co., 6536.—Observer, Wood.—Date, August 22, 1874.—Index error, (−25″, Ex. + 40″=) + 15″.—Chronometer, Bond & Sons, 202.—Computer, Wood.

Observed double altitudes.			Corresponding times.		
°	′	″	h.	m.	s.
92	27	20	19	18	45.5
	28	55		19	35.0
	29	20		20	41.5
	29	40		21	22.5
	30	15		22	57.5
	30	50		23	38.5
	31	10		24	17.0
	31	30		25	09.5
	32	05		25	59.0
	32	20		26	39.5
	33	10		27	30.5
92	33	30	19	28	11.0
92	30	50	19	23	43.9
	+	15			
92	31	05			
46	15	32			
		52			
46	14	40			

log cos p	=	9.1591467	log sin p	9.99543
log △	=	3.6909046	log △	3.69091
log △ cos p	=	2.8500513	log △ sin p	3.68634
	=	708″.03		
			log $\overline{△ \sin p}^2$	7.37268
1st term	=	11′ 48″.03	log a	4.38454
Alt. = A	=	46° 14′ 40″.00	log tang. A	0.01887
2d term	=	59″.72	log 2d term	1.77609
			2d term	59.″72
Latitude	=	46° 27′ 27″.75		

Refraction	− 52″
Chron. correction	− 43m 52s.6
Dec	88° 38′ 12″ △ 49′ 08″.0

	h.	m.	s.
Æ Polaris	1	13	02
Sid. time at mean noon at this station			
Sid. interval from mean time of culmination			
Retardation of mean on sidereal time			
Mean time of culmination of star			
Error of chron. at time of observation		43	52.6
Time by chron. of culmination	1	56	54.6
Sid. time of observation	19	23	43.9
Hour-angle p, in sid. time	6	33	10.7
Sidereal equivalents in arc.			
p in arc	98°	17′	40″

Summary table of daily instrumental observations, with deduced altitudes, the latitude and longitude of each camp, distances traveled, &c.

Date.		Location.	Start.	Arrive.	Thermometer.					Barometer.		Elevation.	Latitude.	Longitude.	Day's march.	Total distance.	Heights of peaks above sea-level, in feet.
					Max.	Min.	No.	Total.	Mean.	Evening.	Morning.						
1874.					°	°						Feet.	° ′ ″	° ′ ″	Miles.	Miles.	
July	2	Buck Creek	8.00 a. m.	8.45 p. m.	94	79	3	260	86.6	....	....	....	46 40 50	101 03 08	15.1	15.1	
	3	....	8.00 a. m.	3.00 p. m.	98½	83	3	272	90.6	27.66	27.60	2,169	46 35 25	101 08 43	14.1	29.2	
	4	Dog's Teeth Creek	5.00 a. m.	11.30 a. m.	102	64	5	434	86.8	27.85	....	1,939	....	....	14.7	43.9	
	5	Creek "where bear winters"	4.45 a. m.	1.00 p. m.	78	59	5	342	68.4	27.74	27.68	2,090	....	....	16.9	60.8	
	6	Cannon Ball River	4.50 a. m.	10.00 a. m.	94	60	5	392	78.4	27.56	27.56	2,251	46 19 52	101 47 43	12.9	73.7	
	7	Cedar Creek	4.00 a. m.	10.00 p. m.	84½	64	4	308.5	77.1	27.36	....	2,459	46 03 20	102 06 07	30.4	104.1	
	8	Hidden Wood Creek	7.00 a. m.	4.30 p. m.	82	67	4	308	77	27.34	27.32	2,345	45 57 20	102 25 01	19.0	123.1	
	9	Grand River	4.45 a. m.	2.30 p. m.	100	46	5	384	76.8	27.45	27.57	2,305	45 54 58	102 45 42	20.0	143.1	
	10	......do	4.50 a. m.	4.00 p. m.	83	45	4	270	67.5	27.20	27.15	2,608	45 58 00	103 01 42	24.0	167.1	
	11	Cave	4.45 a. m.	1.00 p. m.	90	56	6	476	79.3	26.50	26.45	3,439	45 49 10	103 26 46	19.7	186.8	
	12	....	5.00 a. m.	3.00 p. m.	87	62	5	374	74.9	26.61	26.63	3,225	45 43 20	103 29 10	11.0	197.8	
	13	Sage Brush Camp	5.00 a. m.	1.00 p. m.	90	62	5	405	81.0	26.61	26.76	3,189	45 35 50	103 38 05	15.5	213.3	
	14, 15	Prospect Valley	4.45 a. m.	2.00 p. m.	78	50	5	336.5	67.3	26.61	26.57	3,271	45 28 56	103 47 25	13.0	226.3	
	16	Border Camp	4.45 a. m.	8.30 p. m.	82	56	5	357.5	71.5	26.38	26.36	3,488	....	....	30.0	256.8	
	17	Bad Lands	4.45 a. m.	2.15 p. m.	84	60	5	382	76.4	26.09	....	3,858	44 58 10	104 02 39	17.7	274.5	
	18, 19	Belle Fourche	5.00 a. m.	4.30 p. m.	93	63	4	328	82.0	26.73	26.84	3,054	44 48 05	104 08 57	17.5	292.0	
	20	....	4.45 a. m.	5.00 p. m.	78	65½	37	2,644.6	71.5	26.14	26.16	3,734	44 38 35	104 15 27	18.3	310.3	
	21	Red Water Valley	4.45 a. m.	4.30 p. m.	88	50	26	1,811.5	69.7	25.80	25.71	4,226	44 30 18	104 15 52	14.3	324.6	
	22, 23	Inyan Kara Camp	4.45 a. m.	4.30 p. m.	91	73	16	1,333.3	83.3	24.85	24.85	5,318	44 13 00	104 15 57	22.2	346.8	Inyan Kara, 6,500.
	24	Floral Valley	4.45 a. m.	5.00 p. m.	88	62	11	842.7	76.6	24.09	24.09	6,196	44 12 40	104 11 30	11.0	357.8	
	25	......do	4.45 a. m.	3.15 p. m.	86	86	1	86	86.0	23.73	23.73	6,459	44 08 35	104 03 34	11.5	369.3	
	26, 27	Castle Valley	4.45 a. m.	5.00 p. m.	66	40	11	591.2	53.7	24.03	24.03	6,136	44 01 45	103 51 20	14.0	383.3	
	28	Indian Camp	4.45 a. m.	2.00 p. m.	....	....	....	....	....	23.92	23.92	6,285	44 00 52	103 48 27	10.0	393.3	
	29	....	4.45 a. m.	3.00 p. m.	82	64	9	646	71.8	24.25	24.10	5,903	....	....	15.0	408.5	
	30, 31	....	7.00 a. m.	1.00 p. m.	93	46	12	895	74.6	24.50	24.51	5,664	....	....	10.2	418.7	
Aug.	1–5	Permanent Camp	7.45 a. m.	9.30 a. m.	70	66	4	268	67.0	24.60	24.60	5,488	43 46 10	103 33 02	3.5	422.2	Harney's Peak, 9,700.
	6	....	4.45 a. m.	7.30 p. m.	71	65	2	136	68.0	23.53	23.53	6,768	....	....	23.2	445.4	
	7	....	4.55 a. m.	5.30 p. m.	....	....	....	....	....	24.24	24.25	5,877	44 08 53	103 45 50	16.2	461.6	
	8	....	4.45 a. m.	....	89	63	2	152	76.0	24.49	24.49	5,633	44 15 10	103 38 08	14.7	476.3	
	9	....	5.00 a. m.	....	....	....	....	....	....	24.60	24.61	5,481	....	....	7.5	483.8	
	10, 11	....	5.00 a. m.	....	72	68	6	416	69.3	24.96	25.35	4,807	44 09 53	103 30 16	7.5	491.3	
	12	....	4.45 a. m.	7.00 p. m.	57	46	5	261	52.2	25.64	25.58	4,368	44 07 35	103 26 04	5.7	497.0	
	13	....	12.00 m.	2.00 p. m.	90	88	4	355	88.7	25.45	25.45	4,518	44 07 46	103 23 48	4.7	501.7	
	14, 15	Bear Butte Camp	4.45 a. m.	6.00 p. m.	90	66	14	1,100	78.5	26.30	26.30	3,624	44 23 43	103 25 19	26.0	527.7	Bear Butte, 4,800.
	16	....	4.45 a. m.	7.00 p. m.	86	66	11	1,849	77.2	26.87	27.02	2,889	44 47 35	103 28 02	29.5	557.2	
	17	....	4.45 a. m.	7.00 p. m.	84	54	11	730	66.4	26.75	26.85	3,067	45 09 30	103 37 45	28.2	585.4	
	18	Prospect Valley	4.45 a. m.	5.30 p. m.	86	62	10	786	78.6	26.27	26.27	3,675	45 31 05	103 52 35	30.2	615.6	
	19	....	7.20 a. m.	7.30 p. m.	79	62	4	291	72.7	26.63	26.63	3,225	....	....	35.3	650.9	
	20, 21	Little Missouri River	5.00 a. m.	7.15 p. m.	74	66	22	1,534	69.7	26.80	26.84	3,023	46 08 30	103 51 30	29.9	680.8	
	22	....	5.00 a. m.	....	84	61	15	1,088	72.5	26.59	26.59	3,256	46 27 20	103 42 54	28.5	709.3	
	23	Little Missouri River	4.45 a. m.	....	75	59	16	1,070	66.9	27.28	27.28	2,554	46 34 55	103 29 25	19.0	728.3	
	24	Heart River	4.45 a. m.	....	81	52	17	1,132	66.6	27.13	27.13	2,718	46 44 45	103 07 51	24.7	753.0	
	25	....	4.45 a. m.	12.00 m.	86	58	11	751	68.3	27.15	27.00	2,779	....	....	17.7	770.7	
	26	Young Men's Buttes	4.45 a. m.	5.00 p. m.	87	64	25	1,910	76.4	26.90	26.90	2,965	46 52 20	102 15 49	32.2	802.9	
	27	....	4.45 a. m.	12.00 m.	68	62	13	829	63.8	27.23	27.25	2,608	....	....	17.1	820.0	
	28	Little Muddy Creek	4.45 a. m.	10.50 a. m.	69	64	12	795	66.2	27.30	27.55	2,384	....	....	16.0	836.0	
	29	White Fish Creek	4.30 a. m.	....	78	58	13	865	66.5	27.82	27.80	1,998	46 52 00	101 16 18	20.0	856.0	
	30	Fort Abraham Lincoln	4.00 a. m.	....	90	58	20	1,507	75.3	27.65	....	2,211	46 46 10	100 50 57	27.3	883.3	

RECONNAISSANCES.

Date.	Name.	Distance.	Total.
July 31	Colonel Ludlow	20	136 miles.
Aug. 3 to 5	......do	100	
10	......do	16	
July 27	Lieutenant Godfrey	8	104 miles.
31	......do	20	
Aug. 2 to 5	......do	70	
7	......do	6	

Date.	Name.	Distance.	Total.	
July 25	Mr. W. H. Wood	10	28	322 miles.
27	......do	18		
July 27	Sergeant Becker	11	22	
31	......do	11		
July 27	Sergeant Wilson	16	32	
31	......do	16		

Wagon-train traveled	883.3 miles.
Reconnaissances, traveled	322.0 miles.
Total	1,205.3 miles.
Camps	47

CHIEF ENGINEER'S OFFICE, *Saint Paul, Minn., April* 23, 1875.

O